The Adventurous World of
PARIS
1900-1914

The Adventurous World of
PARIS
1900-1914

Nigel Gosling

William Morrow and Company, Inc.
New York 1978

A NOTE ON CURRENCY

An approximate guide to rates of
exchange during the period 1900–1914:

4.9 French francs = U.S. $1.00
25.2 French francs = £1 sterling

Printed in Great Britain.

First Edition
1 2 3 4 5 6 7 8 9 10

ISBN 0-688-03366-0

Library of Congress Catalog Card Number
78-52477

Contents

Introduction

AN ATTEMPT TO ISOLATE a particular group of years is like trying to cut a slice out of a river; it can never wholly succeed, for it cannot accommodate the prelude and the reverberations which give the period its shape and meaning. But occasionally a span of time seems made for encapsulation, and the opening decade and a half of this century is one of them. In that short period the modern world suddenly materialized, like a cell forming in the womb. The exact moment of conception is unidentifiable, but at least we can pinpoint when and where the new life became visible inside the body of the old. The time was between 1900 and 1914, and the place was Paris.

It had to be Paris, because the city was at that moment the vessel which held the whole of western civilization within its twenty *arrondissements*. After the Renaissance France had inherited the parental role in Europe, and its capital status was further entrenched by Napoleon. During the nineteenth century, with the flowering of the Romantic movement and the outpouring of creativity that followed it – with painters like Delacroix, novelists like Balzac, and poets like Victor Hugo flooding France with masterpieces – it became the undisputed dynamo from which western culture drew its power.

There was a semblance of material strength, too; but that received a devastating blow in 1870 when Prussia, about to become the head of a united Germany, manifested its growing power by knocking out the French Second Empire in a few weeks. The cracks in the national structure split open. The brief take-over by the Commune in Paris – put down with bloody brutality – uncovered a pit of discontent beneath the gilded bourgeois crust; and the rivalries of the other great European powers, Britain, Germany and Russia – together with alarming far-off newcomers like Japan and America – began to blow round the heads of succeeding French governments like thunder clouds.

At home the débâcle of General Boulanger's bid for power in 1889 indicated weakness in the constitution and instablity in the national mood. The Panama scandal which followed it disclosed a vein of festering anti-semitism which exploded in 1894 when the Dreyfus Affair revealed a violent social dichotomy – one half of the nation supporting the army, the other the unassuming Jewish officer whom the army had accused of treachery.

OPPOSITE A kiosk on the boulevards, *c*. 1910.

The end of the century found France uncertain and isolated in a threatening world, drawing what solace she could from Britain's discomfiture in her war against the Boers. But in its last years a kind of exhausted lull was established. The President, Félix Faure, died and was succeeded by the anodyne Emile Loubet, who was incongruously to preside over the revolutionary years to come. A commercial treaty was signed with Italy, a potentially useful ally, and a settlement reached with Britain over the Sudan. Dreyfus was re-tried, and pardoned. The new government under Waldeck-Rousseau embarked on mildly reformist measures at home. As the nineteenth century moved majestically to its close there was a pause like the hush before the curtain goes up.

The concept of a dramatic historical break is misleading. As in animal birth, there is always a period of co-existence while a new age forms in the framework of the old. In the last decade of the nineteenth century there were clear indications of the twentieth. The Lumière brothers staged the first cinema show, to thirty-five terrified spectators in a café basement, as early as 1895. Two years later Georges Méliès was shooting a space film in a trapdoor-studded studio, and by 1900 he was turning out a film a week. Electricity had replaced gas in the streets. Haussmann's vast avenue network which turned Paris into a modern city was finally completed. Wagner was undermining the cheerful French tunefulness of Offenbach and Bizet. The Impressionists won official approval with the opening of the Caillebotte collection in the Luxembourg Museum in 1897, and even a few Symbolist artists were recognized by the art establishment. Cézanne's monumental achievements forced their way into the respect of at least educated taste. And the supreme symbol of rebellion, Alfred Jarry's *Ubu Roi* with its wild theme and four-letter words, had been launched in Lugné-Poé's Théâtre de l'Oeuvre as early as 1896.

If signs of our own age were already visible in the nineteenth century, shadows of the past stretched well into the twentieth. At this moment two worlds shook hands and took their leave of each other. In 1900 Paris was still not vastly different from the city of Molière, with its teeming poor and its luxurious *salons*, its hand-wrought wealth (wine and silk were still at the top of France's exports) and horse-cluttered streets. It still preserved the character of a cluster of connecting villages, with a busy centre housing the administrative and economic headquarters and monuments like the Opéra and the Louvre, and an elegant residential area round the Boulevard St-Germain spreading up the Champs Elysées towards the Bois de Boulogne. This prosperous core was flanked by backwaters to the north and south, Montmartre and Montparnasse, where cheap lodgings and quietness attracted writers and artists.

There was no sense of bursting expansion, in spite of a healthy prosperity. The population of Paris had risen from one million in 1851 to almost three million by 1891, but mainly as the result of extending the city's boundaries. For the next twenty years it was to remain virtually unchanged. Paris remained a small community where it was easy and natural to meet people with shared interests; bread and wine were cheap, and you could get a meal at a modest restaurant for two francs. Friends still walked or – a new fashion – cycled to visit each other, and wrote copious letters, though the telephone was widely used by the better-off. You could rattle across the whole city from the Théâtre de l'Odéon to the top of La Butte in half an hour in the regular bus, drawn by three horses abreast. A *bateau-mouche* would carry you down the river from the Bois de Vincennes to the Bois de Boulogne for twenty-five centimes; or you could risk yourself (even if you were a lady, who could not be seen on a bus) in one of the new steam trams.

Life in Paris was still stamped ineffaceably with the paternalistic ambitions of the monarchy and the empire; they had merely been transferred to the new democratic officials. Diplomacy was signalled – even engineered – by royal visits and exchanges; cavalry clattered through the streets at every important occasion. Medals were pinned, toasts drunk, speeches declaimed. The rich lived massively and comfortably, while the poor went hungry and flexed their political muscles. Recognized in 1884, the trades unions mustered 140,000 members in 1890; by 1902 there were over 400,000.

The art world seemed to be resting, like everything else, in the comfortable arms of officialdom. Its main manifestation was the Salon; art came but once a year, but then in gargantuan plenty, served up with pomp and discussed with long-winded respect. Until the very last years of the century the Salon gave artists their only chance to exhibit their work; here reputations and fortunes were made, commissions handed out, and prizes distributed. Even Cézanne and Degas pined to be included. The Salon was the giant against which the puny champions of revolt declared war, and its size and quality are a measure of their achievement.

It had been founded in 1831 as a sign of regal approval of the arts, with a jury appointed by the Académie des Beaux Arts. But inevitably jealousies arose, and in 1863 Napoleon III, after inspecting the rejects, boldly sanctioned a rival exhibition, the Salon des Refusés. Shocked by Manet's *Le Déjeuner sur l'Herbe*, he did not repeat the exercise, which marks the birth of anti-establishment art. But in 1884 a more successful attempt to set up an opposition to official taste resulted in the foundation of the Salon des Indépendants by a group of artists which included Georges Seurat, Odilon Redon and Paul Signac. The first show was torpedoed by scandals and quarrels (a fishing rod was found to have been included in one member's expenses), but in 1886 two hundred paintings were hung in a large temporary building which had been erected for the Post Office in the Tuileries Gardens. They included Rousseau's *Evening Carnival* and a sketch for Seurat's *A Summer Afternoon on La Grande Jatte*, and from then on the exhibition was taken seriously every year, though usually held in that long, low, inelegant shed.

In 1881 the Salon itself was reformed, giving artists who had exhibited the right to elect their own jury the following year. It was renamed the Salon des Artistes Français, and took place every spring in the Palais de l'Industrie, off the Champs Elysées. But even such a strongly entrenched fortress of the establishment was liable to schism. In 1890 Ernest Meissonier, the most famous and most expensive artist in Paris – piqued, it was said, because he could not be President of the Salon, the office being already filled – led a revolt. His fellow-renegades included some of the top names in official art – Eugène Carrière, Carolus-Duran, Albert Besnard, Gervex, Giovanni Boldini and the advanced but respected Puvis de Chavannes, besides the now venerated sculptor Auguste Rodin. But the youngsters from the Indépendants did not join; Meissonier died; and soon the new group, the Salon National, was reabsorbed, exhibiting side by side with the old Salon, though insisting on different opening times.

The opening of the Salon (or Salons) was a combination of social flutter and artistic anticipation. In the morning the President would arrive with his entourage and go round the galleries. He and his party would then repair to a restaurant to fortify themselves with salmon and *tournedos* before the exhibition was opened to a favoured crowd in the afternoon.

In 1900 the Palais de l'Industrie was pulled down to make way for the International Exhibition, and the Salon moved across the river to the Place de Breteuil behind the Invalides, but this only added to the interest. Fashionable crowds mingled with the artists, their wives, friends and models, decked out in expensive and inexpensive varieties of the new Art Nouveau fashions. Rivalling the works of art was the usual sprinkling of theatrical celebrities. People stared breathlessly at Sarah Bernhardt, Réjane or Mounet-Sully.

There were usually about three thousand oil paintings besides pastels, watercolours and drawings, and a huge array of sculptural nudes and notabilities in bronze or livid white marble. Many of the artists were well known to the public, and very conscious of their eminence. Stars like Bouguereau and Bonnat always wore frock-coats while painting, while Detaille put on full uniform to work on his battle pictures. Their studios – mainly in the smart seventeenth *arrondissement* – looked like banqueting halls fitted out by a junk merchant, with medieval and oriental bric-à-brac filling the spaces between posing thrones and easels. Their output was immense and the quality distinguished by high technical competence. The most favoured portraitists were Carolus-Duran, who could ask 50,000 francs for a sitting (but stoutly championed the Impressionists) and the more serious Bonnat, a teacher at the Ecole des Beaux Arts and a friend of Degas. ('I don't like to talk too long with him,' he admitted. 'After leaving I feel tempted to change my style.') There were the dashing La Gandara; Besnard; Helleu, the recorder of the smart set; Lévy-Dhurmer, 'pastellist of pale people'; Sargent (a pupil of Duran); and the bold Boldini, whom Degas called 'a monster of talent' and Gertrude Stein was paradoxically to announce as father of the modern school. Carrière was their doyen, with his tender, blurry domestic scenes – 'The model must have moved,' remarked Degas tartly of one of his pictures. Gérome was a respected teacher as well as a popular idol; Gervex shocked the public with his scenes of seduction; the aged Bourguereau remained popular with his cloying nudes and religious subjects. And there were innumerable landscapists in the manner of Corot and of the Barbizon school.

They made a formidable team, and were backed by an enormous machine armed with medals, prizes, commissions and nationwide publicity. To set beside one of their huge, crowded canvases one of Cézanne's tiny studies of a plateful of apples is to realize the nerve of the rebels and the measure of their victory. The rebels' main weapon was the Salon des Indépendants, which ran concurrently with its rivals and was even more of a hotch-potch. Anybody could contribute four works on payment of a ten-franc fee. In 1901 just over a thousand pictures were on show; by 1908 they had swelled to six thousand, so that in the April of that year Parisians had over ten thousand paintings on view. That a handful of artists were to drive a way through this enormous mass and impose their new vision on the professional art world seems almost a miracle.

The big Salons were not quite the only showcase for an artist. But right up to the turn of the century they obliterated the little exhibitions at one or two private galleries which were beginning to spring up. The Galerie Goupil, founded soon after the restoration of the monarchy in the 1830s, was the most serious; in its lavish premises in the Rue Chaptal it sold furniture, tapestries and porcelain, as well as paintings. It was frankly a shop, leading its one-time salesman, Vincent Van Gogh, to comment that 'the buying and selling of works of art is nothing but organized robbery'. In 1882 a rival had sprung up, the Galerie Georges Petit in the Rue de Sèze near the Madeleine. This was another large establishment, whose private views and sales soon turned into social occasions which the gallery developed by organizing tea-time meetings and recitals. One of its big *coups* was the handling of Millet's *The Angelus*, which it resold several times, finally achieving the price of one million francs. More go-ahead than Goupil's, it was soon handling the Impressionists in competition with another new gallery, Durand-Ruel, from whom it seduced one or two artists such as Sisley. Renoir showed his *Les Grandes Baigneuses* there, and it held a Monet retrospective in 1889.

Other small dealers began to open their premises at the end of the century – Begnet, Gérard and Tempelaere. Almost all of them sold Salon pictures by painters like Henner, Ziem, Fantin-Latour and Boudin. There were one or two exceptions, such as the second-hand dealer Le Père Tanguy, immortalized by Van Gogh; Le Barc de Bouteville, a rich dealer in the Rue Le Peletier who handled Toulouse-Lautrec, Bonnard, Vuillard and Maurice Denis; and Ambroise Vollard, whose support for Cézanne, and later for even more daring artists, has passed into history. His little shop in the Rue Laffitte, on the lower slopes of Montmartre, became in the 1890s the nucleus of a whole row of galleries in that street, earning it the nickname 'Rue des Artistes'.

If one place can be picked out as the birthplace of modern art, it is here. In the Rue Laffitte and in the run-down old houses on the hill above it, La Butte, the art of the twentieth century can be said to have first taken shape. At the time it would have seemed incredible that such a humble neighbourhood and such a ragged, ill-disciplined crew would inherit the noble mantle of Parisian art tradition. Outwardly, they were nothing but a bunch of ragamuffins, but within less than a generation they had overthrown a whole cultural dynasty and founded a new race of artists and a new kind of art. To the superficial eye Paris might seem to be foundering in the extravagant confusions of an empire sinking under the weight of centuries of domination. Paradoxically, it was to be the bitter and irreverent enemies of its traditions who were to work the miracle of its resuscitation, turning the sunset of one age into the dawn of another.

*** N° 1
PUBLICATION HEBDOMADAIRE
Prix : 50 cent.
ENCYCLOPÉDIE DU SIECLE
L'EXPOSITION
DE
PARIS 1900
LOIR.LUIGI
PARIS
MONTGREDIEN & Cie
LIBRAIRIE ILLUSTRÉE
8, Rue St Joseph, 8

1900
The Great Divide

THE WINTER which carried the old century into the new was cold and dismal. 'Dear Robbie,' wrote the forty-six-year-old Oscar Wilde on 2 January from a little hotel on the Left Bank to his friend Robert Ross, 'I have to acknowledge with thanks the two cheques you have sent me for my income for December and January, £27.10 in all. Paris has been cold and wet but I had a very pleasant Christmas.' The French papers were not interested in a disgraced and impoverished British playwright. They were understandably concerned with nostalgic ruminations on the achievements of the past century, and hopeful estimates of the future one. 'The year 1900 was the culmination of the period between the two wars [1870 and 1914], of its illusions and its mistakes,' commented the novelist Léon Daudet later. 'It would be instructive to re-read the newspaper articles of the period. . . . Writers were competing to celebrate the marvels of the mewling new-born century which was succeeding to the age of Hugo and Pasteur.'

Culturally the year opened cheerfully. The newly gilded Eiffel Tower gleamed against the skies, grey and humid after storms. Portraits of the American dancer Loie Fuller and the *demi-monde* actress La Belle Otéro were everywhere, recorded the Director of the Théâtre Français, Jules Claretie. *Voortrekker* felt hats and music sheets of *La Marche des Boers* flaunted ill-concealed popular delight at British difficulties in South Africa. The Galerie Georges Petit was showing gallant war pictures by the Russian artist Vassily Vereschagin. Offenbach's *La Belle Hélène* was playing at the Variétés. And on 2 February the curtain at the Opéra rose on a tuneful, pleasingly sentimental new work by the forty-year-old composer Gustave Charpentier, *Louise*. It struck exactly the right note for the moment – a sympathetically idealized vision of picturesque poverty, a kind of gently socialist *La Bohème*. Though the American accent of the heroine, sung by Mary Garden, was teasingly commented on, the vivid impressions of Montmartre, the nostalgic views over the city at dusk summoned up by the designer, Jussaine, and the romance between Louise and her lover Julien scored an immediate success.

But the mood of well-being was short-lived. On 8 March André Antoine, the celebrated founder of the Théâtre Libre, which, in 1887, had launched Naturalism into the French theatre, made his way to a rehearsal at his own new theatre.

OPPOSITE The spirit of the Universal Exhibition.

13

An actress escapes from the fire at the Théâtre Français which killed one of her colleagues. The artist has seized the chance to show a peep of feminine legs.

Hardly have I arrived ... when I hear a shout coming from the Boulevard de Strasbourg: 'The Théâtre Français is on fire!' It is five minutes past twelve. I ask at once if there is anybody in the theatre. ... A group of firemen come out of the stage door carrying something black covered with soot. Suddenly among the ambulances there appears my lodger Henriot, bare-headed, running towards the theatre and crying out: 'My daughter! I tell you my girl is in there!'

She was right. Antoine took her off to the actor Albert Lambert's house to wait for news, but none came. Finally he went off to the morgue where he found the actor Coquelin junior. Together they confirmed that the body lying there was that of Jeanne Henriot. The death of the young actress (and the temporary closure of the theatre) cast a gloom over the public.

It was, however, soon to be distracted by a major, long-awaited première – a new play by the most popular dramatist of the moment, starring the most popular actress. Edmond Rostand, now thirty-two, had jumped into the public eye in 1895 when the famous Sarah Bernhardt had consented to play in his Symbolist romance *La Princesse Lointaine*. Two years later he had confirmed his reputation with a huge success which exploited current historical nostalgia, *Cyrano de Bergerac*. Now, after the Dreyfus Affair, the general mood had changed to one of suppressed nationalism. Rostand, who had taken the side of the accused officer, came up with an idea which harked back to the glorious days of Napoleon, and offered to Bernhardt the role of the Emperor's ill-fated son in *L'Aiglon*. Fired with the desire to outshine Coquelin's success in *Cyrano*, she accepted at once; Lucien Guitry took the part of the gallant General Flambeau.

Rehearsals would begin, so Guitry's son Sacha relates, every day at 1.15. About ten minutes to four Bernhardt used to make her entry; everybody rose to their feet and kissed her hand – a lengthy operation, since about sixty people were present. Bernhardt then changed into her rehearsal costume, and work began. But after not much more than an hour the proceedings were disrupted by 'Madame Sarah's cup of tea'.

Interruptions were frequent. At one point in the play Guitry had to cry: '*Le ciel blanchit vers l'Est!*' to which Bernhardt responded: '*J'empoigne la crinière – alea jacta est.*' What, she asked one day, did the '*crinière*' (mane) signify? A comet, perhaps? No, just a horse, explained Rostand, so a horse was duly summoned. The first one was too frisky. The second replied to her cry of '*Vive l'Empereur!*' with a loud stomach rumble. Rostand called for another, but Bernhardt had decided there would be no horse.

Not surprisingly, rehearsals dragged on for six weeks, but the first night was a triumph. Bernhardt, her ripe fifty-five-year-old figure corseted into a tight uniform, moved Parisians to tears as her golden voice played with the patriotic and pathetic sentiments of the doomed young Duc de Reichstadt. Her position as queen of the Parisian stage was established impregnably.

From the literary point of view it was to be a quiet year – with one exception. A strange, unheralded little novel appeared one day in the Paris bookshops. 'I am called Claudine and I live at Montigny; I was born there in 1884 and probably I won't die there,' it began. *Claudine at School* related the adventures of an innocently corrupt country schoolgirl; it was an account of adolescent lesbianism described with the lightest and most elegant of pens. The author was ostensibly the columnist and music critic Henri Gauthier-Villars, who wrote under the name of 'Willy', but the book had actually been written by his wife. In 1893 the sophisticated, middle-aged man-about-town had surprisingly married a young girl from Burgundy, Sidonie-Gabrielle Colette. Willy suggested that she should write down some of the stories she had been telling him of her schooldays. She dutifully shut herself up in their dark little flat in the Rue Jacob and filled six exercise books, but Willy was not impressed when he first read them. However, two years later he came across them again and, after three failures, placed them with Messrs Ollendorf, claiming, as he did with his ghost-written articles, that he was the author. Madame Rachilde, wife of the magazine's proprietor, wrote in the *Mercure de France*: '*Claudine* – vital, original and marvellously spirited – places Willy in the front rank of French novelists.' The book sold forty thousand copies in the first two months, and became the start of a whole series of dazzlingly successful novels which blended charm, sexual titillation and the purest of styles, though it was not until after her marriage had broken down that Colette was to reveal herself as the real author.

But all artistic disasters and delights were overshadowed by the slow, irrevocable approach of an event which was to absorb public attention all through the summer and autumn – the Universal Exhibition, which was to provide as distinctive a milestone at the start of the century as the Great War was at its abrupt extinction. The last exhibition, which had been held in 1889, had produced a feature which outraged educated taste. A letter of protest to the Press was signed by such eminent names as Dumas *fils*, Maupassant, Gounod, Sardou, Bouguereau and Meissonier: 'For twenty years to come we shall see stretching over the entire city – still quivering with the genius of so many centuries – we shall see, like an ink blot, the hateful shadow of the odious column of riveted steel metal.' But the Eiffel Tower had crept up ineluctably into the sky, and there, eleven years later, it still was. Many people were apprehensive. Would something even more offensive grow up alongside it?

But threats of a competitive show in Germany overcame the opposition. The huge operation of earth-moving and demolition began in 1896, and in October of that year the President of France and the Tsar of Russia jointly laid the foundation-stone of a new bridge across the Seine, the Pont Alexandre, joining the two halves of the site. As the spring of 1900 drew on with relentless rains the site began to look like a battlefield, dominated by the vast Grand Palais and its smaller counterpart, the Petit Palais, which faced each other across the avenue leading to the bridge. The Dreyfus Affair and the Panama scandal of 1893 had shaken public confidence, and the building was interrupted intermittently by strikes. A few days before the opening a commentator wrote: 'France has invited the whole world to a festival and will be able to offer only a muddy building-site.' But the great day arrived, and, flanked by armies of officials, escorted by cavalry, saluted by cannon fire and serenaded by a choir singing Saint-Saens' *Hymn to Victor Hugo*, the diminutive President

Sarah Bernhardt, aged fifty-five, impersonates the Duc de Reichstadt in Edmond Rostand's play about Napoleon's son, *L'Aiglon*.

processed across the new bridge and ceremoniously mounted the dais in the Salle des Fêtes. 'Soon', he declared, 'we may have completed an important stage in the slow evolution of work towards happiness and of man towards humanity. It is under the auspices of such a hope that I declare the 1900 Exhibition open.'

It was to stay open until mid-November and be seen by 50,860,801 visitors – fewer than anticipated, but still greater than the whole population of France. There was plenty for them to see on a site two and a half miles across. The principal entrance was the Porte Binet, a monumental gateway leading off the Place de la Concorde – it had a multicoloured dome embedded with coloured lights, housing fifty-six ticket offices, and was surmounted by a fifteen-foot-high plaster statue symbolizing Paris, with a massive bosom and a robe designed by Paquin. The wits derided her as 'the triumph of prostitution' but 'La Parisienne' was typical of the naive use of sculptured allegory throughout the grounds. Everywhere there were muscular athletes, prancing horses, lions, cherubs and buxom women clutching torches or baskets of fruit piled up in front of the buildings. The Exhibition has sometimes been hailed as a high point in the history of Art Nouveau, but the general flavour was unremittingly neobaroque at its most florid, with excursions into music-hall fantasy when some local flavour was called for. The Grand Palais, the most considerable building in the show, was characteristic, with its heavily ostentatious façade and interior enlivened by fine ironwork in Art Nouveau style. The Petit Palais, by a different architect, was more traditional, and its entrance was decorated by two noted Salon painters, Albert Besnard and Paul-Albert Laurens.

The most obviously picturesque sections of the Exhibition lay along the banks of the Seine. A cluster of make-believe houses with spires and gables representing 'Old Paris' lay on the Right Bank; complete with costumed actors, it resembled a film set. On the Left Bank, rather overshadowing it, was the Rue des Nations, a row of pavilions erected in evident competition by the bigger foreign powers – which still did not include America, whose modest building, noted for its business centre, was squeezed in between Turkey and Australia.

The foreign quarter produced a splendid *macédoine* of style. The Germans dominated the area with a massive pavilion topped by a lighthouse which made rival illuminations 'look like oil lamps'. Britain offered a pastiche by Sir Edwin Lutyens of an Elizabethan manor house. The Turks went in for Alhambra-style Moorish. China entertained its visitors to tea in a fanciful building of dark red wood with porcelain tiles and dragons snarling from the roof. Most admired by the intellectuals was Eliel Saarinen's Finnish pavilion.

The Russian exhibit was so large that it was removed to the site in front of the Trocadéro, where it formed a whole 'village'. There were mountains of crystal and porcelain and piles of furs. In one pavilion visitors were transported through the countryside in a simulated train with views of the countryside appearing on moving scenery behind the windows. Plenty of gold-mines and precious metals were included to bolster the confidence of French capitalists.

Such simple devices were already beginning to look outmoded, relics of the past century. Many other diversions can be seen now as portents of our own age. Steam locomotives and boilers attracted little attention compared with an impressive array of those five-year-old novelties, automobiles, in the Palais de l'Industrie – the first time they had appeared in an exhibition. The Optical Pavilion housed a microscope which magnified a drop of Paris water 1,000 times ('a horrid spectacle', noted one reporter). There were samples, also seen in public for the first time, of x-ray photography and wireless telegraphy. A diorama conducted visitors on a tour round plaster reproductions of the Imperial Palace at Peking and the temple at Angkor Wat. Another presented a voyage through outer space. A cinerama simulated an ascent in a balloon. Visitors could make a round trip of some areas on a three-speed moving platform.

The cinema was everywhere. Lumière showed a film, *Pope Leo* XIII *in Private*, to embellish a panorama of Rome. Pathé had a stand of its own, run by the pioneer Ferdinand Zecca. In the centre of the Machine Gallery hung an enormous transparent screen, dampened so that the image was visible on both sides to 25,000 spectators. Attempts were made to project giant travel scenes on to screens erected on the Eiffel Tower, but the wind proved too strong for satisfactory viewing. There was even a primitive 'talkie' – Léon Gaumont ran a film of Coquelin declaiming his famous *tirade des nez* from *Cyrano de Bergerac*, accompanied by a

Jacques-Emile Blanche:
André Gide and Friends, 1901
(Musée des Beaux Arts, Rouen).
An imaginary meeting of writers
in a Moorish café at
the Exhibition. Gide is in the
large black hat.

synchronized record. The magic lantern was dead, the live theatre was threatened; the film age had arrived.

Another twentieth-century phenomenon scored its first triumph. The entire exhibition was run by electricity and the huge dynamos installed to provide the power were ingeniously made part of the show. By day smoke poured from the chimneys at each end of the power house, while crowds stared in awe at the machinery inside; and at night the Palace of Electricity was transformed by five thousand fairy lights into a magic world surmounted by the Spirit of Electricity in a chariot, showering coloured flames. The stained glass and transparent ceramics glowed like jewels, while floodlit fountains and ever-changing lights turned the gigantic, fan-shaped edifice into one of those twinkling, iridescent wedding cakes dear to designers at the Théâtre du Châtelet – a marriage of fantasy and function wonderfully symbolizing the merging of two ages.

The cheerful vulgarity of most of the buildings was severely criticized by sophisticated commentators. Though such strictures now seem extreme – a streak of commonplace panache is essential to temporary exhibition architecture – it was true that the ensemble symbolized all too well the last frothy eruption of the nineteenth-century volcano of creativity. Yet the discerning eye could find among the plaster and marble bric-à-brac signs of a new, genuine taste and style – Art Nouveau.

It was not quite a novelty; examples from Belgium and Britain and – in the local *Jugendstil* variation – Austria had been seeping into Paris for ten years, and put down a vital root in the Rue de Provence in 1895 in the shop of an American dealer in Japanese antiques, Samuel Bing. Some of the work of the new designers was to be found in the foreign sections of the Exhibition – frescoes by Alphonse Mucha (famous in Paris for his Sarah Bernhardt posters) in the Bosnia-Herzegovina pavilion, and murals by Gustav Klimt in the Austrian section of the Decorative Arts building. Three Parisian shops – Le Printemps, Le Louvre and Le Bon Marché – co-operated in a single pavilion fitted out with elegance and luxury to display jewellery, glass and furniture in the new style, the work of men like René Lalique, Grasset and Emile Gallé.

The most striking evidence, however, of the style which was to dominate the next few years was in Bing's own pavilion. The façade included a panel by Georges de Feure showing two mysterious girls in fashionable frocks; the interior was replete with copper and stained leather, silk and mottled wood, wrought metal and glass, voluptuous mouldings and elegant detail carried out in twilight shades and pale, delicate pastels. The display scored a big success in influential circles and decisively established Art Nouveau as the style of the moment.

The appearance of Art Nouveau in two other, rather unexpected, places helped to suggest that it featured more prominently in the Exhibition than it actually did. The problem of transporting thousands of visitors to the site had raised anxieties, in spite of the introduction of outsize four-horse buses, and great emphasis was placed on the Métro. Work on the opening of the first line, from Porte-Maillot to Bastille, was speeded up and entrance gates were erected over the stations. Designed by Hector Guimard, the serpentine wrought-iron flowers and fancy lettering were

OPPOSITE Electricity came of age in the Exhibition. The central power house (ABOVE, in a photograph by the writer Emile Zola) was cunningly disguised as an exotic palace, lit at night by thousands of coloured lights. Visitors could tour the extensive site either by train or by sailing round on a moving platform (BELOW) with three tiers rolling at three different speeds.

Loie Fuller, the American dancer, was no beauty but obtained fantastic effects by means of flying veils and lighting in a theatre specially built for her.

to become a well-known feature of the Paris streets right up to the present day.

The other essentially Art Nouveau feature was one of the entertainment offerings. Among the buildings on the Right Bank was a large, cube-shaped pavilion awkwardly wrapped in a plaster impression of a half-raised theatrical curtain – a theatre given over to Loie Fuller. Born thirty years earlier in Chicago, she had started at the Folies Bergère at the age of twenty-two, and became the rage of Paris the following year when she danced at the Athénée. She was not especially beautiful, but she had something new to offer. Claude Anet wrote:

Instead of the traditional dancer in tights and muslin skirt, instead of the familiar but ever-entertaining acrobatics ... there appeared one evening at the back of the darkened stage the indistinct form of a woman clothed in a mass of drapery. Suddenly a stream of light issued apparently from the woman herself, while around her the folds of gauze rose and fell in phosphorescent waves.

Inspired, so she later declared, by a chance mishap with the lighting, she had developed an intricate display involving swirling material and ingenious effects that included projections and a glass stage. Her impressions of flames and lilies lent themselves perfectly to Art Nouveau designs, and she figured in countless statuettes and jewels, becoming almost a symbol of the Exhibition.

Among the enraptured audiences at her pavilion was a twenty-two-year-old girl from San Francisco, Isadora Duncan, who had just made her début in Paris society *salons*. Another entranced devotee was the nine-year-old Jean Cocteau, who saw her as 'active and invisible like a hornet in a flower. She stirs up an orchid of light and fabric.'

Only the keenest eye could have detected anywhere in the Exhibition signs of the birth of modern art. There were two huge exhibitions of painting in the Grand Palais. The first was the Décénnale, comprising international works executed in the last ten years. The French section contained over 1,500 paintings selected by a Beaux Arts committee presided over by Léon Bonnat and dominated by the portraits, landscapes and subject pictures favoured in the Salon – historical, symbolic or often slyly

Jean Béraud: *The Châlet du Cycle in the Bois de Boulogne,* *c.* 1900 (Musée de Sceaux). Bicycles had already reached their standard shape by 1900. Cycling was a popular pastime, giving women the opportunity of displaying at least half their legs in fashionable 'bloomers'.

erotic. Some minor Symbolist admirers of Gustave Moreau and Puvis de Chavannes were included, but no Impressionists. The British showed Millais, Lord Leighton, Alma-Tadema, Beardsley and Burne-Jones. The United States had a strong Realist entry, including works by Whistler, Sargent, Louis Eakins and Winslow Homer. Germany had portraits by Lenbach and the young Franz von Stuck. Italy gave a whole wall to the striking portraits of Boldini. Switzerland was well represented by Ferdinand Hodler and Austria introduced a breath of Art Nouveau with three paintings by Klimt. Belgium showed the nightmare visions of James Ensor and Fernand Khnopff. Russia had portraits by Serov, and Spain some by Zuloaga. The huge display was swamped by mediocre academic painting, and was understandably conservative in taste, but it did include a number of accomplished and interesting works, including two by Rouault, who was awarded a bronze medal.

The other massive collection, the Centenary Exhibition of French Art, was restricted to the period 1800–89 so as not to overlap with the other show, and must have presented a spectacle which no other nation could even approach. It ranged from David and Ingres to Delacroix and Géricault. There were thirteen Manets (including his once controversial *Le Déjeuner sur l'Herbe*), twenty-three Corots, eight Courbets, nineteen Daumiers, six Millets, five Moreaus, and an impressive show of living artists – fourteen Monets, a Gauguin, eleven Renoirs, eight Sisleys, two Degas, a Seurat, seven Pissarros, and, surprisingly, three controversial Cézannes. Here was indeed a triumphant accolade to the last century, with, had the organizers known it, the seeds of the future one's achievements.

The sculpture section was less rewarding, mainly for the reason that the figure who dominated its whole world, the sixty-year-old Auguste Rodin, was excluded. His reputation was such that he had been accorded a pavilion of his own, on a site on the Right Bank rented for him by the city. Rodin himself paid for the building and its upkeep, which cost him 80,000 francs. 'If things don't work out I shall have no choice but to sign up at the Institute to get commissions,' he recorded anxiously. This was the largest assembly of his work so far. Carrière designed a poster and wrote a catalogue tribute together with Besnard and Monet, and the opening – three weeks late – was carried out by the Minister of Fine Arts.

The exhibition attracted little publicity, however, and some disapproved. 'Alongside works of profundity are examples of pure childishness,' noted Proust's beloved composer, Reynaldo Hahn. 'The naive arrogance of the man! He exhibits some drawings of unsurpassed ugliness and insignificance.' However, the effect on influential opinion was decisive. 'My exhibition has been very successful from the prestige and financial point of view,' Rodin wrote. 'I should meet expenses. I have sold 200,000 francs' worth and I hope a little more.' He raised his prices to 40,000 francs for a bust – enough even for him, spendthrift though he was. When the exhibition finally closed the pavilion was dismantled and re-erected in the sculptor's new property at Meudon.

The only other feature to survive was the complex formed by the Grand Palais and the Petit Palais leading to the sumptuous new Pont Alexandre.

Rodin at work modelling one of his sculptures. Eugene Carrière's poster for the Rodin Pavilion, built as an annexe to the 1900 Exhibtion.

The rest disappeared, to become a memory of a century which had been as prolific in invention and achievement as any in the history of France, with a richness which turned only towards the end into vulgarity. The plaster picturesqueness of the colonial section below the Trocadéro, where Javanese nymphets (aided by Cléo de Mérode, celebrated dancer and courtesan) vied with devil dancers from Ceylon, Chinese violins, Spanish castanets, African drums and the wails of Algerian singers; the fanciful restaurants and fun-palaces; the Upside-Down Hall where chandeliers stuck up from the floor and furniture hung from the ceiling; the Swiss village with its mountains and waterfalls; the whole jamboree of official functions (there were 127 international congresses and in September 20,777 French mayors sat down together for a gigantic lunch); all faded away on the final day, 12 November.

Three hundred and sixty-nine thousand visitors had come to have a last look, and, as night fell, gathered on the Champs de Mars. 'Suddenly the cannon on the Eiffel Tower reverberated,' wrote a correspondent, 'repeating its death-knell every quarter of an hour, then the last explosion burst forth like a last lament: all the lights were extinguished and the drums ominously beat the retreat; it was all over and the crowd, gripped by an unconquerable emotion, roared "*Vive la France!*"'

Were they saluting the death of the nineteenth century or the birth of the twentieth? Visitors had been excited by the scientific marvels which seemed to herald an age of comfort and prosperity. Even international politics took on a sinister glamour. 'The engines of destruction used by the civilized nations are real gems,' wrote a Negro observer. 'Shells cut in two show what they are like inside; the bullets are arranged in the most orderly manner in compartments of polished copper. The cannons and machine guns are very clean, even luxurious.' The wonders of electric power were magnificently, and those of the combustion engine agreeably,

An artist's fantasy about the sophisticating effect of the Exhibition on simple visitors from the country. Denizens of the woods enjoy their version of the popular '*five o'clock*' tea.

ABOVE A *bateau-mouche* takes a party of visitors up the Seine past the Eiffel Tower, a survivor of the 1889 Exhibition, and a giant globe.

LEFT A general view of the Sculpture Hall in the Grand Palais. It was against these massive displays of well-publicized traditional art that the youthful rebels of Montmartre and Montparnasse had to pit their puny efforts.

suggested (though the aeroplane had still not replaced the popular balloon). In material terms the future could be clearly discerned.

Only the eye of hindsight, however, could detect traces of the way the
arts would develop. Architecturally the Exhibition was unadventurous
and undistinguished. The decorative arts established Art Nouveau as a
popular style but at the same time marked the beginning of its vulgariza-
tion and decline. The pullulating clusters of symbolic sculpture were uni-
formly mediocre. The painting exhibitions illustrated the achievements
of the past rather than potential for the future. The thirty-one-year-old
Henri Matisse, still unknown and poor, was employed to help his friend
Albert Marquet paint a decorative frieze round the ceiling of the Grand
Palais.

Meanwhile the foundations of twentieth-century art were being laid
elsewhere. The Salon had shown 1,379 pictures, ranging from Carl Rosa
and Bouguereau to Le Sénéschal de Kerdeoret and Miss Fanny Plimsoll,
but had included Braque's *Salome*. The most seminal painting exhibition,
though, was in Vollard's gallery – a retrospective show of the work of
Cézanne. At sixty-one a confirmed recluse in his home near Aix, Cézanne
had grown into a mysteriously powerful figure. 'The exhibition currently
at the Galerie Vollard excites the curiosity of painters and art lovers
about this enigmatic painter, solitary, nomadic, so superbly instinctive
that he seems among the men of today more like a legend,' wrote *La Revue
d'Art*. Like Rodin's, his artistic presence dominated his juniors. 'One
never sees him. He moves across the face of France. He wanders and
watches, sniffs, exposes his sensibility to the bewitching surprises of
nature, the radiant marvels of heaven. . . . The thirty canvases exhibited
chez Vollard are enough to make us love this robustly open and truthful
art.'

Two other exhibitions that year must have excited inquisitive young
painters. By some accident the entries of the forty-two-year-old Italian
sculptor Medardo Rosso arrived in Paris too late for inclusion in the
Décénnale Exhibition at the Grand Palais. In recompense his dealer
arranged a show at the Galerie Ségantini. Here Parisians could see for
the first time a collection of the strange Impressionist sculptures which
had so impressed Rodin. Rosso's *Bookmaker* of 1894, which was included
in the show, must have supported his claim that he had influenced the
great French sculptor in his conception of *Balzac*, which Rosso had seen
and admired at the 1898 Salon. A more obviously impressive exhibition
had taken place in April in the offices of the enterprising magazine *La
Revue Blanche* at 23 Boulevard des Italiens. For two weeks the secretary
of the magazine, Félix Fénéon, presented a generous selection of the work
of Georges Seurat. No collection of his paintings had been seen since
the retrospective included in the Salon des Indépendants of 1891, immediately after his death. On that occasion forty-six of his paintings and
drawings were exhibited, though none was sold; this time there were fifty
works, including the magisterial *A Summer Afternoon on La Grande Jatte*.
The sixteenth Salon des Indépendants, at 5 Rue du Colisée, did not take
place until mid-December and seems to have been a modest affair with
only 164 exhibits.

The old years were visibly passing. Ruskin had died in January in London – the twenty-nine-year-old Proust was moved to write a tribute to him. In August Nietzsche had died in the asylum in Weimar where he had lived for the last six years. Degas, aged sixty-six, was now practically blind and only rarely left his house in the Rue Victor Massé. Toulouse-Lautrec was temporarily out of hospital but manifestly approaching the end. And in a narrow street on the Left Bank another figure from the nineties made his exit.

Oscar Wilde, who had rung in the new year with a letter of thanks from Paris for his meagre weekly allowance, and had felt well enough to visit the Exhibition several times, was failing at last. Since his conviction for homosexuality five years before, and his two years in prison, he had allowed his health to go to seed through drink as he wandered about Europe. He had settled in Paris, where he was now living in the Hôtel d'Alsace. Towards the end of November he had fallen ill, probably with an abscess in the inner ear. On 29 October he got up and went to drink an absinthe in a café with his friend Robert Ross, who noticed that he suddenly looked older. Ross wrote later:

On 12 November I went to the Hôtel d'Alsace with Reggie [Turner] to say goodbye as I was leaving for the Riviera. . . . About 10.30 I got up to go. Suddenly Oscar asked Reggie and the nurse to leave the room for a minute as he wanted to say goodbye. He rambled at first about his debts in Paris and then he implored me not to go away. . . He broke into violent sobbing and said he would never see me again because he felt that everything was at an end.

He was right. On 28 November Ross and Turner slept at the hotel.

We were called twice by the nurse who thought Oscar was actually dying. About 5.30 in the morning a complete change came over him, the lines of the face altered and I believe what is called the death rattle began but I had never heard anything like it before; it sounded like the horrible turning of a crank. . . . From 1 o'clock we did not leave the room; the painful noise from the throat became louder and louder. Reggie and myself destroyed letters to keep ourselves from breaking down. . . . At 1.45 the time of his breathing altered. I went to the bedside and held his hand, his pulse began to flutter. He heaved a deep sigh, the only natural one I had heard since I arrived, the limbs seemed to stretch involuntarily, the breathing came fainter; he passed at 10 minutes to 2 pm exactly.

Next day the district doctor arrived after much signing of papers (Wilde had booked in under a false name; 'Dying in Paris is really very difficult and expensive for a foreigner,' complained Ross). The doctor asked if the dead man had committed suicide or been murdered. After a series of drinks and unsuitable jests and 'a liberal fee' he left, to be replaced by another official who asked how many collars Wilde had and the value of his umbrella. After the funeral at St-Germain des Prés the coffin was driven to a temporary grave at Bagneux, where it was to remain for nine years.

The jollifications of the Exhibition had half concealed a period of growing violence, international menace and social change. In July the French legation in Peking had been besieged by fanatical Chinese Nationalists. In August King Umberto I of Italy was assassinated. The Shah of Persia, one of the few royal visitors to the republican-sponsored Exhibition, had

Pablo Picasso: *Self-Portrait Arriving in Paris*, 1901 (Mrs E. Heywood-Lonsdale Collection). Picasso was nineteen when he made this drawing of himself arriving from Barcelona. He had paid a brief visit the previous year: this time he would stay.

a bomb thrown at him. In October there were two huge Socialist congresses in the Salle Wagram, and on almost the last day of the year the Socialist minister Jean Jaurès made a fiery speech at the première of Romain Rolland's *Danton* at the Théâtre Nouveau, dedicating the play to the working people of Paris.

But the germs of the new age were already sprouting in many different fields. In Vienna Sigmund Freud had just published his *Interpretation of Dreams*. In the *salon* of the Comtesse de Greffulhe Isadora Duncan gave one of the first of her recitals of modern dance. The twenty-nine-year-old poet Paul Valéry wrote to the thirty-eight-year-old Claude Debussy: 'Since Sunday I have been dreaming a little about dancing matters ....

In my opinion one must make the most lucid ballet in the world, one without a story, for it would convey only what legs and instruments permit.' In Banyuls Aristide Maillol abandoned weaving for sculpture. Guillaume Apollinaire wrote his first poem. André Derain, aged twenty, met Maurice de Vlaminck, aged twenty-two, in a train crash near Chatou outside Paris, and began a friendship which would blossom into the Fauve movement. The eighteen-year-old Georges Braque moved to Paris from Le Havre and entered an art school. From Barcelona in Spain arrived Julio Gonzales, and from the same city came a stocky nineteen-year-old with pitch-black eyes, knickerbockers, and a portfolio of drawings and ideas which were to overthrow the whole history of art. Earlier that year he had published his first drawing in a Barcelona periodical, *Juventad*. Rather hesitant and indecisive, the vision of a plump girl and her dream lover was signed 'P. Ruiz Picasso'. He had set out with his friend Carlos Casagemas – originally on his way to London – and they alighted in a studio which had belonged to a Catalan painter, Isidro Nonell. It was at 49 Rue Gabrielle, a narrow street on the steep slopes leading up to the new church of the Sacré Coeur. Picasso was not to desert either Paris or Montmartre until he had made his name irrevocably linked to theirs.

He did not stay long this time, but his visit was decisive. There was a small colony of Spanish painters in the district, and friends like Ricardo Canals and the exuberant sculptor Hugue Manolo (who liked to introduce his shy, youthful companion as his 'daughter') soon made Picasso at home in the cafés of La Butte. He painted several pictures of his new environment, adopting the style of Toulouse-Lautrec who had recorded the same scenes so often. He showed three bullfight paintings to Berthe Weill, known as 'La Merveille' (La Mère Weill), who ran a tiny gallery nearby. She offered him 100 francs for the three, and immediately sold them for 150 francs. Even more important, a Catalan industrialist and connoisseur called Manach happened to be in the gallery; seeing Picasso's work he offered him at once a contract for all the work he produced – 150 francs a month. This was a big step forward for the impoverished youth, giving him freedom. He made use of it straightaway. The last week of the year found him back in Spain. But he would return.

Pablo Picasso: *La Diseuse*, 1900–1 (Museo Picasso, Barcelona). One of Picasso's drawings of Montmartre music-hall artists made soon after his arrival in Paris. It is much in the style of Toulouse-Lautrec.

1901
Symbols and Salons

AN EVENT WHICH can be seen now to symbolize a fundamental change in international politics and social styles began the new year. On 23 January the news flashed across the new telephone cable between London and Paris that the eighty-two-year-old Queen Victoria – the seemingly unshakeable foundation-stone of half the royal courts of Europe and guardian of British power – was dead. In Paris grief was moderate in public and minimal in private. Anti-British feelings were strong; devastating caricatures of the Queen had appeared regularly in the comic papers, alongside reports of Boer successes in South Africa. The new king, Edward VII, was a different proposition. Already a familiar figure in Paris Jockey Club society, his affable, pleasure-loving personality was less alarming than that of the formidable little queen. Edward represented perfectly the character of the *belle époque* which had supplanted the uneasy languors of the *fin de siècle*.

But for a time a strange blend of the two moods persisted, colouring the last reflections of the Symbolist movement which, apparently so delicately ephemeral, was to linger on obstinately, turning up again later in the dreams of the Surrealists. The figure dominating the whole Symbolist approach was Gustave Moreau, who had died three years before, in 1898, at the age of seventy-two. Reclusive, outwardly conventional, single-minded, he had become a kind of counterpart to Cézanne, gaining the respect of his colleagues through his unworldly integrity and a kind of notoriety by the opulence and fantasy of the paintings which he showed in the Salon and at the Galerie Goupil. With a curious magic he blended many of the most preposterous accoutrements of the period – its omnivorous appetite for the exotic, its extravagance, its sentimentality – into visions infused by an elusive poetry. He believed he was carrying on the tradition of historical painting, but in fact he was moving into the rich, dark world of the subconscious. He became a cult among the rich and the eccentric – particularly after his sumptuous fantasies, which often resembled the hallucinations of an opium-smoker, were publicized in the wildly *fin-de-siècle* novel *A Rebours* by J.-K. Huysmans in 1884. This overtly decadent work complemented the Christian mysticism of Joséphine Péladan's *Le Vice Suprême*, published the same year; together they represented the two wings of the French Symbolist movement. Moreau himself lived a rigorously private and celibate life, and became the much

OPPOSITE Giovanni Boldini: *Young Woman Undressing*, c. 1900. The fashionable Italian painter, who had settled in Paris in 1892, gave his nudes and portraits a verve and fire which presaged the Futurists.

BELOW A cartoon in the comic paper *L'Assiette au Beurre* reveals the bitter hostility towards 'Shameless Albion' current in Paris. The French were solidly pro-Boer.

loved and brilliantly permissive head of the painting department at the Ecole des Beaux Arts where Marquet, Rouault and Matisse were among his pupils. 'Let him alone,' he had said on seeing Matisse's *Dessert* of 1897. 'His decanters stand steady and I can hang my hat on their stoppers.'

Moreau was curiously convinced of his own importance – when his health began to fail he arranged the rooms in his house as a museum and, in 1897, made his will, leaving the house and all its contents to the state, 'on the express understanding . . . that the collection shall always be kept together'. He died the following year, leaving in the house 800 unfinished paintings and sketches, 350 watercolours and nearly 5,000 drawings.

Moreau's death left the Ecole des Beaux Arts in some confusion. Matisse was asked to go; others, including Rouault, left of their own accord. 'At my very first exhibition in the Rue Laffitte,' wrote the dealer Vollard, 'I noticed a young man with a short red beard wearing a hooded cape adorned, by way of a clasp, with two large silver-plated balls. This, I was to learn, was Georges Rouault, favourite pupil of Gustave Moreau, who had said of him: "You can see he is a pupil of mine, he wears jewel-

The Symbolist writer J.-K. Huysmans (left), photographed in 1900 with some friends. Next to him is Dom Besse; the painter Georges Rouault is in the centre of the back row.

Henri Matisse: *Notre Dame*, 1900
(Tate Gallery, London).
A view of the cathedral painted
by Matisse from his attic studio
on the Quai St-Michel.

lery."' Rouault was to move towards the idealist wing of the group which
had grown up round Moreau, together with painters belonging to the
Catholic Rose-Croix movement; others, such as Matisse, Marquet, Manguin and Camoin, developed in a less mystical direction, preferring landscapes and still lifes. They were to carry art in the new direction of Fauve
painting, thus forming the next wave of avant-garde assault. But for the
moment it was the dreamy, spiritual visionaries who commanded most
attention.

The most striking of these was Odilon Redon, who had been a friend
of the Symbolist poet Mallarmé and was much admired by the literary
world. He did not deal with mythical or religious subjects, but created
nightmare visions, often conceived as illustrations for poetry. Unlike
many of the Symbolists, he was not interested in the occult or super-
natural: 'My dreaming stems from the visible,' he declared. But his dark,
alarming lithographs, usually connected only tenuously to their texts,
seemed to arise from some deeply disturbing unconscious (or 'soul', as
it was called then) and provided delicious thrills which Huysmans advertised in *A Rebours*.

Redon had had a one-man show at the Galerie Durand-Ruel in 1900, and this year he was given an exhibition at the Galerie Vollard called 'Mystical and Decorative Panels', which revealed a change of style, or at least of range. He seemed to be emerging from a secret and shadowy world into a luminous paradise filled with flowers and birds and patches of pure colour of jewelled brilliance. Now, at sixty-one, an established figure hospitably entertaining young admirers in his apartment in the Avenue Wagram, he was to abandon the illustrations which had won him such esteem in favour of decorative work – a genre which harked back to the murals of Puvis de Chavannes who had been one of the main sources of Symbolism, and also linked him with other Symbolist artists such as Maurice Denis.

Denis, like Redon, had been a regular visitor to Mallarmé's famous Tuesdays. Much influenced by Chavannes and Gauguin, he had joined with some fellow-pupils of the Ecole Juillard – Bonnard, Vuillard, Roussel and Sérusier – to form the Nabi group; opposed to the current Impressionist style, he was concerned not so much with nature as with 'representing it through plastic equivalents'. It was Denis who announced the theory in a statement which was to become historic: 'Remember that a picture – before being a war-horse, a nude woman or any other anecdote – is essentially a flat surface covered with colours assembled in a certain order.' Paradoxically this approach, while freeing colour from purely representational functions, led to a decorative style, ethereal in hue and harmonious in line, which lent itself particularly to mural decoration. Denis' variety of Symbolism was quite acceptable to the general public, and his personal intelligence and integrity made him a leader of the Symbolist movement.

While particularly admiring Gauguin, Denis joined with most young painters in venerating Cézanne, and this year he found a striking way of paying a tribute to both, as well as to some of his Nabi friends. On 6 June he received a letter from Cézanne: 'I have learned from an article in the Press of the gesture of artistic sympathy for me which you are exhibiting at the Salon National des Beaux Arts. Please accept my sincere thanks and convey them to the artists who are grouped around you.' Denis had painted a group of artists standing in Vollard's gallery in front of a Cézanne still life which Gauguin had bought in his stockbroking days; the artists were Redon, Bonnard, Vuillard, Roussel, Sérusier and Denis himself. Not surprisingly the picture was interpreted as an anti-establishment gesture and attracted attention. One of those who saw it was André Gide, currently in the throes of finishing his influential *L'Immoraliste*. He wrote at once to Denis – whom he had met at Mallarmé's parties – asking if the picture was for sale. It was, replied Denis, and the price was 4,500 francs (a large sum). 'Please consider me from today as a collector, and your temporary debtor,' requested Gide in his characteristically indirect style.

The misty, mysterious mood of the Symbolists crept into the work of apparently unsympathetic artists, such as Seurat, Rodin and Carrière. In March Carrière delivered a curious lecture at the Natural History Museum on 'Man as Visionary of Reality', in which he remarked that

Jean-Louis Forain: *Comtesse Anna de Noailles*, 1907. This flattering portrait of one of Paris's most dazzling poets and hostesses reflects the artist's outlook at this time. Soon afterwards he changed his attitudes, concentrating on savage cartoons attacking social and legal injustice. The Comtesse was by birth half-Romanian and half-Greek.

the skeletons of animals, beautiful as they were, 'lack the caprice, the deceptions of man's'.

Such delicately mystical works appealed greatly to the fashionable connoisseurs of sensitivity. The prince of them all was Marcel Proust, now thirty; conducted to a brothel this year for the first time by his friend Bertrand de Fénelon, he demanded blankets and a hot-water bottle. There were many others, mostly well-to-do, or at least socially acceptable, living around the aristocratic district of St-Germain. This was the society depicted by Helleu, Boldini and La Gandara. The painters themselves frequented the Café Voltaire and the basement of the Soleil d'Or in the Place St-Michel, or attended the artistic and literary parties given by publications like *La Plume*, the *Mercure de France*, *La Revue Contemporaine* and *La Revue Blanche*. Their patrons gathered in the *salons* of the Comtesse de Saint-Marceaux, Comtesse Caraman-Chimay, Madame Strauss – hostess to Réjane, Proust, Degas and the ubiquitous Jacques-Emile Blanche – and the poetess Comtesse Anna de Noailles ('I shall have been useless, but irreplaceable.'). They admired the incredible collection – fifty Renoirs, forty-seven Van Goghs, twenty-eight Cézannes,

The poet and dramatist Catulle Mendès, whose felicitous verse-plays were much admired. Jean Cocteau described him as 'part lion, part turbot'.

forty Monets, twelve Manets and eleven Degas – amassed by a young cavalry officer, the Prince de Wagram, before he was twenty-five. They would attend Lugné-Poé's Théâtre Libre, whisper gossip about the lesbian beauties Liane de Pougy and Cléo de Mérode, or listen to drawing-room concerts by Debussy, Fauré, Ravel or even the sixty-year-old Massenet. 'Come, Monsieur Massenet, play us something!' demanded the hostess (according to Léon Daudet) at an evening party.

... whereupon the composer of *Manon* began to hum 'Rututu, rututu' to a battered and bedizened old Jewess. Then, bounding up to the piano, he began to play a few chords, clutched his head declaring that he had a sudden migraine, engineered some entreaties, recovered, and finished by playing an 1830 polka, crying to the young girls, 'Dance, dance!'

The more esoteric disciples of the Symbolists often ventured into excesses of which their demi-gods would have disapproved – notably spiritualism and a belief in the occult which sometimes went so far as satanism, for exaggerated aestheticism turned easily into the cultivation of decadence. Discreet homosexuality was fashionable for both sexes.

To maintain any kind of ascendancy in these competitive circles a mixture of intelligence, push and charm was essential. All three were manifest in a minor poet whose social qualities were to earn him a second-hand celebrity as the model for two literary characters – Huysmans' des Esseintes and Proust's Baron de Charlus. Robert, Comte de Montesquiou was well-born, well-off and blessed with a quick wit, ambition and a genuine flair for spotting talent; he became a powerful arbiter of fashion among would-be patrons of the arts, was a passionate champion of Art Nouveau, and owned a tortoise set with jewels. He had been a friend and benefactor of Verlaine as well as an intimate of the more socially acceptable Mallarmé, Whistler and Fauré. A brother-in-law of the Duke of Padua, he was a dandy in the old style, cultivating what he called 'the pleasure of astounding and the satisfaction of never being astonished'. Demurely homosexual – he was too discriminating to become involved in the practices of some of his companions – and nattily attractive, his friendship had been courted by Mallarmé, Hérédia, Paul Bourget, Proust and the creepy Catulle Mendès (whom Cocteau described as 'part lion, part turbot'). He was one of those figures, half formidable and half ridiculous, who help to change a whole climate of taste by their example.

Robert de Montesquiou carried to extremes the Art Nouveau doctrine of extending a style into every corner of one's life and surroundings: he admitted that at his receptions the guests were only the most troublesome

Paris society had its own celebrities. One of them was the notoriously effete Jean Lorrain (ABOVE LEFT), here caricatured by Sem. The gentleman adjusting his white tie (ABOVE) is boasting to his valet, 'I lunched with Liane de Pougy, I shook hands with Rostand, and Mendès said "Good morning" to me ... I'm really somebody.' Liane de Pougy was a famous courtesan, Rostand was the most popular dramatist, and Mendès a highly esteemed poet.

A society lady walking her dog in the Bois, by the well-known photographer Lartigue.

part of the décor. In his Pavillon des Muses at Neuilly the library contained books specially bound for Edmond de Goncourt in Japanese silk, a copy of Montesquiou's own poems, *Les Paons*, with a cover designed by Lalique, a lock of Byron's hair, Baudelaire's drawing of the eyes of his mistress Jeanne, and a portrait of Beardsley by Sickert. On the first floor were the *salon des roses* and the *salon empire*. Oriental and Renaissance knick-knacks lay in profusion; the bathroom was dominated by a gigantic pink marble urn – 'a rose of joy opening in the tender air', as Anna de Noailles described it. Blue hydrangeas filled every corner.

This was the kind of ultra-precious interior caricatured in Huysmans description of the home of des Esseintes. Here Montesquiou composed his scented verses, entertained selected celebrities and carried on vigorous campaigns on behalf of his friends and against his many enemies. Among these was his only rival as aesthetic dictator, Jean Lorrain, whose outrageous exhibitionism and openly decadent tastes – drugs, sado-masochism, and aggressive homosexuality – horrified the inhibited and fastidious aesthetes like Montesquiou and Proust, who was driven to unexpectedly courageous action. 'Today', the composer Reynaldo Hahn confided to his diary, 'Marcel fought a duel with Jean Lorrain, who had written an odious article on him in *Le Journal*. He has shown a cool fortitude in the last three days which seems incompatible with his nervousness but which does not surprise me at all.' Lorrain's extravagances were condoned

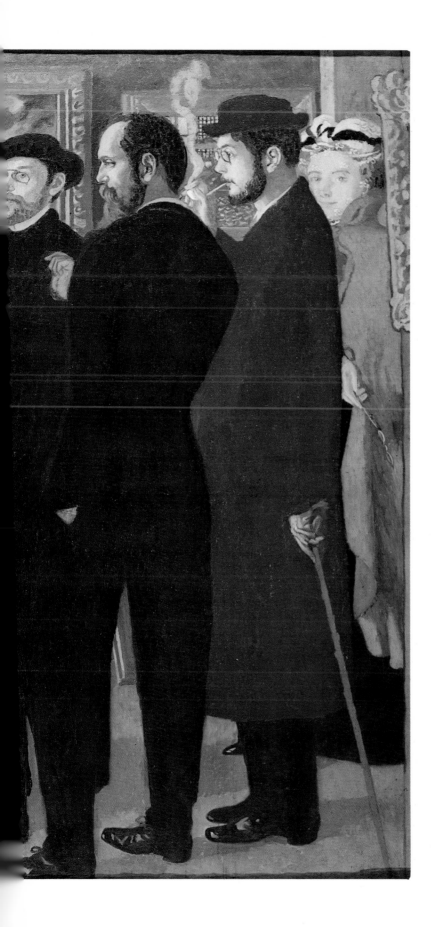

by friends like Sarah Bernhardt, who sailed through the scandals of the time like an unsinkable galleon; Yvette Guilbert, the popular music-hall star; and exotic, eccentric devotees of decadence such as the writer Pierre Loti and the actor Edouard de Max with his bevy of delicate young admirers (among them Jean Cocteau), and the largely homosexual clan who so enraged the right-wing Léon Daudet (but whose son Lucien was passionately admired by Proust and others). Lorrain left fierce descriptions of some of them, such as the painters Boldini: 'a louse not exempt from talent'; Helleu: 'dark, slim, frail and venomous'; and Jean Tissot: 'his conversation was an exquisite twilight'.

The extreme wing of the aesthetic set (which embraced both Symbolism and Art Nouveau enthusiasts) merged into less fanciful, more serious circles. There were the poetry readings under Bernhardt's patronage in her own theatre, where she would intone Victor Hugo while de Max read aloud from Baudelaire to fellow-poets like Cocteau and Catulle Mendès. At the Duchesse de Rohan's Tuesdays André Mauriac, Charles Péguy and Lucien Daudet would recite their own works. The masterful Princesse de Polignac (*née* Winnaretta Singer from New York) offered champagne and chamber music. There were lively evenings with the Comtesse de Noailles who had opinions of her own: 'One evening,' wrote Lucien Daudet,' after a dispute arising from a letter I had written to Jacques Maritain, the countess pursued me in a long nightgown brandishing a chair. She leaned over the banisters, crying: "It's perfectly simple. If God existed I would be the first to be told!"'

More serious still were the *soirées* organized by Madame Nathanson, director of *La Revue Blanche*, the monthly dinners of the by now rather scattered members of the Nabi group – Bonnard, Roussel, Maurice Denis and Edouard Vuillard – and the literary *salon* of Anatole France's mistress, Madame Arman de Caillavet. The last of these was attended by writers like the now silent Paul Valéry, Proust, Gide, Pierre Louÿs and Paul Fort, founder with Lugné-Poé of the Théâtre d'Art which had commissioned designs from Maurice Denis and Vuillard and put on Maeterlinck's Symbolist play *Pélléas et Mélisande*.

In February the eighty-eight-year-old Verdi died in Milan, and in the autumn a symbol of the nineties in Paris passed from view. Toulouse-Lautrec had been half-paralysed for months and on 9 September he died, aged only thirty-seven, in the arms of his mother in the south of France. His father wrote to the critic Maurice Joyant, ceding him all rights in his son's work. 'I have no intention of becoming converted to his art and publicly parading, now that he is dead, the work which I looked on as no more than daring studies. . . . You believed in his work more than I did and your judgment was right.'

The Symbolists did not monopolize the non-establishment art world; other currents were beginning to run, leading into the main stream. On 15 March 1901 the prestigious Galerie Bernheim-Jeune had opened a large retrospective exhibition of Van Gogh, who had died eleven years before. It made a tremendous impression on some of the young painters who went to see it, among them Derain and Vlaminck. They went back several times, excited by the dashing style and bold colours; on one of

OPPOSITE Pablo Picasso: *Seated Nude*, 1905 (Musée National d'Art Moderne, Paris). This sensitive nude is characteristic of the short 'Pink Period' in Picasso's early development – a wistful pause before he plunged into the rigorous disciplines of Cubism.

Pablo Picasso: *Self-Portrait*, 1903. (Apollinaire Collection). He was evidently trying out the fashionable droopy moustache.

their visits they found Matisse there. 'I saw Derain', Matisse wrote afterwards, 'accompanied by a young giant who was voicing his enthusiasm in authoritative tones and declaring that one must paint with pure vermilion, pure Veronese green and pure cobalt. Derain was a little afraid of him, I think, while admiring his ardour and enthusiasm.' The two young men asked Matisse to come down to Chatou to see their work. 'I was happy to find that there were young men with convictions similar to my own,' he wrote. He visited them again with his wife, called on Derain's parents, and convinced them that art was a respectable profession. Derain, in turn, had just met Othon Friesz. The Fauve movement had been born.

With railways making travel both easy and cheap, more and more aspiring young students were pouring into the acknowledged capital of the art world. From London came a brilliant young man called Gerald Kelly, well armed with introductions, who stayed at the relatively comfortable Hôtel de l'Univers et Portugal. He visited Monet at Giverny with the dealer Paul Durand-Ruel, and was unimpressed by his garden: 'Nice and large, it was covered with common rambling roses which you know you get, practically speaking, in any suburban garden all over England. And there was a little piece of water where there were some common or garden water lilies.' Kelly also met Manet ('frightfully handsome, huge beard, ever so tall and beautiful daughters, oodles of them'); Degas ('a funny little man, rather irritable'); and Maillol. The sculptor explained to him how he worked. ' "Sometimes I get lost. I call for Clothilde. She comes. What do I do?" And he stooped down and picked up her skirt, he just tranquilly raised it above her head and then you saw her legs, of a massive construction, covered with hand-knitted stockings. "Then I find the marble again." '

Meanwhile, outside the circle of dreaming artists and decadent dandies history was pressing in uncomfortably. From China came accounts of appalling atrocities committed in the Boxer Rebellion; photographs of beheadings and mutilation in *L'Illustration* made macabre subjects of discussion in the fashionable *salon*s. President McKinley was assassinated in America. A child was killed by a competitor in a motor race, resulting in a rule forbidding such contests on the open road now that cars could attain 100 kilometres an hour. The airship belonging to the indomitable Santos-Dumont, trying for a prize, collapsed on a house near the Trocadéro, and two months later another fell into the Baron de Rothschild's lake. In an effort to cement Franco-Russian relations the Tsar and Tsarina paid a visit, accepting bread and salt at Dunkirk after a rough sea-passage. The right-wing Dreyfusards were defeated in the elections, and the new Premier, Emile Combes, began a vigorous anti-clerical policy which included the seizure of all church property. A new game, ping-pong, arrived in Paris from across the Channel.

Invisible still in the humming swarms of the French capital, the young men who were to overturn the old artistic order were taking up their positions. Matisse exhibited his first painting in public at the Salon des Indépendants, a big show this year, with a thousand exhibits including Cézanne, Bonnard and the gentle Henri Rousseau, who had just moved into his last apartment at 2 *bis*, Rue Perrel. Fernand Léger, aged twenty, enrolled at the Ecole des Beaux Arts, and Picasso was back in Paris. He had returned from Spain in the spring with an armful of pictures and taken a room at 130 Boulevard de Clichy in Montmartre. When his patron, Manach, took him along to Vollard's gallery he already had a hundred paintings to show. Vollard was instantly impressed by the talent of the twenty-year-old youth, 'dressed with the most studied elegance', and offered him an exhibition. It opened on 24 June, but had no success. It did, though, attract the first favourable – indeed enthusiastic – review, from the critic of the *Gazette d'Art*, Félicien Fagus:

Picasso is a painter, absolutely and beautifully. Like all pure painters he adores colour in itself and to him each substance has its own colour. Also he is in love with every subject and to him everything is a subject.... Danger lies for him in this very impetuosity which can easily lead him to a facile virtuosity. The prolific and the fecund are two different things, like violence and energy. This would be much to be regretted since we are in the presence of such brilliant virility.

The paintings did indeed already display Picasso's gift of inspired borrowing from the discoveries of other painters; his portraits, cabaret scenes, nudes and racecourse scenes echoed those of his colleagues. But before he returned to Spain again after six months, a new personal note crept into his work, which perhaps began to be influenced by the Symbolist imagery which he saw all around him in Paris and which was to set the key of his painting in the next few years. A close friend, Carlos Casagemas, had recently shot himself in a Paris café. Picasso was deeply disturbed and, in the autumn of 1901, he began work on a large allegorical canvas in which grieving figures surround a rider on a white horse above a corpse. The mood of melancholy compassion was far removed from his previous exuberant canvases and from the idyllic never-never land nostalgia of the majority of Parisian Symbolists. The image of Paris as a good-time city, the home of fashion, fun and refined feelings was fading. A change was in the air.

Henri de Toulouse-Lautrec: *Cocyte in 'La Belle Hélène'*, 1900 (Musée Toulouse-Lautrec, Albi). This drawing of a singer in Offenbach's operetta was one of the last drawings made by Toulouse-Lautrec.

1902
Exotic Flowering

THE NEW YEAR OPENED HOPEFULLY. On the home front President Loubet was observed to shake the hand of the arch-champion of the violently oppositional Boulangists, the Duchesse d'Eze, at the opening of a Salon of Women Artists – in itself a sign of the times – of which she was President. And abroad, the death of the unpopular Cecil Rhodes in South Africa was greeted with gloating detail – an event soon to be followed by the declaration of peace between the British and the Boers. Friendship with Britain – much to be desired on strategic grounds – was becoming possible, and in April the King, Edward VII, was observed by a French correspondent to be 'much superior to his reputation as a *bon vivant* and a jolly companion. He is tidy, punctual and incapable of an incorrectitude.' The Shah of Persia and the King of Portugal boosted official confidence with visits, President Loubet went off on a return trip to Russia, and at home the anti-Dreyfus group was soundly defeated at the elections.

The big artistic event of the spring was the première of Debussy's opera *Pélléas et Mélisande*. In 1892 Debussy had bought a copy of Maeterlinck's Symbolist play at a bookstall on the *quais* and, encouraged by his friend Erik Satie, decided to set it to music. Already in 1901 it had been accepted for the Opéra Comique by the director, Albert Carré, supported by the composer André Messager. It was arranged to mount it the next year, but some patriotic doubters began a muttering campaign, pointing out that the libretto was by a Belgian and the proposed designer was a German. Then, on 14 April, just two weeks before the opening, the venture suffered a serious blow. *Le Figaro* published a letter from Maeterlinck, dissociating himself from the new version, which he found strange and hostile. 'From now on it is in the hands of the enemy,' he declared, and concluded with the hope that it would be 'a resounding flop'.

The reason for Maeterlinck's rage was not so much artistic as personal. Instead of choosing for his heroine the singer who was Maeterlinck's mistress, Debussy had picked the Scottish-American star Mary Garden. Maeterlinck worked himself into such a fury that he ended by challenging Debussy to a duel. But the drama blew itself out. According to the (unreliable) evidence of Maeterlinck's mistress, the poet merely advanced upon the composer brandishing a walking-stick, whereupon Debussy collapsed and had to be revived with smelling salts.

OPPOSITE Poster for the 1902 dramatic adaptation of Colette's novel *Claudine in Paris*, ostensibly by her husband 'Willy' (Henri Gauthier-Villars). The real author was much amused to see herself portrayed in the uniform of a schoolgirl.

Claude Debussy, composer
of *Pélléas et Mélisande*.

A typical cartoon by Steinlen,
who championed the Parisian
poor. 'What have they done?'
asks the girl.
'Slept – without paying.'

Finally, on 28 April, the opera had its dress rehearsal – to the mocking accompaniment of touts hawking parodies of the text outside the theatre – and two days later the curtain rose on the first performance. The opera's reception was decidedly unenthusiastic. It was described as 'morbid and spineless'; one writer compared the music to the sound of a squeaking door, while others poked fun at Mary Garden's accent. But Colette's husband, Willy, evoked the Impressionists in a favourable review, and Debussy's colleagues Paul Dukas and Vincent d'Indy both praised it, though Gabriel Fauré did not. The opera was given fourteen performances during the next few months, and there was even talk of reviving it with a woman in the part of the hero. Debussy received an official decoration but it did not make him pompous. Soon afterwards he was writing to the twenty-seven-year-old Maurice Ravel, who had just composed his Quartet and heard it severely criticized by Fauré: 'In the name of all the gods don't alter a note of what you have written.'

Pélléas was the last important bloom in the exotic garden devised by the Symbolists as a refuge from a society in which the beefy pleasures of the middle class were offset by the miseries of the proletariat. One of the great witnesses to the seamy realities of Parisian life died in October. André Antoine – who had been producing a play derived from Zola's novel *Earth* in January – heard the news in his theatre. 'On arriving, one of the stage hands called out to me: "Zola is dead!" .... After returning from Meudon he had woken up in the night feeling ill and jumped out of bed; his wife, also ill, heard him fall down but did not go to his assistance .... Fumes of carbonic acid, apparently issuing from a nearby stove, had passed through the wall and asphyxiated them.' Madame Zola was

saved by remaining on her high bed, but the writer died. A few days later Antoine was recording: 'Zola's funeral this morning. A fear of riots at the Montparnasse cemetery. Anatole France delivers a magnificent oration, calling Zola "the incarnation of a moment in the movement of the human conscience".' Dreyfus, whom Zola had championed so bravely, was among the crowds but withdrew discreetly before the service was over, avoiding the clash between the police and anti-semetic gangs.

The big event of the year in the arts was the retrospective devoted to Toulouse-Lautrec in the Salon des Indépendants in May, concurrently with an even bigger show containing two hundred paintings at the Galerie Durand-Ruel, arranged by his friend Joyant, and with a tribute by the critic Arsène Alexandre. Offered a choice of all the paintings after the exhibition closed, the Luxembourg Museum accepted one, *Woman in a Feather Boa.*

Motoring was popular but roads were dusty. L. Sabattier's impression of a Sunday afternoon at the entrance to the bridge of Suresnes.

ABOVE Henri Matisse: *Studio under the Eaves*, 1902 (Fitzwilliam Museum, Cambridge). Though giving magnificent views over the Seine, the little attic on the Quai St-Michel was often so cold that the painter had to work in overcoat and hat.

OPPOSITE Albert Marquet: *Matisse Painting*, 1904–5 (Musée National d'Art Moderne, Paris). If it was cold for the painter, it must have been considerably worse for the model.

A fellow exhibitor at the Indépendants, showing in public for the first time, was Georges Rouault, now just beginning to change his style, and turning to savage studies of prostitutes and clowns in place of the Symbolist biblical visions he had derived from Moreau. Paradoxically, the change came just as he was appointed as the first curator of the Moreau Museum. After much hesitation, Moreau's gift had finally been accepted by the state, which was nervous of creating a dangerous precedent; thus it became the first private museum in France.

The appointment at least gave Rouault financial security, which was rare among his companions. Even Matisse, who was now thirty-three, found life so difficult that, after a show with Marquet at the Galerie Weill, he had to withdraw to live for a time with his parents in the country. Braque was called up to do his military service. Maurice Utrillo, poorer than any and already an alcoholic, was painting his first impressions of Montmartre as a kind of remedial exercise. On the other side of Paris an almost equally ragged young twenty-two-year-old, Jacob Epstein, arrived from New York and moved into a humble studio behind the Gare Montparnasse. He briefly joined the Ecole des Beaux Arts, but spent his time eagerly drinking in his first impressions of Europe; he listened to Paderewski playing the piano, watched Richard Strauss conduct, and was permanently impressed by the Egyptian rooms at the Louvre.

A little further to the south more portentous projects were being plotted. One evening there were three knocks on the door of a modest apartment near the Parc Montsouris; it was opened by a bald young man

OPPOSITE The actress Polaire in her schoolgirl's costume as heroine of the play *Claudine at School*. The reputed author, 'Willy', used to parade her and his wife, Colette (BELOW), dressed up as twins.

EXPRESS DETECTIVE NADAR, PARIS.

with dark, oriental eyes. The tenant was Lenin and his visitor was Trotsky, on his way to London. 'It is like Odessa – but Odessa is better,' was Trotsky's first impression of Paris. He and Lenin went out together and sat in the top gallery of the Opéra Comique, with Trotsky squeezed painfully into a pair of Lenin's shoes, and Lenin clutching his inseparable briefcase.

But the twentieth century and the nineteenth still overlapped. In October a young Pole was killed at Viroflay in a pistol duel with his closest friend, and in November two Deputies were clashing swords ostentatiously in front of the cameras at Neuilly; while at Montreuil Georges Méliès was making a film of men landing on the moon. The wily Willy joined with Lugné-Poé in a stage presentation of Colette's *Claudine in Paris*, parading the star, Mademoiselle Polaire, in public 'dressed up as a boyish twin' to the author. In July the campanile in Venice collapsed punctually, according to scientific calculations.

The state reception for Tsar Nicholas II and the Tsarina on their visit to Paris. Close relations with Russia were important, both militarily and financially. Much French money was invested in that country.

1903
Faces of Poverty

UP TO THIS TIME writers and musicians had played at least as prominent a part as painters in the artistic life of Paris. Symbolism and the Nabi approach were very much a literary movement – a reaction to the Impressionists' cult of the innocent eye, while Art Nouveau expressly spread its influence over every field. From now on, however, painting became the dominant art.

One particular change became evident. In recent years artistic Paris had been shaped by relatively affluent circles. The Impressionists had mostly been comfortably off; their successors in the Salon were positively rich, and even the serious-minded Symbolists tended to move in respectable social circles. Now the young were to take over, and even when they grew older they would not adopt bourgeois fashions or appear in the smart *salons*. The first wave of impoverished young men who were to transform the whole face of art was beginning to arrive.

One of these down-at-heel foreigners was, in fact, a writer. James Joyce, aged twenty, had left Dublin at the end of 1902 and moved into the Grand Hôtel Corneille, next to the Théâtre de l'Odéon. On 2 February 1903 he wrote to his mother in Ireland:

Dear Mother, Your order for 3s 4d of Tuesday last was very welcome as I had been without food for 42 hours. Today I am twenty hours without food. But these spells of fasting are common with me now and when I get money I am so damnably hungry that I eat a fortune (1/–) before you could say knife. . . . If I had money I could buy a little oil stove (I have a lamp) and cook macaroni for myself with bread when I am hard beat. . . . I hope the carpet that was sold was not one of the new purchases that you are selling to feed me. If this is so, sell no more or I'll send the money back to you by return of post. . . . With the utmost stretching your last order will keep me until Monday midday (postage half a franc probably) – then, I suppose, I must do another fast. I regret this as Monday and Tuesday are carnival days and I shall be the only one starving in Paris. Jim.

Two months later he was to receive a telegram: 'Mother dying come home father.' He borrowed three pounds and took the boat-train for Ireland. His dream of fame in Paris was over.

Over on the other side of the city another young visionary was eking out an almost equally precarious existence. Max Jacob, a young poet, painter and art critic born in Brittany of Jewish parents, had moved up

OPPOSITE Pablo Picasso: *Life*, 1903 (Grand Palais, Paris). Painted soon after a visit to Barcelona, the picture combines Symbolist overtones with a new sympathy towards the miseries of the poor, typical of what was to be christened his 'Blue Period'.

59

to Paris and taken a room in Montmartre. He had visited Picasso's first exhibition at the Galerie Vollard, and had liked it enough to leave a note expressing his admiration. Within hours he had received from Manach an invitation to visit the painter. Jacob wrote:

Already this first day we felt a great sympathy for each other. He was surrounded by a swarm of poor Spanish painters who sat on the floor eating and chatting. He painted two or three pictures a day, wore a top hat like me, and spent his evenings in the *coulisses* of the music-halls drawing portraits of the stars.... He talked very little French and I no Spanish but we shook hands.

While away in Barcelona in the summer of 1902 Picasso had written affectionately to his new French friend, and shortly after his return to Paris he moved in to share Jacob's apartment in the Boulevard Voltaire in the eastern industrial district. There was only one bed. Jacob slept on it at night while Picasso painted; Picasso used it by day while Jacob worked as a shop assistant. Six months later Picasso was writing from Spain: 'I think of the room in the Boulevard Voltaire, of the omelettes, the beans and the fried potatoes and I think also of those days of poverty and I become sad.' It was all a long way from the refinements of the Symbolists and their exquisite admirers.

Whistler died this year in London, and Gauguin, a few weeks after being condemned to three months' imprisonment for libelling a policeman, died in the Marquesas, aged fifty-five. The Gustave Moreau Museum opened and proved a flop. Degas found it so depressing that he changed his mind about leaving his own studio to the state. *La Revue Blanche*, principal mouthpiece of the Symbolists, went bankrupt.

On 20 March the nineteenth exhibition of the Société des Artistes Indépendants opened at the Cours-la-Reine. It was a huge affair, containing three landscapes by Matisse, who had deserted the Salon for this more congenial company, where he was now showing for the third time. He had also completed his first sculpture, *The Slave*; when he showed it to Rodin, the great man rebuffed him by suggesting that he should 'fuss' over the piece a little more. There were also paintings by the two friends Derain and Vlaminck; by Albert Marquet, Matisse's companion; and by Henri Manguin and Charles Camoin. All were to join soon in the Fauve movement, and in fact in May this year the Galerie Weill showed what amounted to the first show by this group – a collection of drawings and pastels by eleven artists.

A more immediately important collection opened later in the year, the first of the immensely influential Salons d'Automne. Its founder was the architect and writer Fritz Jourdain, who had designed the shop La Samaritaine and the pedestal for Rodin's *Balzac*. Jourdain, who was to remain President of this Salon until its disappearance in 1925, had been considering the idea ever since the Universal Exhibition. He recorded:

One morning I went to the Rue de Valois to ask from the state the use of the Galerie des Machines, which the vandals had not yet sold off to the scrapyard and which was unoccupied.... Becoming very red in the face, the Director of Fine Arts [Roujon] told me drily that in his opinion there were already two

Salons too many and that he would formally oppose the organization of any new group. . . .

Two or three years later I received, to my great surprise, a visit from Yvanhoé Rambosson, the distinguished poet and keeper of the Petit Palais, whom I hardly knew. He outlined to me with warm and generous enthusiasm the project for a lively, ingenious and bold artistic organization about which he wished to have my opinion, and he very kindly offered me the position of President of the new Salon. . . . I agreed to take on the control of this major gallery . . . and I launched myself into the unknown.

Jourdain had as honorary Presidents the prestigious Eugène Carrière and the respected Salon painter Albert Besnard. The Secretary-General was Georges Lopisgish, himself an artist; and there were ninety-one founder members including the painter Jules Chéret, the writer J.-K. Huysmans, and the Belgian poet Emile Verhaeren.

The first exhibition took place in the basement of the Petit Palais, with a grand opening graced by smart society in white ties and tails; Proust,

Pablo Picasso: *Two Women Seated at a Bar*, 1902 (Walter Chrysler Collection, New York). Poverty and dejection are conveyed in this picture, whose strong outlines and full, sinuous forms recall some of Gauguin's paintings. Though his work at this time was consistently sad, Picasso himself remained lively, cheerful and mischievous.

The death of Queen Victoria and
the succession of Edward VII,
already well known in Paris as
the pleasure-loving Prince of
Wales, facilitated a new
rapprochement between France
and Britain. It was celebrated
by a state visit in 1903.
The Rue Castiglione is seen here
decorated for the occasion.

Jean Lorrain and Léon Blum rubbed shoulders with the Comtesse de Noailles and important critics like Louis Vauxcelles, Roger Marx, Camille Mauclair and Arsène Alexandre. As a kernel the exhibition contained a small 'Homage to Gauguin', including four landscapes, three genre studies and a self-portrait. There were 990 exhibits comprising paintings, drawings, sculpture, architecture and the decorative arts, and it was all a decided success. Jourdain was an able and articulate organizer and the new institution offered a more coherent group than the Indépendants with their free-entry system, and a more lively one than the establishment Salons. But it was not greeted with delight everywhere. In the *Mercure de France* Charles Morice, champion of the Symbolists, found it confused and superfluous:

In order that people should not be able to claim they were condemned to silence, they are allowed to talk all at the same time. . . . If art is no longer to be confined to one month in the year, there is no sound reason to refuse it the whole year. After the 'Autumn Salon' we shall be having the 'Winter Salon' . . . and finally the 'Summer Salon'!

He defined the exhibition as 'advanced but correct, something like the Indépendants without the good Monsieur Henri Rousseau'. He picked out for praise the Gauguin group and pictures by Carrière and Gustave Moreau – the last obviously a posthumous entry.

The year 1903, which had opened with the usual stories of trouble in the Balkans – in February the papers were full of pictures of bloody massacres in Macedonia – saw the beginning of the important drawing together of France and Britain in the face of Germany's growing power. In May Edward VII arrived in Paris on a state visit and received a warm welcome from crowds who seemed by now to have forgotten the sufferings of the Boers. His popularity must have cheered the hearts of three English witnesses – Gerald Kelly, who had now spent two years in Paris; Somerset Maugham, who had been born there twenty-nine years before; and the young Arnold Bennett, who had arrived in March and described the scene enthusiastically: 'Hat-waving. Cries of "*Edouard! Edouard!*" Then the breaking of the line of *gendarmes* and a huge hum of excited conversation. It was all over in thirty seconds, but the symbol and figure of the Majesty of England had passed by!'

Debussy was in London and, in April, filed reviews of *Parsifal* and *The Ring* at Covent Garden for *Gil Blas* – he was temporarily music critic both of that magazine and of *La Revue Blanche*. He found Amfortas a 'melancholy Knight of the Grail who whines like a shop-girl and whimpers like a baby', while Kundry seemed to him 'a sentimental draggle-tail', yet he considered *Parsifal* 'one of the most beautiful monuments ever raised to music'. *The Ring* bowled him over; 'It is difficult', he wrote, 'to imagine the effect made on even the toughest mind by the four evenings of *The Ring*. Wagner, if one may express oneself with some of the grandiloquence which belongs to him, was a beautiful sunset which was mistaken for a dawn.'

Musical life in Paris was less serious. In a neighbouring column in *Gil Blas* 'Claudine' (alias Colette) remarked of Beethoven's *Missa Solemnis*, 'To believe in God like that for thirty-five minutes without snoring is too much for my mediocre faith.' The eccentric and impoverished Erik Satie had just moved all his belongings to an apartment in the suburb of Arcueil-Cochan, pushing them in a wheelbarrow. He was supporting himself by writing songs for the music-hall, and this year finished a short work in seven movements which he chose to call *Three Pieces in the Form of a Pear*.

Another eccentric was entrenching himself in Paris – the Polish-Italian writer Guillaume Apollinaire, whose real name was Wilhelm Kostrowitsky. He had arrived in Paris the year before, aged twenty-two, having left his mother's comfortable villa at Vesinet, and moved into an apartment in the Rue Henner in Montmartre where he began to hold weekly receptions. He was a brilliant talker and an inventive poet, but he was also neurotically mean and fussy – woe betide the visitor who sat on his bed. In this year he wrote a peculiar work called *Le Jim-Jim-Jim des Capussins*, and in the preface used the prophetic adjective '*sur-réel*'. In October he founded his own magazine, *Le Festin d'Esope*; the first number contained a curious article on the modern orchestra, in which the French Romain Rolland appeared alongside the British critics Ernest Newman and Edward Dent.

Apollinaire himself contributed gossip notes on Isadora Duncan, who had just given a recital at the Théâtre Sarah Bernhardt supported by her whole family. There were titters at her unaccompanied dances. 'Miss Duncan danced a lot and talked even more,' wrote the critic of *La Revue Illustrée*. 'Since she tells us so much, why did she not tell us that Loie Fuller was her teacher, from whom she learned these tragic Botticelli poses, these da Vinci cadences and Pausippa manners?' This autumn, in New York, Loie Fuller was exhibiting her huge private collection of sculpture by Rodin – his first one-man show in America. But in Paris an apparently trivial event had just taken place which was to pass into the history books: a tiny café in Montmartre was taken over by a bar-keeper called Frédéric Gérard.

Isadora Duncan, the American dancer, made her début in Europe first at private parties, then in large theatres in Paris.

1904
The Montmartre Mob

FOR THE NEXT SIX YEARS Montmartre was to become the dynamo charging the revolution which overturned the whole European art world, and Frédé's café was its core. It stood at the junction of the Rue St-Vincent and the Rue des Saules, on the steep northern slopes of La Butte – the little hill which had recently been crowned with the dazzling white dome of the church of the Sacré Coeur. Known as the Cabinet des Assassins because of the ferocious murals that decorated its walls, the café – a haunt of local artists and writers for many years – was not prospering and in 1903 was in danger of being demolished. The famous cabaret singer Aristide Bruant, for whom Toulouse-Lautrec had designed posters, bought it for sentimental reasons and leased it to the ex-proprietor of a little night-club called the Zut. The comic artist André Gill drew a sign for it representing a rabbit dancing in a frying pan, an animal soon christened the *lapin à Gill*; in no time the café's nickname changed to the Lapin Agile, a title which was to become famous in art history through the records of the writers who gathered in its cluttered inner room or sat around the wooden tables outside – Francis Carco, André Salmon, Roland Dorgelès and Pierre MacOrlan.

The precipitous slopes of Montmartre had been a feature of Paris for centuries, the rough common land broken by quarries, vineyards, little houses and gardens, and dotted with windmills such as the Moulin de la Galette, which appear in countless paintings of this period. In the nineteenth century the rustic charms of the district had appealed strongly to the bohemian students of the Romantic movement, who found there attractions of the kind symbolized by Musset's sentimental seamstress Mimi Pinson. It became as well known for its entertainments as for its healthy air and superb views over the city. By the beginning of the twentieth century the lower slopes had already been taken over by city night-life. Around the Place Pigalle the streets were filled with dance-halls like the Moulin de la Galette and the Moulin Rouge, night-clubs, *café-concerts* like the Chat Noir with its silhouette shows, and, inevitably, prostitutes. In 1892 there were fifty-nine brothels in the district; by 1900 they had increased to 127, each with its characteristic large, illuminated street number. Some of them were expensively fitted out, like the Chabanas which boasted 'the prettiest torture chamber in Paris'. But few revellers climbed the steep steps to the summit, which remained a quiet little

OPPOSITE The modest inn sign painted by the caricaturist André Gill, which gave its name to the Montmartre café frequented by Picasso and his friends. The *lapin à Gill* soon turned into the Lapin Agile.

Montmartre at the time of
the birth of Cubism. It was in
these humble surroundings that
the revolution which was to
overturn the whole art scene
of the modern world was born.
OPPOSITE ABOVE The slopes of
La Butte crowned by the Moulin
de la Galette.
OPPOSITE BELOW The Moulin de
la Galette dance-hall (hats
appear to be obligatory).
ABOVE A street market in
the Rue Lepic. RIGHT The Rue
Laffitte, running up to the
foot of La Butte, and
containing the galleries where
the Montmartre artists hoped
to show their pictures.

OPPOSITE Two aspects of
13 Rue Ravignan, the cluster
of artists' studios known as
the Bateau-Lavoir.
ABOVE The northern slopes of
La Butte, c. 1906, still covered
with vines and vegetables,
showing the studios on the right
and the dome of the Sacré Cœur
beyond. BELOW The single-storey
façade giving on to the Place
Emile Goudeau. The old wooden
building was burnt down in 1970,
but the front wall survives.

tumbledown village, while the northern slopes were still half wild. Rooms were cheap, if uncomfortable, and a kind of sheltered intimacy easy. The amenities of the big city were not far away; the galleries in the Rue Laffitte were just at the bottom of the hill. It was a perfect haven for poor but hard-working young artists.

Most of them could be found in the evenings at the Lapin Agile, and many came from a group of studios nearby, at 13 Rue Ravignan. It was a big, lopsided, wooden structure with a low frontage which opened on to a tiny, sloping square, the Place Emile Goudeau. The studios were not all of the same size, and some of the rooms were occupied by simple artisans and tradesmen, but all were equally austere, without electricity or water – a tap in the courtyard served the whole building. Rents were around 450 francs a year. The dealer Daniel-Henry Kahnweiler wrote a few years later:

I often used to climb up to No. 13 Rue Ravignan . . . to the little sloping square planted with trees . . . the curious wooden structure which was variously nicknamed the Trapper's Hut or the Laundry Boat [le bateau-lavoir]. . . . The door was always open – the concierge lived in the house next door – and one went downstairs to reach the inhabitants of any but the two studios which faced the square. For the house, which hung on the sheer side of the hill of Montmartre, was entered by its upper storey.

The most lively of the artist tenants was Picasso, who had returned to Paris in April 1904, this time for good. He sent several cases of pictures ahead, borrowed some money from the dealer Durand-Ruel immediately on arrival, and settled into a studio in the Bateau-Lavoir. Its furnishings were simple, wrote the girl who soon moved in with him, Fernande Olivier:

. . . a mattress on four legs in one corner. A little rusty cast-iron stove with a yellow earthenware bowl on it which was used for washing; a towel and a piece of soap were on a white table next to it. In another corner, a poor little black trunk made a rather uncomfortable seat. A wicker chair, easels, canvases of all sizes, tubes of paint scattered around the floor . . . no curtains. In the table drawer there was a tame white mouse, which Picasso looked after lovingly and would show to everybody.

Picasso had probably heard of the studios through one of the Spanish artists in Paris. They had been popular among young artists for some time. A young Dutch artist from Rotterdam, Kees Van Dongen, had moved in four years before and quickly acquired a girlfriend and a child. There were several other Spaniards in the neighbourhood; they were mostly poor, but none poorer than Picasso, whom they sometimes helped by bringing presents of a loaf of bread, a tin of sardines or some wine. Picasso's studio was often filled with friends – poets rather than painters, though Picasso was never seen reading a book. Among the most faithful was the bald, nervous Max Jacob, who now lived nearby with a young poet but was equally fond of Picasso. Jacob's own apartment was dark and bare, the walls decorated with the signs of the zodiac in green chalk (he told fortunes for money), and it smelt of ether, to which he was addicted.

RIGHT Picasso in 1904.

BELOW Pablo Picasso: *Portrait of Max Jacob*, 1904 (Marcel Lecomte Collection). A sketch made in a café in the Boulevard de Clichy.

FOOT OF PAGE Max Jacob: *Pablo Picasso*, c. 1904 (Modern Art Foundation, Geneva). This sketch was made by Jacob in the Place Pigalle.

'How little money we needed then!' wrote Fernande Olivier later, 'when fifty francs could last a month. . . . The shopkeepers of the quarter were trusting and prepared to open accounts which ran into formidable amounts; fifteen or twenty francs, which we often found difficult to pay.' Sometimes they had recourse to deception. 'We would order a lunch at the shop in the Place des Abbesses asking them to deliver it exactly at midday. At midday the delivery boy would arrive, knock in vain and finally leave his basket at the door, which would be opened as soon as he had left. We would pay several days later, when we had the money.' The money came from selling drawings for a few francs to local junk dealers like Sagot or Soulier.

Another friend who became a regular visitor at the Bateau-Lavoir at this time was Guillaume Apollinaire, whom Picasso had met in a café near the Gare St-Lazare and who loved to join in the nocturnal excursions of the 'Picasso gang'. 'They would come back at night frequently drunk,'

Fernande Olivier recalled, 'shouting, abusing one another, singing and declaiming in the little square. . . . They would wake up the neighbours with revolver shots: Picasso had a mania for this. He always carried a Browning.' She first met Apollinaire after one of these outings.

[He] was dressed in a suit of heavy beige English cloth of which he was particularly fond. His coarse straw boater seemed too small for his skull. He had a rather pear-shaped head, the features pointed, kindly and distinguished, with small eyes very close to his long, thin hook of a nose and eyebrows like commas. He would deliberately purse his lips to make an already diminutive mouth smaller, as if to give bite to what he was saying. He possessed a mixture of nobility and a sort of vulgarity, which came out in his crude, childish laugh. His hands were the hands of an unctuous, gesturing priest. . . . All this was disguised and softened by a charming, childlike quality, which made him seem calm, serious and tender so that one listened confidently to him when he talked – and talk he certainly did.

Imaginative and perceptive, a free-flying poet, Apollinaire was to be the first to write a book on the Cubists. Some of his literary activities at this time, however, were rather obscure – he referred to them as 'mysteries', but actually they were introductions to pornographic books. One day he challenged a fellow-writer to a duel – the journalist had rashly compared Apollinaire to Apollinaris soda water at a banquet – and called on Picasso and Max Jacob to be his seconds. The affair was settled amicably but Jacob sent in a bill for his services:

9 am: coffee for 2nd witness 10 fr.
10 am: one box matches for 2nd witness who had left his at home 10 fr.
11 am: bread for 2nd witness who had not yet breakfasted .05 fr.
12 midday: morning paper for 2nd witness who was getting bored .05 fr.
5 pm: 2nd witness offers coffee to 1st witness 1.20 fr.
Apéritif to enemy to reduce his martial ardour. . . .

Another frequent but irregular guest at the uproarious evenings when the bearded Frédé would entertain his guests by singing to a guitar was the twenty-one-year-old Maurice Utrillo – 'Monsieur Maurice', as he liked to be called. After a chaotic childhood he was already an alcoholic. His mother was Suzanne Valadon, a circus performer who had become a model for Degas and Renoir and taken up painting on her own. His parents did not marry, and until the age of seven he was called Maurice Valadon. Then a Monsieur Utrillo, a Spanish engineer friend of the painter Zuloaga, offered to recognize him as his son. Maurice resented this and signed his first pictures 'Valadon U' before changing to 'Utrillo V'. While he was still a child his mother had married and moved out of Paris. Maurice used to stop off on his way home from school and drink with the local labourers. When his stepfather objected, Suzanne Valadon left him and took up with a boy of the same age as Maurice. Hoping to cure Maurice of his neurotic drinking, his mother gave him some paints, and at nineteen he had begun to sell impressions of the neighbourhood to which they had returned, usually working from postcards in a little room above a bar run by its kindly owner, Le Père Gay.

Alfred Jarry sets off from his home in Corbeil to cycle to Paris.

A natural friend for Picasso was Alfred Jarry, the success of whose iconoclastic play *Ubu Roi* eight years earlier had brought him notoriety but not money. 'He inhabited a miserable, dilapidated hut on the edge of the river,' wrote Sacha Guitry later. 'You could still read on the walls the words "Cleaning and Mending".' It had an earth floor, and a bicycle hung from the roof, 'to stop the rats from eating the tyres,' explained the seedy-looking writer, a 'proud little Breton' with a droopy moustache and long hair which had a greenish tinge acquired from drinking strange concoctions. Like Picasso, to whom he had given a revolver, Jarry was given to alarming pranks. He sometimes used to shoot at the apples in a neighbouring garden with a bow and arrow. 'You will kill my children!' complained the owner's wife. 'Never mind, *madame*,' shouted Jarry, 'I will give you some more.' He was to die, still penniless, in 1907.

A newcomer to Paris this year was a twenty-eight-year-old sculptor from Romania, Constantin Brancusi. He moved into the Impasse Ronsin in Montparnasse, and studied briefly at the Ecole des Beaux Arts.

Poverty and unconventionality bonded this seminal little band of artistic explorers, living in the flank of fashionable Paris like a nest of microbes who would soon destroy their host culture. It is hard to imagine their material miseries existing alongside the kind of lifestyle carried on a mere kilometre away, as it appears in Colette's description of the home of the notorious actress Otéro:

112. PARIS
Montmartre Pittoresque
(Rue des Saules)

Fine old pieces of furniture were anchored in a sea of satin which was probably embroidered with Japanese storks and probably foaming with appliqué lace ... a serene and delicate blue stretched over the walls, falling from the testers of the beds, draped in festoons round windows and doors ... strawberry pink and dawn-coloured brocades which 'stood up by themselves' as the saying is. ... Two *salons* were better than one, three better than two, even though grandeur had to be sacrificed to quality. ... Automobile designs were worked out in humble collaboration with the great milliners. .... I can still see Madame Otéro's blue Mercedes, a hat-box for aigrettes and ostrich feathers which was so narrow and high that when it rounded a corner it drooped and sank gently on its side.

This was the world of café society and high society, of the art snobs and the Jockey Club, through which writers like Proust and Gide moved with observant eye. While the snobs were at the Opéra or the first night of Henri Bernstein's *La Rafale*, and the aesthetes were admiring Antoine in *King Lear* at his own theatre or Isadora Duncan at the Trocadéro, Picasso and his friends were more likely at the local cinema or at the circus, reigned over by Footit and Chocolat, the famous clowns.

The same contrasts were beginning to appear in the art exhibitions. The two Salons took place as always in May at the Grand Palais. There were the usual canvases by Bouguereau and Carolus-Duran, Boldini and La Gandara, de Laszlo and Mucha – joined this time by Gerald Kelly (whose picture was bought by the state); G. F. Watts; the Alma-

OPPOSITE ABOVE The interior of the Lapin Agile. On the right Frédé plays his guitar. At the end of the table is a battered plaster Christ and to the left of it hangs a painting of a harlequin by Picasso.

OPPOSITE BELOW Pablo Picasso: *Portrait of Frédé*, 1905 (J. Warnod Collection, Paris). A lightning sketch of the owner of the Lapin Agile.

ABOVE The Lapin Agile at the start of the century. It remains much the same today.

OPPOSITE The world of official art. ABOVE A lady admiring some drawings – *Woman at a Gallery*, an etching by the Salon artist Paul-César Helleu. BELOW Jules Alexandre Grun: *Friday at the Salon*, 1911 (Musée des Beaux Arts, Rouen).

Pupils in the studio of the popular painter Adolphe Bouguereau.

Tademas, husband and wife; the Pre-Raphaelite John Brett; and Don Carlos, King of Portugal. The sculpture included the inevitable Rodin, Bourdelle, the English Thorneycroft and the Italian Rosso. There were the usual smart crowds and the usual state purchases.

But works at the Salon des Indépendants in February and March were beginning to command high prices. Edvard Munch's *Madwoman* was priced at 10,000 francs, while Maurice Denis asked 2,500 francs for a beach scene. Henri Rousseau's *Scouts Attacked by a Tiger* could have been bought for 600 francs and a *Young Girl* by Bonnard for the same price. Matisse, who showed six paintings, asked 450 francs for his *Monk Meditating*, and Van Dongen (showing for the first time), Dufy, Friesz and Robert Delaunay were in the 200–300 francs range.

What was to prove an even greater threat to the established exhibitions was the second Salon d'Automne, at the Grand Palais, home of the Salons. There were now 156 ordinary members including Bonnard, Matisse and Redon; over two thousand entries; and a new section, for photography.

Jean Béraud: *The Night Moths*, 1905
(Musée Carnavalet, Paris).
One aspect of Paris society
in the early 1900s.

The catalogue, which had a caricature of an Academician on its back cover, included no fewer than fourteen paintings by Matisse, ten by the Russian Constantin Kusnetsov, eight by Rouault, nine by Vuillard, seven by Bonnard, four by Friesz, three by Jean Metzinger, Francis Picabia and Marquet, and two by John Lavery. To add to the stature of the exhibition, there were five substantial one-man retrospectives. The first was devoted to Cézanne. It contained thirty-three paintings and drawings including a portrait of his wife, a view of the Montagne Sainte-Victoire, and several loaned pictures – *The Abandoned House*, belonging to Vollard; a flowerpiece from Monsieur Blot; and the *Portrait of Monsieur Chocquet* – Chocquet was a collector – lent by Durand-Ruel. The exhibition made a deep impression on the younger artists, but many critics were still hostile. *L'Univers* called his pictures 'false, brutal and mad', and the *Petit Temps* described the artist as 'a great incompetent with defective eyesight which renders him unable to see anything except as a tangle of straight lines'. Cézanne had just written, in a letter to Emile Bernard, a sentence which was later to become a famous text for the Cubists: 'Everything in nature is modelled after the sphere, the cone and the cylinder.'

Another gallery was devoted to the Symbolist painter Puvis de Chavannes, who died six years before. It contained the cartoons for several of his large public commissions, such as the decorations in the Panthéon, the Hôtel de Ville and the Sorbonne; his touching *The Fisherman's Family*; and two displays of his well-known caricatures. Chavannes was a popularly respected artist, and the other retrospective displays were also relatively accessible. Renoir had a show of thirty-five paintings, including another *Portrait of Monsieur Chocquet* as well as *La Loge*, *Le Déjeuner des Canotiers* and a *Portrait of Jane Samary* – all loaned by Durand-Ruel; and Toulouse-Lautrec, who had died in 1901, was represented by twenty-eight paintings including three views of the Moulin Rouge, two portraits of a Miss Bedford, and his charming *Jane Avril*.

These four collections rather overshadowed the fifth, by the Symbolist Odilon Redon. Now aged sixty-four, he was fairly well known to the gallery public – he had first exhibited in the Salon of 1878 and enjoyed one-man shows at Durand-Ruel and Vollard, and his lithograph illustrations for poems by Baudelaire, Flaubert and Poe were familiar to connoisseurs. But this collection attracted hardly any comment, perhaps because it emphasized his new style; he had abandoned his dark, mysterious images for a more lyrical and colourful world evoking visions of airy flowers and luminous skies, which one critic compared to oriental carpets. Answering an article by Emile Bernard, he declared: 'My soul is not black, for I glorify life which makes me love the sun, flowers, and all the splendours of the external world.' He was certainly no rarified visionary. 'The best things for work', he confided to Maurice Denis, 'are wine, walking and continence.' He seemed, in fact, to be moving towards the Impressionist approach. Possibly he had visited a recent show at Durand-Ruel, where the sixty-four-year-old Claude Monet exhibited views of the Thames which he had painted in London during the two previous years.

Other notable exhibitions this year included another 'fauvish' group at the Galerie Weill in March: a Nabi exhibition at Bernheim-Jeune in April; the British Walter Sickert there in June; and, in the same month, the first one-man show by Matisse at Vollard, of which Charles Morice wrote in the *Mercure de France*:

I accused him last year of unnecessary distortions, for these assaults added – or so it seemed to me – neither beauty nor expressiveness. Today, in front of these latent important manifestations, I do not hesitate to announce the growing sympathy he inspires in me.... Monsieur Matisse's painting reveals a delight in colour and tone and in the relationships between them; but these relationships are important only in themselves. This artist certainly has a taste, even a passion, for his medium; but perhaps not a complete sense of his art.

It was a favourable beginning, a portent of changes to come in the next year. The general public must have been hoping for a respite from the general agitations. The year 1904 had opened with the outbreak of the Russo-Japanese War which was to demolish all hopes of help for France from the Tsar against the might of Germany. The rout of the Russian troops was reported and illustrated weekly and even filmed by news-cameramen. The beloved Kruger, ex-President of the Transvaal, died in retirement in Switzerland. Science marched on relentlessly, with the winning car in the Gordon Bennet cup reaching 130 kilometres an hour and Madame Curie winning the Nobel Prize for her radium discoveries. 'Radium can never be vulgarized nor used from day to day, except in medicine or surgery,' she declared firmly, describing theories that it could be applied to energy, light or heat as 'childish'.

Odilon Redon: *Pegasus, c.* 1905 (Private Collection). Redon was the doyen of the Symbolist painters.

Public morale was nervous. There was well-founded alarm at the increasing discrepancy between the strengths of France and Germany. 'Only the memories of Alsace-Lorraine', wrote Léon Daudet in *Le Gaulois* in January, 'have prevented the Jews, the Freemasons, and the politicians in their pay from carrying out their plan for French disarmament.' At home Daudet and his friends on the right – soon to be crystallized in the Action Française group – were disturbed by the irresistible emergence of working-class power.

The change was vividly symbolized by the birth of the new artistic energy-centre in Montmartre. Apart from Van Dongen – who did later fall victim to patronage by the rich – none of the writers and painters who frequented the Lapin Agile dreamt of money; fame was their spur, and the images which appeared in their poems and pictures accurately reflected their new vision. We are no longer in the company of the Impressionists' picnickers with well-filled baskets and pretty frocks; the cosy, firelit parlours of Bonnard and Vuillard; nor the jewelled, languid fantasy world of the Symbolists. The Montmartre artists painted their own humble surroundings. Utrillo depicted its deserted streets and crumbling houses. Steinlen and Poulbot left faithful records of its inhabitants. Braque, who had just taken a studio further down the hill in the Rue d'Orsel, was the poet of its frugal meals.

While he was away in Barcelona Picasso had begun a series of pictures of beggars and underdogs, compassionate and even sentimental studies in emotional blue colours which used the elongated figures of the Pre-

Pablo Picasso: *The Two Sisters*,
1904 (Private Collection).
Long, emaciated limbs,
partly derived from the
Pre-Raphaelites, and melancholy
expressions are characteristic
of Picasso's 'Blue Period'.

Raphaelites to express misery rather than spirituality. Back in Paris, he continued the same approach – now labelled his Blue Period. Even when he tackled the subjects of his predecessors, such as the artistes of the Cirque Médrano, his angle is different. Instead of presenting the dashing spectacle, the acrobats or bareback riders, he looked behind the scenes to the drab, hard life of the performers after the show. His *Actor* of this year – a forerunner of the pathetic, half-starved harlequins and seedy clowns of the following months – stands not only for the artist's conception of himself, an impoverished outsider, but for the whole underside of Parisian society which, in the next few years, was paradoxically to become its secret treasure and, later, its pride.

1905
The Triumph of the Beasts

JUST AS THE SEINE separated the contrasting social worlds of Montmartre and St-Germain, it also ran between the studios of the two artists who were to become the leaders of different branches of the School of Paris. With his workman's clothes and nocturnal habits – he mostly painted at night, by the light of an oil lamp or a candle held in his free hand – Picasso was perfectly at home near the Place Pigalle, though on Tuesdays he and his friends sometimes ventured across the river to Paul Fort's poetry readings at the Closerie des Lilas in the Boulevard Montparnasse. But Henri Matisse, as he was always labelled at this time to distinguish him from a well-known academic painter with the same surname, was a natural inhabitant of the Latin Quarter – the district on the Left Bank of the river, near the university. With his steel-rimmed glasses and bushy beard, his quiet manner and conventional clothes, he would have cut an incongruous figure in the Lapin Agile. And surely he would have been shocked by a practical joke perpetrated by Dorgelès, who entered for the Salon des Indépendants a picture painted with the tail of Frédé's donkey, Lolo; since there was no selection committee it was, of course, hung, and seems to have passed unremarked. At this time, in fact, Picasso and Matisse had not yet met, though they had friends in common.

Matisse had been a slow starter, in the sense that he deliberately hesitated after initial success. The son of a grain merchant in Picardy, he had begun to paint during an illness at the age of twenty. At twenty-two he enrolled as a pupil of the arch-Academician Bouguereau at the Académie Julien – a private art school attended by professors from the Ecole des Beaux Arts. Quickly dissatisfied with their teaching, Matisse put himself under the admirably open-minded Gustave Moreau, one of the teachers at the Beaux Arts. Moreau encouraged rather than instructed, and Matisse flourished under his tuition. He also enjoyed the company of the lively youngsters who were attracted by Moreau's approach; they included Georges Rouault, who had been there for two years; Albert Marquet, who became a close friend; Charles Camoin, Henri Manguin and Jules Flandrin – all destined to become members of the movement of which Matisse was undisputed leader, the Fauves.

They were already very much in evidence at the 1905 Salon des Indépendants. It was the biggest ever, with no fewer than 4,269 entries. The Neo-Impressionist painter Paul Signac was Vice-President this year.

OPPOSITE Henri Matisse: *Nude in the Studio*, 1905 (Private Collection). Matisse was evidently under the influence of the Pointillist style of Paul Signac, who also led him to use lighter, brighter colours.

Lolo, the donkey belonging to Frédé, proprietor of the Lapin Agile. A picture painted with its tail was entered for an exhibition, using the pseudonym 'Joachim Raphael Baronali'. It is seen here on the verandah in front of the bar, with some of Frédé's customers.

As the centrepiece of the show, he had organized handsome retrospective collections of his master, Georges Seurat, and of Van Gogh, and had persuaded Matisse to be chairman of the hanging committee. It must have been an overwhelming display – all the future Fauvists exhibited, and there was even a tapestry woven by Madame Matisse to a design by Derain – but the public was used to mammoth shows, and some of the critics, at least, were enthusiastic. 'What a vibrant atmosphere of life and youth one breathes there!' wrote Charles Morice in the *Mercure de France*. He remarked that both the retrospectives were by young painters – Van Gogh had died at thirty-seven and Seurat at thirty-two – and he divined another presence:

Above all you will observe that above their shades there rises and diffuses, ubiquitous and irresistible, the spiritual reality of a living man.... You will quickly sense – ten paces, ten will be enough – this hidden and at the same time obvious presence which is not that of a former master nor even one of yesterday. The twenty-first Salon des Indépendants is a complete homage to Cézanne.

A place of honour was given to a portrait of the veteran of Aix by a caricaturist, Hermann Paul; and Matisse's companions, Camoin and Van Dongen, declared in Morice's magazine that he was 'a genius ... the finest painter of his age'.

Cézanne's classical influence may have been detected in the Pointillist paintings ('confettist', Morice called them) which had already been given prominence in two shows at the Galerie Druet – paintings by Signac in December and by Henri Edmond Cross in March. The Seurat retrospective was certainly a massive show of classicism, and to this was added – somewhat unexpectedly – a big picture by Matisse in the same style, *Luxe, Calme et Volupté*. Matisse's paintings during recent years had been sombre and relatively anonymous. He was working in an apartment high up on the Left Bank, and wrote later:

I lived on the Quai St-Michel above Vanier's, the editor of Verlaine. I had two windows which looked straight down from the fifth floor on to the channels of the Seine. A fine view: on the right Notre-Dame, on the left the Louvre, the Préfecture and the Palais de Justice opposite. On Sunday mornings there was always terrific activity on the *quai*; barges were moored there, fishermen came and planted their little rods, people browsed in the boxes on the bookstalls. It was the real heart of Paris.

Here, in a tiny room containing just a table, a bed, an easel and a big cupboard, doubtless stacked with canvases, he and his friend Albert Marquet had been painting still lifes, flowers, nudes and, above all, views of Paris, in darkish tones and gentle colours.

For the summer of 1904, however, he had taken a studio at St Tropez in the south of France, near to where Signac and Cross were staying. Always patient and modest, and still searching for a language of his own, he was seduced by their approach, and the carefully composed *Luxe, Calme et Volupté* was the result. Signac was so delighted with it when he saw it at the Indépendants that he bought it himself. In truth it was not, as it happened, the discipline and order of this picture which were to hold the secret of Matisse's future development, but the brilliant palette which he had adopted in St Tropez – perhaps borrowed from Signac and Cross – and which was closely related to the Van Gogh retrospective in the Indépendants. Van Gogh's influence was to emerge overpoweringly in October, when the Salon d'Automne opened – in spite of opposition from the established Salon – at the Grand Palais. 'We are at the end of something, which leads one to believe that we are at the beginning of something,' Morice remarked of the Indépendants. He was to be proved right.

During the summer of 1905 Matisse returned to the south of France, this time to Collioure near the Spanish frontier. Here he was joined by Derain, who in turn kept in touch with Vlaminck. When they returned to Paris they brought with them canvases which were to start a revolution in painting. What had occurred was simply that, by loosening up the dabs of bright paint which the Pointillists used to create a vibrant effect, they had incidentally established each larger patch as an independent statement. Colour was no longer merely descriptive; it was an expressive tool in its own right.

In the Salon d'Automne Matisse exhibited ten paintings, Derain nine and Vlaminck five. Marquet, Camoin, Friesz, Louis Valtat, Jean Puy and Van Dongen sent in pictures painted in the same strong style. They were hung together in gallery seven. Matisse wrote afterwards:

In the Salon d'Automne all the canvases which were a bit brightly coloured were hung in one large room. In the centre there stood a sculpture by Marque, who specialized in pleasant things in the spirit of the Renaissance. Marque was

The cover of the 1905 Salon d'Automne catalogue, the Exhibition which launched the Fauve movement.

showing a group of dancing babies – cherubs. When the hanging had been completed, the critic Vauxcelles entered the gallery beside me and, looking at the saccharine piece by Marque, he remarked: 'Ah, Donatello surrounded by wild beasts' [*Donatello au milieu des fauves*].

The effect of this mass demonstration was immediate and the label stuck. The Fauve movement – if the word 'movement' can be used of a small, disorganized group which never issued a manifesto – had developed largely in an art school in the Rue de Rennes, the Atelier Calillo, where Carrière sometimes taught. 'We didn't want to react deliberately against Carrière's painting, but ours was done with fresh, pure colours instead of dull or "muffled" colours,' Matisse explained. Rouault, who was soon to be lumped by critics in the same group, had three large pictures nearby, including a huge triptych entitled *Prostitutes*, inspired by a book by Léon Bloy. Bold and freely handled, it was certainly as savage in its way as the garish, flat, patterned paintings of Matisse and his colleagues. Bloy was not pleased. 'This artist, whom one thought capable of painting seraphim, no longer seems to be able to conceive anything but atrocious and vindictive caricatures.' He confided to his diary: 'It's a sorry sight. He's seeking a new path. What a pity! Bourgeois filth has wrought such a violent and horrified reaction in him that his art seems to have received a death blow.'

The sudden eruption of deliberately bright, brash colour made a lasting effect on the young artists who saw it and aroused shocked amusement

Some Fauve manifestations.
OPPOSITE Albert Marquet: *The Fourteenth of July at Le Havre*, 1906 (Private Collection).
ABOVE Charles Camoin: *Portrait of Marquet*, 1904 (Musee National d'Art Moderne, Paris).

BELOW Matisse out riding with Camoin (on the grey horse) and Marquet (right). They are posed in front of a dirigible.

A few months spent in the south of France in 1905, with Signac staying nearby, introduced a new luminosity into the paintings of Matisse and Derain.
LEFT Henri Matisse: *The Open Window, Collioure*, 1905 (John Hay Whitney Collection, New York). BELOW André Derain: *Collioure*, 1904–5 (Pierre Lévy Collection, Troyes). OPPOSITE A page from the magazine *L'Illustration* of 1 November 1905, reproducing some of the pictures in the current Salon d'Automne.

HENRI MANGUIN. — La Sieste.

M. Manguin : progrès énorme ; indépendant sorti des pochades et qui marche résolument vers le grand tableau. Trop de relents de Cézanne encore, mais la griffe d'une puissante personnalité, toutefois. De quelle lumière est baignée cette femme à demi nue qui sommeille sur un canapé d'atelier !

LOUIS VAUXCELLES, Gil Blas.

GEORGES ROUAULT. — Forains, Cabotins, Pitres.

Il est représenté ici par une série d'études de forains dont l'énergie d'accent et la robustesse de dessin sont extrêmes. Rouault a l'étoffe d'un maître, et je serais tenté de voir là le prélude d'une période d'affranchissement que des créations originales et des travaux définitifs marqueront.   THIÉBAULT-SISSON, le Temps.

M. Rouault éclaire, mieux que l'an passé, sa lanterne de caricaturiste à la recherche des filles, forains, cabotins, pitres, etc.   GUSTAVE GEFFROY, le Journal.

M. Rouault... âme de rêveur catholique et misogyne.   LOUIS VAUXCELLES, Gil Blas.

HENRI MATISSE. — Femme au chapeau.

ANDRÉ DERAIN. — Le séchage des voiles.

M. Derain effarouchera... Je le crois plus affichiste que peintre. Le parti pris de son imagerie virulente, la juxtaposition facile des complémentaires sembleront à certains d'un art volontiers puéril. Reconnaissons cependant que ses bateaux décoreraient heureusement le mur d'une chambre d'enfant.   LOUIS VAUXCELLES, Gil Blas.

LOUIS VALTAT. — Marine.

A noter encore : ... Valtat et ses puissants bords de mer aux abruptes falaises.   THIÉBAULT-SISSON, le Temps.

M. Louis Valtat montre une vraie puissance pour évoquer les rochers rouges ou violacés, selon les heures, et la mer bleue, claire ou assombrie.   GUSTAVE GEFFROY, le Journal.

HENRI MATISSE. — Fenêtre ouverte.

M. Matisse est l'un des plus robustement doués des peintres d'aujourd'hui. Il aurait pu obtenir de faciles bravos : il préfère s'enfoncer, errer en des recherches passionnées, demander au pointillisme plus de vibrations, de luminosité. Mais le souci de la forme souffre.

LOUIS VAUXCELLES, Gil Blas.

M. Henri Matisse, si bien doué, s'est égaré comme d'autres en excentricités coloriées, dont il reviendra de lui-même, sans aucun doute.

GUSTAVE GEFFROY, le Journal.

JEAN PUY. — Flânerie sous les pins.

... M. Puy, de qui un nu au bord de la mer évoque le large schématisme de Cézanne, est représenté par des scènes de plein air où les volumes des choses et les êtres sont robustement établis.   LOUIS VAUXCELLES, Gil Blas.

among the public. Matisse paid one visit to the exhibition and then, disgusted at the public reaction to his work, from visitors 'doubled up with laughter before it', stayed away. Few of the critics noticed the new group at all, and those who did were not much impressed. 'Matisse, so greatly gifted, has been misled like the others into eccentricities of colour from which he will doubtless recover,' wrote Gustave Geffroy in *Le Journal*, and Jean Puy later recorded that the group were nicknamed 'The Incoherents' or 'The Invertebrates'. According to Vollard the Salon's President, Jourdain, was so alarmed by one of Matisse's pictures that he urged the jury to reject it so that they might save the artist from embarrassment.

But some voices were raised in defence of the new school. *Le Temps*, *La République Française*, *Gil Blas*, *Le Figaro* and the *Mercure de France* were favourable to the exhibition as a whole, though they did not pick out Matisse and his friends. One of the few who did was an amateur critic, the writer André Gide, in the *Gazette des Beaux Arts*:

Paul Cézanne in front of one of his paintings of *The Bathers*. He showed a male bathing scene in the 1905 Salon d'Automne.

I stayed quite a time in this gallery. I listened to the visitors and when I heard them exclaim in front of a Matisse: 'This is madness!' I felt like retorting, 'No, sir, quite the contrary. It is the result of theories....' When Matisse paints the forehead of this woman apple-colour and the trunk of a tree an outright red, he can say to us, 'It is because – .' Yes, this painting is reasonable, or rather it is reasoning.

The painter Maurice Denis, whose *Homage to Cézanne* Gide had bought some years earlier, wrote a long review of the exhibition in *L'Ermitage*, picking on the Matisse group as 'the most alive, the newest, the most debated'.

When one enters the gallery devoted to their work, at the sight of these landscapes, these figure studies, these simple designs, all of them so violent in colour, one prepares to examine their intentions, to learn their theories; and one feels completely in the realm of abstraction.... Here one finds, above all in the work of Matisse, the sense of the artificial ... it is painting outside every contingency, painting in itself, the art of pure painting. All the qualities of the picture other than the contrasts of line and colour; everything which the rational mind has not controlled, everything which comes from our instincts and from nature, finally all the factors of representation and feeling are excluded from the work of art. Here in fact is a search for the absolute.

The artists who appeared to the public as wild beasts were treated by the critics, on the contrary, as intellectual theorists; but even they were off-target.

An ambiguous but telling comment was mounted by the editor of the popular *L'Illustration*, which ran a double-page spread showing twelve of the paintings together with quotes from laudatory critics. This has been seen as a satirical exercise – and was so interpreted by some at the time. But it is possible that it was a friendly gesture. The editorial introduction ran thus:

People have asked why *L'Illustration*, which devotes a whole number each year to the traditional Salon, pretends to ignore the Salon d'Automne? Its provincial and foreign readers, exiled far from the Grand Palais, would be glad to have at least some idea of these little-known masters whom serious papers, even *Le Temps*, praise so warmly. Surrendering to these arguments we devote two pages to reproducing, as well as we can, a dozen striking works from the Salon d'Automne.... If some of our readers are surprised at some of our selection, let them read the texts printed beneath each picture. They are the opinions of the most notable writers on art and we retire behind their authority. We would only remark that if in the old days critics reserved all their praise for established celebrities and their sarcasm for beginners, things are very different today.

The paintings selected included those of Cézanne, Rousseau, Vuillard, Rouault, Derain, Manguin, Valtat, Jean Puy and Matisse – an extraordinarily acute choice, especially since the picture by the last painter which was chosen for reproduction was the most shocking of all his canvases, the *Woman in a Hat* (it alone was shown without any textual protection). As if to restore confidence, the magazine illustrated on the following page a striking example of Russian Socialist-Realist painting, *The Education of the Russian People* by Bogdanov-Belsky.

OPPOSITE Henri Matisse:
Portrait of Madame Matisse
(*Portrait with the Green
Stripe*), 1905 (State Art Museum,
Copenhagen). It is easy to
imagine the shock aroused by the
violently unnaturalistic colours of
this painting.

FOLLOWING PAGES Fauve
portraits by Fauve painters.
LEFT ABOVE Henri Matisse:
André Derain, 1905 (Tate Gallery,
London).

LEFT BELOW André Derain:
Portrait of Vlaminck, 1905
(Private Collection).

RIGHT ABOVE André Derain:
Self-Portrait in a Black Hat,
1905 (Musée de Chambourcy).

RIGHT BELOW Henri Matisse:
Self-Portrait, 1906 (State Art
Museum, Copenhagen).

The dashing painting by Matisse had impressed one vitally influential family – the Steins from Pennsylvania. The two brothers and a sister – Leo, Michael and Gertrude – had settled in Paris three years earlier and become enthusiasts for modern painting. They had seen Matisse's show at Vollard's and were not much impressed; but his *Woman in a Hat* at the Salon d'Automne struck them forcibly. 'There were a number of attractive pictures, but there was one that was not attractive,' wrote Gertrude later. 'It infuriated the public, they tried to scratch off the paint.' Exactly who tried to buy the picture is uncertain; there was evidently much family discussion. 'I would have snatched it at once if I had not needed a few days to get over the unpleasantness of the putting on of the paint,' confessed Leo afterwards. Finally an offer of 400 francs was made for the painting. The artist stuck to his catalogue price, 500 francs. It seems to have been Madame Matisse, the subject of the picture – doubtless wearing one of the confections run up in the milliner's where she worked – who held out, in spite of their poverty, and the deal was made. It was to mark a turning-point in Matisse's fortunes, and the picture became the foundation-stone of the Stein collection.

It was not altogether surprising that the Fauve group was overlooked by most of the critics. The Salon was huge and contained many other eye-catching features. There were two big retrospectives. One was devoted to Ingres. He had been out of favour as a dry, cold academic during the Impressionist years, and even now his *Turkish Bath* raised doubts; 'There is no orgy,' complained *La Grande Revue*. 'It is nothing more than a timid and almost decent rehearsal of tomorrow's gestures and poses.' The other one-man show was by Manet – the first big retrospective of an artist whose direct, flat, tonal style had much influenced the early Matisse and Marquet. The acceptance of this once alarming artist and his treatment as an equal of the arch-traditional Ingres was taken by the critic of *Le Figaro* as 'a warning to look carefully at those who show daring, and to have sympathy and even compassion for those who, in all sincerity, deceive themselves while mumbling their profession of faith'.

Not all the critics were so cautious. Cézanne had sent ten paintings, mostly landscapes but including one of his *Bathers* (singled out by *L'Illustration*) and a *Portrait of Madame Cézanne*. 'Let others admire the Cézanne-style scarecrows painted with mud or something worse,' wrote the critic of *La République Française*; while *L'Intransigeant*'s critic declared: 'Of M. Cézanne I will say nothing; his art – since it seems that it is art – is beyond my humble comprehension.'

Renoir, now honorary President of the Salon, sent up some figure paintings from Cagnes – the Impressionists by now presented few difficulties – and Odilon Redon, the doyen of the Symbolists, was given a place of honour in the first room. Bonnard and Vuillard represented the Nabis. Rodin, who continued to exhibit each year in the Salon de la Nationale, was given a room of his own, and there was a special gallery for Russian painters, among whom were Kandinsky and Jawlensky. The British contingent included John Lavery, Sickert and Gerald Kelly; and there was an American group with such painters as Putnam Brinley,

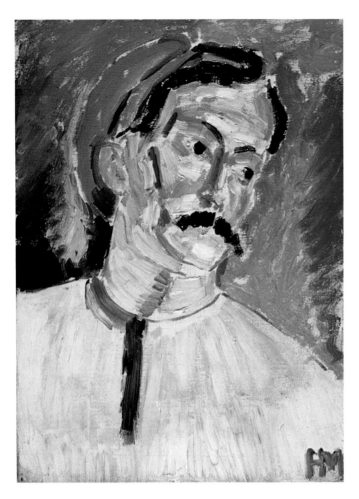

Patrick Bruce and Theo Butler. And of course there was the inevitable, and by then almost legendary, Henri Rousseau, whose painting this year was prominently hung. It bore the title *The Lion, Being Hungry, Leaps upon the Antelope and Devours It; the Panther Waits Anxiously for the Moment When It Can Have Its Share. Carnivorous Birds Have Pecked off Pieces of Flesh from the Back of the Poor Beast which is Shedding a Tear! Setting Sun.* Surprisingly, the sheer conviction of Rousseau's innocent visions had won a kind of patronizing critical respect, while the freshness of his inspiration and the impact of his apparently simple images filled some of his young and highly professional colleagues with wonder and admiration.

The twenty-three-year-old Braque was still isolated and tentative at this time, and his first sight of the Fauves at the Salon d'Automne proved to be the trigger to set his talent loose. 'They opened the way for me,' he declared later, and briefly he became associated with Matisse and his friends. The seven pictures which he submitted to the Salon des Indépendants the next spring were all to be in the Fauve style. Dufy too joined the Fauves after being bowled over by Matisse's *Luxe, Calme et Volupté* at the Indépendants. 'In front of this painting I understood all the new reasons for painting. . . . I understood instantly the new pictorial mechanics.'

Picasso sent nothing to these mixed shows – neither to the Salon d'Automne nor to the Salon des Indépendants, in which Braque had this year made his début. Picasso was absorbed in his melancholy world of half-starved acrobats and jugglers – though he was abandoning the pervasive overall blue coloration for warm, tender pinks and orange, and a brief visit to Holland this summer awakened a liking for fuller, rounder forms which aroused, perhaps, his budding interest in sculpture.

His emaciated figures, described by Apollinaire as 'beggars worn out by life, cripples, the disabled, scoundrels, grown old the way oxen die at twenty-five, young men carrying children suckled by the moon', were perhaps a last distorted echo of the *fin de siècle*. It was disappearing fast. Jean Lorrain, the apostle of decadent aestheticism, died this year, as did the actress Eleonora Duse, whom Arnold Bennett and Gerald Kelly had shortly before been admiring in a Russian play. Debussy got divorced – and so did Madame Bardeck, mother of his adored 'Chouchou'. During the Salon d'Automne his *La Mer* was played and compared to Impressionist painting, but had unfavourable reviews. The Protestant André Gide was flirting with the Catholicism of Claudel, and wrote about him thus in his journal:

'I have not seen him in three years. As a young man he looked like a nail, now he looks like a sledge-hammer. . . . He gives me the impression of a solidified cyclone . . . a jacket that is too short and makes him look even more thickset and lumpish. . . . 'But Gide, why don't you become converted?' He talks in a not very loud voice like a man very much in earnest. I notice again how unsuited real passion is to eloquence.

Gide also visited the Luxembourg Museum with Hugo von Hofmannsthal, Richard Strauss's librettist – 'I greatly enjoy seeing him,' Gide

OPPOSITE Henri Matisse: *Luxe, Calme et Volupté.* 1904–5 (Musée National d'Art Moderne, Paris). This first version of the painting shows the artist moving from Neo-Impressionism towards his mature flat decorative style. The hurrying attendant and shimmering mountains seem to belong to the old world; the over-lifesize standing figure to the new.

wrote. 'He speaks rather loudly and lacks hidden qualities, but the words with which he rather stuns you are not at all stupid. Sent a necktie in very good taste.'

From London arrived a wild young bearded artist, Augustus John, who settled in Montparnasse with a wife, a mistress, four children (a fifth was born within a few weeks) and a dog. The thirty-year-old Austrian poet Rainer Maria Rilke presented himself this year to Rodin and was taken on as secretary at 200 francs a month. Proust's mother died at their apartment in 45 Rue de Courcelles, murmuring a quotation from Corneille's *Horace*: 'Even if you're no Roman, deserve to be one!' Colette, now an established writer, exchanged books with the Comtesse de Noailles. 'I expected that each word would be vital and delectable. Everything moves, trembles, agitates, darkens, explodes, relaxes, falls quiet! ... It is the world's landscape in a dewdrop, in a raindrop,' wrote the Comtesse in her letter of thanks. Colette replied: 'Your book ... is so tumultuous and beautiful that it leaves one breathless, as after speeding or making love.'

In Berne a twenty-six-year-old German physicist, Albert Einstein, published a paper on the *Special Theory of Relativity*. In Paris there was a succession of foreign visitors. Edward VII came in the spring to seal the *entente cordiale*. A few weeks later the young King Alfonso of Spain was driving down the Rue de Rohan when a bomb was thrown at him. ('If the king had been less young and less handsome, sobs would not have choked me when I saw him salute the crowd as he passed,' confessed Gide.) In October Paris was fêting Ferdinand of Bulgaria from where the thirty-year-old Julius Pincas – soon to become celebrated under the name of Jules Pascin for his lascivious drawings of young girls – had just arrived. From Russia came a girl who was to marry Robert Delaunay and become known as an artist in her own right – Sonia Terk.

She was about the best thing to come out of Russia at this time, which provided nothing but bad news. The January Revolution had been followed by an anarchist attack on the Russian envoy in Paris, Prince Trubetskoy. In February the Grand Duke Serge was assassinated in Moscow. June saw the final Japanese victory over the Russians at Mukden and in July came the news of the revolt of the battleship *Potemkin*. 'The situation in Russia becomes more tragic every day,' wrote *L'Illustration*. 'Peace may be near in the Far East but when will it be established in Russia?'

As Russia became weaker, Germany became stronger. French nerves were shaken severely in April, when the Kaiser made an unexpected and well-publicized visit to Tangier – a territory considered a French preserve. In June the humiliated Foreign Minister in Paris resigned, while his German counterpart, Count von Bülow, was made a prince.

OPPOSITE Pablo Picasso: *La Toilette*, 1906 (Albright-Knox Art Gallery, Buffalo). This painting shows the new, rather Parisian delicacy and tenderness of Picasso's 'Pink Period'.

1906
Setting the Stage

SAVAGERY WAS THREATENING on the international front, and in the art jungle the 'wild beasts' were at large – a group with aims strikingly similar to those of the Fauves, called Die Brücke (The Bridge), had been founded in Dresden almost simultaneously with the Salon d'Automne display. But it did not yet disturb the peace of establishment artists. The twin Salons still offered the old selection of battlefields and boudoirs, provoking scorn in some circles. 'From year to year bitterness and disappointment turn into grief and then rage. The internationally official character of the two Salons makes them a social danger,' wrote the *Mercure de France* – but they had general support. 'The number of canvases exhibited keeps growing,' remarked *La Revue Illustrée* in its final number, 'and in this lavish production the number of talented artists rises in proportion.' But inflated prices began to raise the magazine's doubts:

Claude Monet fetches 10,000 francs. That adds nothing to his merits, but if it were offered for less nobody would buy it. Modern life has commercialized everything – because the people who buy want to shelter behind the solid doors of the strong-box.... We shall see in a few years the effect of this approach. We shall find that true luxury, the luxury of art, the luxury of which Paris has the monopoly, which it both leads and inspires, will – like ordinary capital flowing abroad – gradually move elsewhere, never to return.

It was a perceptive prophecy, to be borne out at least partially a generation later. But the prestige of these exhibitions died hard. The article continued:

Some eminent personalities cannot dispense with the gesture of attending the openings, that social duty which is still compulsory, however old-fashioned. We find little Sem, dressed in a suit by Poole, entertaining the crowd by pretending to sketch caricatures on the corner of his notebook; the wide-eyed Liane de Pougy accompanied by Yves Lester with his fiery mane; Miss Mary Garden, the wild priestess of the motor-car; Claude Terrasse, even more hirsute than in his portrait by Lumière; Suzanne de Lisery, beautiful in mauve; Princess Tatanoff, who prefers the nocturnal seclusions of the Bois to the electric lights of Armenonville; Blackpot the Parisian Londoner and his friend X. M. Boulestin the London Parisian; L. Gordon-Lennox, on the lookout for another play to translate, the King of Sweden and so on....

This year the distinguished visitors had to pay an extra two francs for entry, but were treated to a portrait of the Russian Tsar by Repin and

OPPOSITE Pablo Picasso: *Self-Portrait*, 1906 (Philadelphia Museum of Art). The simplifications, the slight displacement of the eyes and something angular and bony about the skull and thorax suggest the influence of African woodcarving and the promise of the next stage in his development.

to a new feature, a Salon de la Musique with participation by Camille Saint-Saëns, Charles Widor and Vincent d'Indy.

Convention was still strong. In July the new Minister of Fine Arts, Aristide Briand, declared his intention of decorating the *doyenne* of the French stage, Sarah Bernhardt, with the Légion d'Honneur. But conservative opinion was affronted, and his gesture was foiled on the technical grounds that she was not appearing in a state theatre – she preferred her own. In recompense, perhaps, Dreyfus, eleven years after his false accusations, was made a *Chevalier* of the order – an unobtrusive little figure who seemed a frail centre for such a long, ferocious controversy. Another outsider who this year came in out of the cold was the drama director Antoine, whose production and performance of *King Lear* at his own experimental theatre had won wide praise in 1904. On Christmas Day that year he had confided to his diary: 'The acclaim for this production has been so great that I feel strongly that I have made a big stride towards the Odéon.' And in fact, one day in March 1906, he could write about his ambition to take over the directorship of this prestigious official theatre: 'This evening at 4 o'clock I was summoned to the Ministry of

OPPOSITE Maurice Vlaminck: *The Dancer at the 'Rat Mort'*, 1906 (Private Collection). A night-club study reminiscent of Picasso's first Parisian paintings.

Georges Braque: *The Landing-stage at L'Estaque*, 1905 (Musée National d'Art Moderne, Paris). A painting which shows that Braque too was influenced at this time by the free, vivid handling of Signac.

Education. Briand received me, saying: "Well, there's nothing left except to nominate you."' One week later his own Théâtre Antoine closed.

The march of change was irresistible. The Salon des Indépendants opened the same week that Antoine took theatrical command on the Left Bank, and contained a celebratory canvas by the indomitable Rousseau, now sixty-two; he had been a full-time painter for twenty years, but his lack of formal training and his simple style still lent him the title of 'Sunday painter'. His picture was called *Liberty Inviting Artists to Take Part in the Twenty-second Exhibition of Independent Artists*; the invitation resulted this time in no fewer than 5,552 works. 'Every year the crowd flock to the Cours-la-Reine and every year there are the same cries of stupefaction,' wrote the critic of *La Revue Illustrée*. He had a word or two of praise for some of the Fauves (Vollard had just put Derain and Vlaminck under contract), but Matisse's single big canvas, *The Joy of Life*, was too much for him: 'To be sure, M. Matisse works for his own pleasure and only for his own pleasure. Let us leave him to his solitary diversions and withdraw – or rather let us suggest that he should exhibit among the Sioux. As a canoe decorator he would surely have a big success.' Even Signac, who had bought Matisse's *Luxe, Calme et Volupté* the year before, declared angrily that Matisse had gone to the dogs.

Marie Laurencin, the painter mistress of Guillaume Apollinaire. In this capacity she was sometimes, unjustifiably, included in the Cubist group.

Among the painters exhibiting for the first time were Marie Laurencin, now the mistress of Guillaume Apollinaire and a delegate, so to speak, from Montmartre; and another artist from the same district who was shortly to become closely linked with the 'Picasso set', Georges Braque, who sent seven pictures in the style of the Fauves. He was soon to desert them, however. The sight of a group of Cézanne paintings the next year was to restore to him his basic love of discipline and order. 'You can't stay in a state of paroxysm for ever,' he was to remark, destroying all his Fauve works.

In the commercial galleries the Symbolist tradition still lived on. Durand-Ruel mounted a Redon exhibition in February, and later in the year there was a big Moreau exhibition at the Galerie Georges Petit, with 209 works and a catalogue introduction by Montesquiou. Bernheim-Jeune persisted with the Nabi group, giving shows to Valloton, Vuillard and Bonnard – besides pressing on with an artist they backed doggedly, René Seyssaud. Matisse had his second one-man show at the Galerie Druet in March, coinciding with the Salon des Indépendants.

The Salon d'Automne this year had four impressive retrospectives – of an architect called Dobert, Carrière (who had just died), Courbet and Gauguin. 'We did not know how to profit by the genius of this artist [Gauguin], whose passion for throbbing colours might have endowed stained glass windows with glorious flames and spread grand and inspiring harmonies upon our walls,' wrote Charles Morice in the *Mercure de France*. But the public were still recalcitrant. 'The crowd enters, laughs surreptitiously or loudly, and leaves convinced that the whole thing is a hoax.... The visitor does not pause in front of these absurd and macabre jokes,' recorded *La Revue Illustrée*, and most of the critics were equally hostile. 'In 1906, as in 1905, the Salon d'Automne has been coldly received by the "serious" critics. So it is worth repeating that every year

the Salon d'Automne is the only significant collective expression of contemporary art,' persisted Morice.

An unusual and, as it turned out, significant new feature of the Salon was the large section devoted to Russian art. It occupied no fewer than twelve rooms of the Grand Palais and covered the whole spectrum from modern paintings by the *Mir Iskusstva* (World of Art) School, who were strongly influenced by recent Paris trends – Vrubel, Serov, Bakst, Benois, Roerich and Larionov, among others – to eighteenth-century portraits by Levitsky, and early ikons. These were hung by Léon Bakst on walls covered with gold brocade, creating a theatrical effect which betrayed the man responsible for the show, Serge Diaghilev, who was making his début as an impresario in the west. He introduced a 'winter garden' to display the sculpture, a device he had tried out in St Petersburg with great effect. One of his organizing committee was the rich and influential hostess, the Comtesse de Greffulhe, who was also President of the progressive Société Musicale. Impressed by Diaghilev's playing of some Russian songs, 'altogether wonderful and lovely', she agreed to help his plan for a Russian musical season the following year.

Three weeks after the opening of the Salon d'Automne a serious piece of news reached Paris from the south of France – Paul Cézanne was dead. The sixty-seven-year-old painter had exhibited each year since he had been invited by Maurice Denis to participate. 'It seems to me', he had remarked to Vollard, 'that I can't dissociate myself from the youngsters who have behaved towards me so nicely.' In 1895 Vollard had mounted

Marie Laurencin: *Guillaume Apollinaire and His Friends*, 1906 (Apollinaire Collection). Apollinaire sits in the centre. On his left are Picasso and Fernande Olivier. The seated figure on the poet's right is thought to be Marie Laurencin herself.

a big show of his work which had helped to establish his reputation, at least among painters, but since then Cézanne had almost deserted Paris. His beloved mother had died in 1897, and he had sold their old home near Aix and moved into a house nearby, where he lived the life of a recluse. At the beginning of 1906 he began to suffer seriously from diabetes, but worked on stubbornly. 'At my age', he said to Maurice Denis who called to see him and found him attending mass in the local church, 'one contemplates eternity. One paints to the last, but one must have religion.' He had inherited a certain amount of money, but was frugal to the point of miserliness. At the beginning of October the old man who was accustomed to drive him out with his easel and paints in an old cab, looking for sites to paint, asked for an extra three francs for the outings. Cézanne was furious. 'I have sacked him,' he wrote to his son. 'I now go on foot with only my watercolour box.' A few days afterwards he was returning from one of these expeditions when he was caught in a severe storm. He collapsed and was found some hours later by a passing laundry cart. A week later he was dead.

Though he appreciated Cézanne's pictures ('Yesterday I went to see some paintings. . . . Very beautiful Gauguins, Van Goghs, Cézannes,' he was to write the next year), André Gide made no mention of the epoch-making news in his journal next day. Intellectual life moved on several different levels in Paris, and Gide was absorbed in other questions. 'It hurts me to write to Jammes so flatly. But what else can I do?' he asked himself about the Catholic writer, Francis Jammes. 'His nose is no longer susceptible to anything but incense.' Gide's world was still that of the elegant *soirées*, protocol-conscious dinners and peculiar couplings recorded by Proust. Earlier in the year he had spent a few hours with a young sculptor called Charmoy, an experience which he described in some detail:

A strange evening. In the studio, cluttered with huge statues fantastically lit by a score of candles ingeniously stuck here and there, on the corners of benches, in the folds of enormous angels supporting the monument of Beethoven – in that studio, overheated by a little cast-iron stove, José, his wife and I waited for the Princesse de Broglie and Miss Barney. . . . Around ten o'clock we hear the Princesse's automobile which appears in the blackness of the door. The Princesse is wearing an ermine wrap, which she drops into Charmoy's hands. A gown of black velvet covering only the lower half of her body sets off a vast expanse of lustrous skin; the gown hangs from jet straps. Her face is small and tired. . . . No wrinkles however, but her features are painfully tight. Her intention of charming is flagrant. On the back of a wicker chair, which she considers 'not very inviting', a fur is stretched; on the floor a footwarmer for her little feet, which she also wraps in a shawl. Near her, behind her, Miss Barney takes refuge in an eloquent silence and lets the Princesse strut.

Between these excursions into expensively naughty society, Gide was wrestling with his religious conscience in correspondence with Jammes and Claudel, and preparing to deploy it in a delicate literary composition. 'Have found the right paper for writing *La Porte Etroite* and begun copying,' he noted on 18 April, adding with satisfaction, '. . . Three pages'.

The spring had seen another curious encounter. On 2 April George

OPPOSITE Georges Rouault: *At the Salon*, 1906. A satirical comment on the art establishment. Rouault was soon to turn his savage brush to the ugliness of prostitution and the law courts.

Bernard Shaw posted a letter from his home in Hertfordshire to Rodin in Paris. With characteristic egoism he wrote:

I am always proud to be known as your model. You are the only man in whose presence I feel really humble. There is no-one here who can correct this letter [it was written in French]. Never mind, my mistakes will make you smile, and will help you to recover your health. Extraordinary faculties, ordinary health; that is the fate of a man of genius! We always wear ourselves out.

Whether Rodin shared in this exalted equation is not recorded. He charged Shaw £1000 for the marble bust and £800 for the bronze version. By the summer he was devoting himself to more decorative models, a company of Cambodian dancers who appeared at the Elysée Palace in Paris. He was so delighted with their tiny charms that he followed them to Marseilles. 'Put your foot on that,' he instructed one of the girls, placing a sheet of paper in his lap and tenderly drawing the contours. 'These are religious dances,' he explained. 'I have always confused religious art and art. When religion vanishes, art vanishes too.'

Round about this time, Rodin noticed the work of the young Brancusi in a mixed exhibition at the Luxembourg Museum, and offered to take

BELOW Rodin at work drawing a Cambodian dancer.
OPPOSITE The finished sketch.

him as a pupil. But Brancusi refused, saying: 'Nothing grows well in the shadow of a big tree.' Rodin was to benefit soon after by the separation of church and state, which had agitated public opinion in the last two years. In the catalogue of church properties to be sequestered by the government was the Convent of the Sacred Heart in the Rue de Vaugirard; it reverted to its original name, the Hôtel Biron, and was to become not only Rodin's main studio, but in due course the Rodin Museum. Another of its tenants would be Matisse, who, with Friesz, had just taken a studio in another ex-convent in the Rue de Sèvres. He used the big rooms in the Hôtel Biron for the school he had just opened. Since he refused to take fees for his teaching, his pupils paid for the studios.

Many of these pupils were foreign students attracted by reports of the exciting new ventures in Paris; young painters flocked in from all over the world. Anglo-French relations in particular had suddenly become cordial and work was started on the French coast for the first of many attempts to build a tunnel under the Channel. 'I think I shall be a supernaturalist in Paris and in London a naturalist,' wrote Augustus John from Montparnasse. In London, where he was working in the family stockbroking business, a twenty-one-year-old German, Daniel-Henry

RIGHT Henri Matisse and his class of art students. Instead of paying fees, his pupils used to share the expenses of the studio.

BELOW Amedeo Modigliani soon after his arrival in Paris from Milan in 1906.

Kahnweiler, announced to his astonished uncle that, rather than move to a branch in South Africa, he intended to become an art dealer in Paris. Amedeo Modigliani, a dashing twenty-two-year-old painter, arrived from Milan almost simultaneously with his compatriot Gino Severini; and from Spain came the nineteen-year-old Juan Gris. Kahnweiler wrote later:

The Paris of 1906 which Gris first knew was the Paris of men in top-hats and painted boots, of women in leg-of-mutton sleeves and long, tightly-fitting skirts, of horse-buses and four-wheelers.... How much time he must have spent hawking his drawings from one editorial office to another, how often must he have been snubbed and in the end how poor was the reward! ... The walls of Gris' studio were covered with long columns of figures scribbled in charcoal – they were usually his household expenses.

Gertrude Stein, the dumpy lady from Pennsylvania, became friendly with Picasso, underwent eighty sittings for her portrait, and began to ask him

back to her parties. The players were assembling for the next act in the drama which was being played out in the studios of Paris. The stage was set for the birth of Cubism. 'I find that what interests me is the transformation which renders chaos malleable by man,' wrote the poet Paul Valéry to a friend, prophetically.

1907
The Birth of Cubism

THE CUBIST REVOLUTION can be seen now to have had a logical and almost inevitable gestation, but it arrived like a thunderclap; not fully formed – its first manifestation was rather confused – but dramatically primitive and new. Kahnweiler, who had noticed that Paris art galleries were moving westwards towards the Madeleine, had boldly leased a tailor's shop at 28 Rue Vignon for 2,400 francs a year. He took on an assistant, hung up some paintings, and ran up the metal blind on his first gallery. He wrote afterwards:

One day I was in my shop when a young man came in whom I found remarkable. He had raven-black hair, he was short, squat, badly dressed with dirty, worn-out shoes, but his eyes were magnificent. Without a word this young man began looking at the pictures. He made a complete tour of the little shop which was about twelve feet square, and left. The next day he came back in a carriage with a gentleman who seemed quite elderly to me . . . a rather stout gentleman with a beard. Still without saying a word, the two of them walked around the gallery and left.

Soon afterwards a fellow German, Wilhelm Uhde, who was a writer and art critic and ran a small gallery, told Kahnweiler of a strange picture that a young painter called Picasso was working on – a picture which 'looked Assyrian'. Intrigued, Kahnweiler set off for the Bateau-Lavoir to see it. Later, he put down his impressions of the visit:

I arrived at the door which I had been told was Picasso's. It was covered with scrawls by friends making appointments: 'Manolo is at Azon's. . . . Totote was here. . . . Derain will come this afternoon.'

I knocked on the door. A young man, barelegged, in shirtsleeves with the shirt unbuttoned, opened the door, took me by the hand and showed me in. It was the young man who had come a few days before and the old gentleman he had brought with him was Vollard. . . .

So I walked into that room which Picasso used as a studio. Nobody can imagine the poverty, the deplorable misery of those studios in the Rue Ravignan. . . . The wallpaper hung in tatters from the unplastered walls. There was dust on the drawings and rolled-up canvases on the battered couch. Beside the stove was a kind of mountain of piled-up lava, which was ashes. It was unspeakable. It was here he lived with a very beautiful woman, Fernande, and a huge dog named Fricka. There was also that large painting Uhde had told me about, which was later called *Les Demoiselles d'Avignon*, and which constitutes the beginning of Cubism.

OPPOSITE Georges Rouault: *Girl, a Nude with Pink Garters*, 1906 (Musée National d'Art Moderne, Paris). The plain features and exaggerated hips and buttocks lend a touch of repulsion to Rouault's sensual treatment.

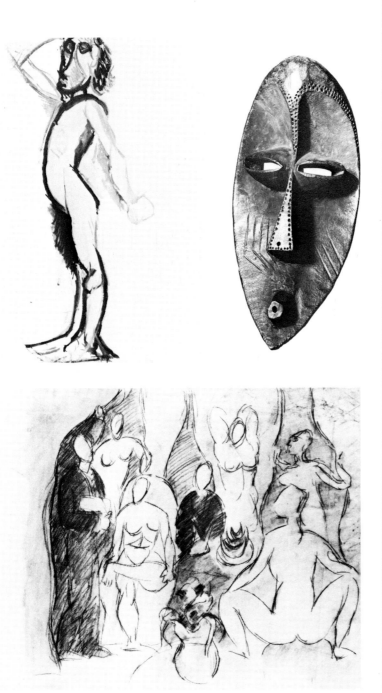

Kahnweiler was overwhelmed by it, as well he might be. It even baffled Picasso's closest friends. Braque, whom he met soon afterwards through Apollinaire, was reminded of somebody drinking petrol and spitting out fire. Derain thought it showed signs of suicidal desperation.

To those who were familiar with Picasso's recent paintings and drawings, the delicate studies of adolescents and theatre folk now called his Pink Period, it must have come as a deep shock. It represented an abrupt change of direction, a reaction not only against his own trends but against most recent French painting, particularly the fleeting, atmospheric, Impressionist-style pictures which still abounded in the various Salons.

In fact *Les Demoiselles d'Avignon* – the title, incidentally, was given to it later, and alludes to a brothel in Barcelona – can be seen now to combine, sometimes rather awkwardly, traces of many current trends in contemporary painting. The subject, a group of five nudes in front of a curtain, is traditional. Originally it was to have included two clothed males and was nicknamed by Picasso's friends 'The Philosophical Brothel'. The painting may have been prompted by Matisse's *The Joy of Life*, shown at the Indépendants the previous year, or by some nudes that Derain was working on at the time. The bold outlines and simplified colours owe something to the experiments of the Fauves. The slightly mysterious atmosphere – the figure on the left was at first planned holding a skull – is Symbolist in feeling. The awkward lines and strange features of the women can be related to Tahitian paintings by Gauguin, and perhaps to early Spanish sculpture, an exhibition of which had recently been shown at the Louvre – Picasso himself owned two small figures which were later to feature in a minor scandal. The sharply faceted modelling of some sections and the enclosed space in which the figures are placed echo Cézanne's *Bathers*. And, lastly, the influence of Negro sculpture is everywhere evident.

Though the painting is tightly composed, it has an almost Fauve disquiet – particularly in the two right-hand figures with their African look. Exactly who first introduced African art into avant-garde Paris is uncertain. Matisse, Derain and Vlaminck were all admiring and collecting it at this time. Picasso was to become a regular collector, and in this painting the primitive energy which he admired in it appeared for the first time.

Not far away another painter was experimenting in a style derived from African art. Braque was already dissatisfied with the Fauve approach, and the big *Nude* he painted in the autumn showed that he had immediately grasped the possibilities opened up by Picasso's new picture. Almost instantly he deserted Matisse and the Fauve group and attached himself to the Picasso circle. Quieter and less volatile than the Spaniard, he set out on a patient exploration of the new style which was to lead directly to Cubism.

In effect the influence which had stamped itself on Braque, over-riding evocations of African primitivism, was that of Cézanne. His presence was already strong – even Matisse, who clung to Art Nouveau curvaceousness and flat decoration, had been affected by him, and in October it became overwhelming. The Salon d'Automne mounted a major Cézanne

ABOVE Henri Matisse: *The Blue Nude*, 1907 (Cone Collection, Baltimore Museum of Art). This painting, with its uningratiating distortions was derived from a sculpture modelled at Collioure which collapsed while Matisse was working on it. The brutal sexuality of the picture shocked visitors at the Salon des Indépendants of that year.

RIGHT Georges Braque: *Nude*, 1907–8. Braque executed this painting directly after seeing Picasso's *Les Demoiselles d'Avignon*, and it shows the same traces of Cézanne and Negro art revealed in that picture.

Georges Braque: *L'Estaque*, 1906
(Musée National d'Art Moderne,
Paris). During a visit to
Cézanne's countryside in the
summer Braque began to develop
a severely disciplined style
which forms a link between
that painter and the budding
experiments of Cubism.

memorial retrospective including forty-eight paintings. The critic Félix
Fénéon, who ran the Rue Richepanse branch of the Galerie Bernheim-
Jeune, near to Kahnweiler's shop, put on a show of his watercolours, and
friends of the artist, like the painter Emile Bernard, published letters and
memoirs; one of the letters included his famous remark that 'everything
in nature is modelled after the sphere, the cone and the cylinder'.

Cézanne had not been a theoretician, but he had a highly developed
sense of pictorial logic and he had pursued with undeviating obsession
the aim of working out a way of translating the visible world into a flat
painting. Like Courbet, but unlike the Impressionists who were concerned with fleeting sensations and reactions, he pursued the reality of
the solid world as we see it and know it. This patient, unhurried probing,
which took as much account of what we know as of what we see, appealed
to painters like Picasso, Braque and Derain. And they took note also of
his firm drawing and the clear, separate touches with which he built up
his equivalents of the material world.

Picasso's sudden revelation of a way to escape from past traditions
opened up a new way of constructing a logical pictorial language built
on Cézanne's marriage of sight and insight, of perceptual and conceptual

knowledge, but carrying it further by stressing a third reality – the flat, painted surface. The fully fledged Cubist landscapes which Braque was to bring back from L'Estaque the next summer were to be as firm and well-carpentered as a painting by Poussin. They represented a reaction against not only the sensitive, ephemeral records of the Impressionists but also against the Fauves with their belief in bold colour as 'charges of dynamite', as Derain described it. Classical and ordered, it was eventually to be labelled theoretical.

Ironically, just as Cézanne had relied entirely on instinct and not on argument, so did Braque and Picasso. Picasso had strong literary sympathies. His friends were mostly poets and he regularly attended the Tuesday *soirées* at the Closerie des Lilas where Paul Fort and André Salmon carried on the Symbolist poetic tradition. One of his friends was Albert Princet, who was a clever mathematician. He may well have discussed with Picasso Einstein's recently published theory of simultaneity and Henri Bergson's famous *Creative Evolution*, suggesting the continuity of time, which came out in Paris this year. Both books now appear very relevant to the syncretic system of Cubism.

Picasso disliked argument about his work – 'Don't talk to the driver,' he used to say – and was never seen reading a book. But his mind was quicker than Braque's, he had a more dominating and adventurous temperament, and he already had something of a reputation. His large output had been handled by Vollard, an established dealer, and fetched good prices. Inevitably it was he who became the leader of what quickly turned into a 'Cubist group' – other members were to be Jean Metzinger, Albert Gleizes, Robert Delaunay and, later, Fernand Léger and Juan Gris. He and Braque never worked together – in fact they were careful to sign their pictures (on the back, so as not to disturb the composition) – but they met regularly, and often their paintings are hard to separate at this period. Later, Braque said:

It was as if we were two mountaineers roped together. We worked a great deal, the two of us.... Museums did not interest us any more.... We were above all very concentrated. We lived in Montmartre, we saw each other every day, we talked. During those years Picasso and I discussed things which nobody will ever discuss again, which nobody else would know how to discuss.... All that will end with us.

Three foreigners proved invaluable supports in the development of Cubism. The Polish-born Guillaume Apollinaire was an instant champion in the Press; he called Cubism 'a new art which will stand in relation to painting as hitherto regarded just as music stands in relation to literature'. The German Kahnweiler not only bought and sold the Cubists' paintings with unshaken confidence but became a lifelong friend and Picasso's sole dealer. And the American Gertrude Stein proved both a regular patron and a skilled and intelligent hostess who acted as a link between the Montmartre painters and the wider world of the arts.

There was a fair sprinkling of American artists in Paris. Like most of the foreign visitors they tended to keep in a group – Picasso, for instance, spoke bad French, and was surrounded by Spanish poets and painters.

OPPOSITE Fernande Olivier, who shared Picasso's studio in the Bateau-Lavoir, takes a walk down one of the steep hills of La Butte accompanied by Dolly, the daughter of the Dutch painter Kees Van Dongen, and Picasso's dog Fricka. This photograph was taken in 1907.

But the Steins' Saturdays at 27 Rue de Fleurus in Montparnasse became a focal point where painters of many groups and nationalities, writers, travellers and collectors met, talked and learned what was new in the arts, both by listening and looking.

The Steins were a well-to-do family who had travelled much in Europe, and were interested in the arts. Michael Stein and his wife Sara settled in Montparnasse first, and began to buy pictures. Leo Stein, his elder brother, a dour, reflective character with ambitions as a painter, followed his example after a trip round the world. He had been joined in 1903 by Gertrude, the youngest. She and Leo leased a tiny house near Michael's with a big studio adjoining, and this quickly became a social centre for the avant-garde and a showcase for young painters. At first it was Leo who set the pace, but Gertrude had views of her own. Their exploration led them naturally to Vollard's shop at 41 Rue Laffitte, where Leo hoped to find paintings by Cézanne, an artist who had been recommended to him by the critic Bernard Berenson. Leo wrote:

It did not look like a picture gallery. Inside there were a couple of canvases turned to the wall, in one corner was a huge dark man glooming. This was Vollard cheerful. When he was really cheerless he put his huge frame against the glass door that led to the street, his arms above his head, his hands on each upper corner of the portal and gloomed darkly into the street. Nobody thought then of trying to come in.

In ten years Vollard's shabby little premises had become famous. In the basement he had served his chicken curry luncheons and suppers –

A postcard dated March 1907 from Picasso to Guillaume Apollinaire at his mother's house in Le Vesinet. The Don Quixote motif was to appear frequently throughout his life, sometimes converted into a picador.

he came from the island of Réunion in the Indian Ocean and the gallery always smelt of spices – to Degas, Renoir, Redon, Forain, Rodin, and, regularly, Cézanne. There was always fine painting talk. Vollard wrote later:

When Degas was dining with me one night in the basement, I asked him, 'Do you know Monsieur Ingres, Monsieur Degas?' 'I went to see him one evening with a letter of introduction. He received me very kindly. Suddenly he was taken with a fit of giddiness and flung out his arms as though seeking for something to hang on to. I had just time to catch him in my arms.' I thought to myself: What a fine subject for a Prix de Rome painting – Ingres in the arms of Degas, the last representative of a dying age borne up by the herald of a new one.

Vollard himself bridged the gap between two generations, with an enthusiasm that stretched from Degas, Manet and Gauguin to Bonnard, who painted a picture of one of his dinner parties, Henri Rousseau and Matisse, to whom he gave his first one-man show, and finally to the young Picasso.

Leo and Gertrude bought several pictures jointly, though Leo was the deciding mind at this stage, with a wide knowledge of art and remarkable perception. After the Steins bought Matisse's *Woman in a Hat* at the Salon d'Automne in 1905 they became close friends of the artist and his wife, who were soon very much at home in the Rue de Fleurus – too much so, indeed, for the cook, who complained of Matisse that 'a Frenchman should not stay unexpectedly to a meal, particularly if he asked the servant beforehand what there was for dinner.' She declared, 'I will not make an omelette but fry the eggs. It will take the same number of eggs and the same amount of butter but it shows less respect, and he will understand.'

Leo in particular became a great admirer of Matisse, and when *The Joy of Life* appeared at the Salon des Indépendants in 1906 it was he who, after initial hesitation, bought it, announcing that it was 'the most important painting done in our time'. It took its place on the walls of the studio in the Rue de Fleurus where it was soon joined by a picture by Picasso. One day Leo was looking at a little gallery in the Rue Laffitte run by a former clown called Sagot. He spotted some paintings by Picasso and brought his sister to see them. The result was the purchase of a lyrical portrait in the artist's 'pink' style, a young girl holding a basket of flowers, and soon afterwards Gertrude and Leo were taken to the artist's studio by a mutual friend.

There seems to have been an instant *rapport* between the twenty-five-year-old Spaniard and the thirty-two-year-old American woman. Gertrude formed the habit of taking him American newspapers featuring the Katzenjammer Kids cartoon strip, which he especially enjoyed. Within a few weeks he had invited her to sit for a portrait. Gertrude later described how Picasso's mistress Fernande read aloud fables from La Fontaine, to keep the sitter amused. When she had taken her pose, she went on, 'Picasso sat very tight on his chair and very close to his canvas and on a very small palette which was of a uniform brown grey colour, mixed some more brown grey and the painting began. This was the first of some

The Steins' studio at 27 Rue de Fleurus, which housed an overwhelming collection of contemporary paintings. Some of them can be seen here among the heavy Renaissance furniture.

eighty or ninety sittings.' The figure took on the heavy sculptural mass that Picasso admired in primitive art, but he was not satisfied with the head. On his return from a holiday in Spain he completely repainted it.

The portrait was hung at 27 Rue de Fleurus and Gertrude Stein became both a patron and – something that Leo was not – a passionate champion of the Cubists. Braque and Derain showed their work at the Indépendants, and Matisse had acquired a reputation through being seen in the various Salons, but Picasso never exhibited in mixed shows, and the Steins' studio and Kahnweiler's gallery were among the few places where his new work could be seen. It was also one of the very few locations where the Left Bank set and the Montmartre set came together. Matisse met Picasso there. The two artists felt a mutual respect for each other, but there was inevitable rivalry and no great intimacy grew up between them. Leo Stein still favoured Matisse, whose thoughtful approach was more sympathetic to his intellectual mind, but Gertrude deserted him for Picasso. 'There is nothing within you which fights itself,' she told Matisse. She went on seeing him – he liked to gossip about the strange foreign pupils at his new school – but she saw very clearly the difference between the two styles. 'The effect of African art upon Matisse and Picasso was entirely different,' she wrote. 'Matisse through it was affected more in his imagination than in his vision. Picasso more in his vision than in his imagination.' Seeing further than her brother, she observed that it was Picasso's Cubist approach which was the more severe.

The Steins' studio became a regular Saturday haunt for the Picasso set. After a visit to the Bateau-Lavoir Gertrude would walk with Picasso and Fernande down the hill and across Paris to her house, wending a leisurely way past the Montmartre music-halls, through the holiday crowds in their bustles and top-hats, and on through smart St-Germain where they might pass Montesquiou or Proust on their way to the fashionable *five o'clock* with some duchess. The studio, entered across a tiny courtyard, was high, square and crowded. Gertrude described it thus:

Against the walls were several pieces of large Italian Renaissance furniture and in the middle of the room a big Renaissance table. On it a lovely inkstand and at one end of it notebooks neatly arranged, the kind of notebooks French children use.... On the walls right up to the ceiling were pictures.... There was a great deal of Matisse, Picasso, Renoir, Cézanne but there were also a great many other things. There were two Gauguins, there were Manguins, there was a big nude by Valloton.... There was a Maurice Denis, a little Daumier, many Cézanne watercolours, there was in short everything, there was even a little Delacroix and a moderate-sized Greco.

Pablo Picasso: *Portrait of Gertrude Stein*, 1906 (Metropolitan Museum, New York). The painting is seen hanging in the centre of the view of the Rue de Fleurus studio (OPPOSITE). After eighty sittings Picasso suddenly wiped out the face and repainted it from memory.

ABOVE Fernande Olivier in Picasso's studio in the Bateau-Lavoir, holding Van Dongen's daughter, Dolly, for whom Picasso used to make paper dolls. Photograph dated 1907. ABOVE RIGHT Kees Van Dongen: *Portrait of Fernande Olivier,* *c.* 1907 (Private Collection).

Gertrude sat by the fire, getting up to answer the door each time the bell rang. If it were a stranger she would greet him with the question, '*De la part de qui venez-vous?*' ('Who introduced you?'); for it was a habit of her friends to send along their friends. There were lots of Hungarians, a few Americans and some Germans, among whom was the sharp-eyed Wilhelm Uhde. Gertrude described him as 'not a blonde German, he was a tallish, dark, thin man with an excellent quick wit'; but he used to bring tall, blonde young men, until one day, to everybody's surprise, he brought a wife – Sonia Terk. She needed marriage lines for an inheritance, and quickly left him for the painter Robert Delaunay, who was a tall, blonde Frenchman. From Bulgaria came Jules Pascin, and Apollinaire would be there with Marie Laurencin.

Sometimes the mood became rowdy:

Picasso, very lively, undertook to dance a southern Spanish dance, not too respectable. Gertrude Stein's brother did the dying dance of Isadora, it was very lively. Fernande and Pablo got into a discussion about Frédéric of the Lapin Agile and Apaches. Fernande got angry and shook him and said, 'You think you are witty but you are only stupid.' He ruefully showed her that she had shaken off a button and she very angrily said, 'Your only claim to distinction is that you are a precocious child.'

Gertrude managed to write as well as to see much of her painter friends. She used to work at night, and during this time finished her first substan-

tial book, *The Making of Americans*. Matisse was taken up by the smart Galerie Bernheim-Jeune; becoming more prosperous, he moved out to Clamart with his family and visited the Rue de Fleurus less and less. Over the next few years it was to be the Cubists, and especially Picasso whom Gertrude rated far ahead of the others, who provided the core of both her parties and her picture collection. 'Outsiders might easily have imagined themselves in a public gallery,' wrote Vollard, who took some friends there. 'People came in and out. Leo Stein never moved from his favourite position, half reclining on an armchair with his feet high up on the shelf of a bookcase. "Excellent for the digestion," he used to say.'

One of Picasso's friends, though never a close one, since his eccentric habits were incompatible with those of the essentially hard-working painter, died in November. Alfred Jarry, the legendary author of *Ubu Roi*, had ruined his health by drink and drugs but his wild spirits had never faltered. He had lived in a peculiar apartment in the Boulevard St-Germain des Prés, in which the rooms were divided horizontally, so that his hair was perpetually white from rubbing against the ceiling. His poverty was equalled only by his honesty. On one occasion, when he was living out in Corbeil, he cycled the whole way into town to repay a debt of 1.50 francs to a little review he was editing. He died a pauper, but representatives of the *Mercure de France* and *La Revue Blanche* followed his coffin.

At this time Picasso and his friends were interested neither in music nor in the theatre, in which Lugné-Poé's Théâtre de l'Oeuvre and Jacques

A photograph taken in Van Dongen's studio in 1907. Left to right: Van Dongen, his daughter Dolly, his wife Guus, and Jean Van Dongen.

Rouche's new Théâtre des Arts remained outposts of quality in a popular art still dominated by figures like Guitry and Coquelin, Bernhardt and Réjane. It is unlikely that anybody from the Stein set would have been present at the Théâtre du Châtelet in May when Richard Strauss conducted the Paris première of his two-year-old opera *Salome*. Its theme and Oscar Wilde's text fitted comfortably into the Symbolist category, but the musical style was too rich for many Parisian palates. A German opera sung in German was in itself a risk, considering the state of French political nerves. In the *Mercure de France* Willy called it 'a colossal piece of biblical elephantiasis', while André Gide found it 'abominable romantic music, with enough orchestral rhetoric to make one like Bellini'. He recorded in his diary a reported remark of Frau Strauss, commenting on the fact that the Parisian audience did not appreciate her husband's music, and threatening to return with bayonets. 'Perhaps apocryphal,' Gide added, charitably.

Strauss, for his part, was not much impressed by the latest French opera, Debussy's *Pélléas et Mélisande*. On his first visit to hear it at the Opéra Comique he turned to his hosts, Maurice Ravel and the novelist Romain Rolland, at the end of the first act and whispered anxiously: 'Does it go on like this all the time?' Afterwards he pronounced: 'Delicate harmonies, excellent orchestral effects in very good taste; but it amounts to nothing at all.'

The German composer's première had been rather overshadowed by a massive success at the Opéra in May. The young impresario Diaghilev had been delighted by the success of his exhibition of Russian art at the Grand Palais the year before; he had been offered the Légion d'Honneur (but had passed it on to Benois and Bakst). Now he determined to introduce to Paris the glories of modern Russian music, and booked the Opéra for an ambitious concert season. He was taking a risk. The music of 'The Five' – Borodin, Mussorgsky, Rimsky-Korsakov, Balakirev and Cui – was already popular in Paris, but Tchaikovsky was regarded as a trivial lightweight by most critics. Only Debussy, who had at one time served in Russia as tutor to Madame von Meck, Tchaikovsky's patroness, admired him. Diaghilev invited the friendly critic of *Le Figaro*, Robert Brussel, to St Petersburg to handle advance publicity. He borrowed ten thousand roubles from a rich music-lover and persuaded even the ailing Rimsky-Korsakov to promise, like Glazunov and Rachmaninov, to conduct his own music. Arthur Nikisch, a world-famous conductor and a Tchaikovsky specialist, was engaged as one of the five conductors taking part.

Apart from a personal *contretemps* between Diaghilev and Scriabin, whose free ticket to hear his own piano concerto nearly failed to appear in time, the season of five concerts was a huge success. The bass Feodor Chaliapin, in particular, caused a sensation in a song from *Prince Igor* – the start of his world career. The programme contained brief biographies, with pictures by Repin. Tchaikovsky, whose Second Symphony formed the core of the first concert, was described as notable for his operas, orchestral music, chamber works and songs; there was no mention of his ballet scores. Diaghilev's interest in music and art – his magazine *Mir Iskusstva* had disseminated French Symbolist ideas in Russia – did

OPPOSITE Léon Bakst: *Diaghilev and his Old Nurse*, 1905. Although Diaghilev was only thirty-three when Bakst painted this portrait in St Petersburg, he already had the characteristic white streak in his hair.

not yet seriously extend to ballet. His experiences at the Maryinsky Theatre, from which he had been dismissed after disagreements, had probably embittered him. And he had not yet met Nijinsky. But he now scored a big success in a highly competitive sphere. On 31 May Romain Rolland wrote to an Italian friend:

Long-distance motor-racing was already a popular sport, combining danger and endurance. This photograph shows Prince Borghese arriving in Paris after a race from Peking in 1907.

In the last weeks we have had an almost uninterrupted succession of concerts, galas, musical evenings and dinners. Never in Paris has there been such an eventful season. The powerful Russian and German composers and conductors have all been here together – Richard Strauss, Rimsky-Korsakov, Glazunov, Rachmaninov, Scriabin, Nikisch, Blumenfeld etc. . . . The ironic situation which emerges – and it is also a little comic, rather sad – is that not one of them understands the other.

The writer Willy was not only busy reviewing – with the aid of anony-

mous helpers – music for the *Mercure de France*. The promotion of his wife, Colette, kept him occupied elsewhere. Temporarily abandoning her 'Claudine' books, she had taken to the stage and was to appear at the Moulin Rouge in a pantomime called *Madame la Marquise de Morny*. The author was actually a well-known lesbian lady known as Missy, married to the Marquis de Belbeuf, whose coat of arms appeared on the poster. During the play *Le Rêve d'Egypte*, the two ladies embraced passionately. The Marquis and Willy came to blows in the auditorium, and the police forbade a second performance until Missy had been replaced by a man. The change was made, the title changed to *Un Songe d'Orient*, and soon afterwards Colette and Missy retired together to the country. Meanwhile the Press had enjoyed itself with 'The Scandal of the Moulin Rouge'.

More serious citizens were troubled throughout the year with fresh signs of international discord. There was trouble again in North Africa, with bombardments at Casablanca. Edward VII was back in Paris, this time with his Queen, but soon afterwards he was chatting with the Kaiser at Wilhelmshöhe. There were pictures in the illustrated papers (which now began to feature good-quality colour photographs) of riots in the Midi against Clemenceau's firm application of anti-clerical measures; of the German Zeppelin airship alarmingly covering 300 kilometres in six hours; and of a new war weapon called a tank. The Eulenburg scandal in Berlin, revealing homosexuality among the Kaiser's entourage, was gratefully seized on as a sign of weakness in Germany. The year ended with depressing news of a financial crisis in New York. France still led in the development of the motor-car and in aeronautics – in November Henri Farman's biplane attained a speed of 88 kilometres per hour at Issy-les-Moulineaux. French sporting, social and artistic activities had never been more active nor more inventive. But both at home and abroad shifting currents hinted at a turn in the tide. Most intellectuals preferred to ignore them, to narrow their eyes and concentrate on small events of private significance.

1908
A Banquet of Innocents

NOBODY COULD REPRESENT the power of privacy and non-commitment more completely than a figure who wanders through these years like a child in the jungle – the naïve painter Henri Rousseau. Effortlessly he eluded every pressure of period or place, all attempts to fit him into a group or category of art. He sprang up like a wild flower in a well-dug garden, to stand as a happy symbol of the brave new permissiveness. Naïve art had never before featured as the equal of, indeed an influence on, the professional mainstream. The recognition of Rousseau's gifts by younger contemporaries like Picasso is both a tribute to their perspicacity and an illustration of the creative benefits of their apparently destructive processes. There is no forerunner of Rousseau, because no previous age would have accepted him.

Rousseau, however, did not regard himself as in any way eccentric. He was fifty-six when the century was born, already a dedicated artist innocently aspiring to be accepted as a rival to the great names in the Salon. Petit-bourgeois to the backbone, he was a revolutionary by accident. Nothing would have pleased him more than to know that today his name appears in dictionaries of art on the same page as those of Raphael, Rembrandt and Rodin. His sweet-tempered originality and integrity disarmed even the dourest critics and charmed the public. Half-mocked but greatly enjoyed, Rousseau's paintings penetrate their period through the force of his vision. He remained on the fringe of the Parisian art world, yet he was an essential part of it.

He was born in Laval, a small town in the west of France, and joined the army as a bandsman. His gentle, dreamy disposition must have made poor military material and at the age of twenty-five he left the army – though he rejoined it for the brief 1870 campaign against Prussia. He moved to Paris, settling in the district south of Montparnasse, where he was to remain all his life. He married and fathered nine children, seven of whom died young. To support them he worked as toll-keeper at the nearby Porte de Vanves, collecting duties from people bringing their wares into the local markets.

In 1885 his wife died and he applied for a retirement pension. He was awarded 600 francs a year and settled down to devote himself to his favourite hobby, painting. To eke out his pension he acted as local sales inspector for the *Petit Parisien* newspaper. He also fixed a notice on his

Henri Rousseau, nicknamed 'Le Douanier', posing in
appropriate costume in his studio at 2 *bis* Rue Perrel.
The painting beside him is *Scouts Attacked by a Tiger* of 1904.

door: 'Henri Rousseau. Academy of drawing, painting and music. Residences visited. Moderate prices.' In the afternoon he would receive music pupils from the neighbourhood; he played the flute and clarinet, and specialized in the violin. There is no record of any art pupils, though that is where his own interests lay. What had been a hobby soon became a passion, and he took it up as his profession. It was to remain so for the next twenty-five years – though his lack of formal training always branded him as an amateur, with the affectionate, if slightly inaccurate, nickname 'Le Douanier' ('customs official'). Filled with ingenuous ambition, he began to submit his work to professional exhibitions. He must have had disappointments, but fortunately there existed the Salon des Indépendants which had no selection committee. In 1886 he paid his fee and sent in his first canvas; thereafter he showed there regularly.

In 1895 Rousseau wrote his own entry for a proposed artists' guide:

In view of his parents' lack of wealth he was obliged at first to follow a career other than that to which his artistic taste called him. It was only in 1885 that he made his beginnings in art after many mortifications, alone with only nature as teacher, and some advice received from Gérome and Clément. His first two works were sent to be exhibited at the Salon in the Champs-Elysées; they were entitled *An Italian Dance* and *Sunset*.... It was only after hard experience that he managed to make himself known from the hundreds of artists that surrounded him. He has perfected himself more and more in the original manner that he has adopted and is on the way to becoming one of our best realist painters. As a characteristic sign he wears a bushy beard and has long since joined forces with the Indépendants, believing that all liberty to create must be left to the inventor whose thoughts are elevated to the beautiful and the good.

He added, with characteristic politeness: 'He will never forget the members of the Press who have understood him, who have upheld him in times of discouragement and who have helped him to become the man he should be.' It was certainly remarkable that a few critics, such as Wilhelm Uhde, did manage to single him out among the thousands of canvases at these enormous shows, particularly since many of the exhibits must have been equally unsophisticated, if not equally inspired – the Salon des Indépendants achieved a record entry this year, 6,701, among which were Modigliani's first contributions.

Rousseau's admirers included Toulouse-Lautrec, Renoir, Redon and Gauguin, who, however, mischievously took advantage of his trusting simplicity by sending him off one day to the Ministry of Fine Arts to discuss a non-existent official commission, and on another occasion 'to meet the President' at the Elysée Palace. By 1900 he was a licensed oddity whose regular contributions to the Indépendants had become a kind of institution. In 1905 he had made his first appearance in the Salon d'Automne, with one of the 'jungle' pictures which he declared were inspired by his service with the army in Mexico. Fact and fantasy were often indistinguishable in his mind, and it now seems likely that inspiration came from the Jardin des Plantes with its caged animals and exotically decorated tea-rooms. Oddly, no dealer ever offered Rousseau a one-man show.

His ambitions were set high, humble though his circumstances

remained. In 1889 he submitted a 'Vaudeville in Three Acts and Ten Scenes' to the director of the Théâtre du Châtelet, the home of spectacular musical shows. Ten years later he tried again, with a 'Drama in Five Acts and Nineteen Scenes called *The Vengeance of a Russian Orphan*'. In 1886 he had solemnly submitted to the Academy of Literature and Music a waltz of his own composition, playing it himself in the Salle Beethoven. It was named *Clémence* after his beloved wife, and afterwards used to figure in the little *soirées* which he gave in his modest apartment, evenings attended by local tradespeople who mingled with his friends from Montmartre – Picasso, Robert and Sonia Delaunay, André Salmon, Max Jacob, Marie Laurencin and Apollinaire. The last of these did not at first take much to Rousseau's work; 'He is lacking in general culture. . . . He ought to have remained a mere artisan,' he wrote. But in 1909 he was to give Rousseau a commission to paint a portrait of Marie Laurencin and himself – though it took a long time for Rousseau to extract from him his fee, 300 francs. The picture was entitled *The Muse Inspiring the Poet*. Rousseau used to invite guests to his *soirées* with phrases like: 'My

Henri Rousseau: *The Artist Painting His Wife*, 1900–5 (N. Kandinsky Collection, Paris).

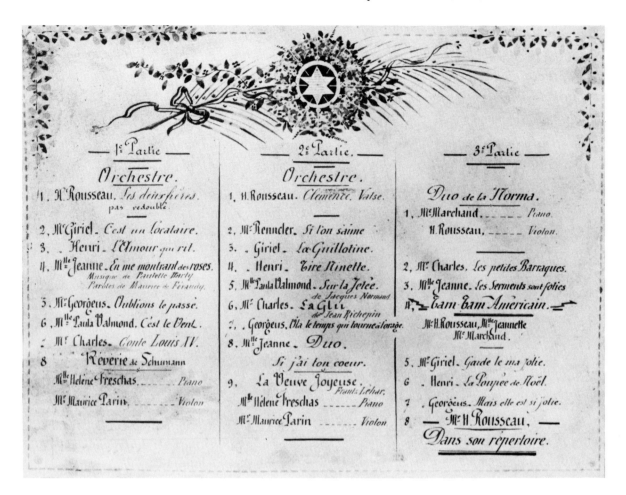

The hand-written programme for one of Henri Rousseau's musical evenings, attended by artists from Montmartre and local shopkeepers and performed by the painter and his pupils.

literary and artistic gathering will take place tomorrow Thursday the 11th inst. I expect you and your muse, who will sing us some gay and charming songs.'

Picasso was a particular admirer, and one day he came across a canvas by Rousseau among the pictures in the junkshop-*cum*-gallery of Père Soulier in the Rue des Martyrs. Delighted with his find, he and his friends decided to celebrate the occasion with a party in honour of the painter. The motive seems to have been a mixture of genuine affection and respect and mischievous teasing; the temptation to pull the leg of the incorrigible innocent must have been irresistible to the more boisterous members of the gang.

Thirty people were invited and met for drinks beforehand in a café at the end of the Rue Ravignan. When Gertrude Stein and her companion, Alice B. Toklas, arrived, spirits were already high and Marie Laurencin was dancing a solo. A big trestle table was set up in Picasso's studio, together with a seat of honour for the painter, a chair mounted on a packing case, surrounded by flags and lanterns and a banner proclaiming 'Honour to Rousseau' – a true Douanier scene. The company assembled in the studio. Max Jacob's room below was used as a kitchen and a cloakroom for the men; the women put their coats in a front studio on the ground floor which had once belonged to Van Dongen. Frédé from the

Lapin Agile called by with his donkey for a drink. Braque and André Salmon arrived, and finally Apollinaire, conducting the guest of honour.

After a somewhat improvised meal (Picasso had ordered it for the wrong day) the ceremonies began. André Salmon recited a eulogy, finishing it by drinking a toast so generous that he knocked himself out. Some of the guests sang songs. Finally Apollinaire got to his feet and recited a poem which can roughly be translated:

> You summon up the Aztec scene, Rousseau,
> The fields where mangoes and bananas grow,
> While apes spill melon-blood upon the floor,
> And scatter the blonde, shot emperor's gore.
>
> Your brush revives Mexican memories,
> A russet sun bedecks banana trees,
> And gallantly you swapped your soldier's coat
> Against the customs-man's blue redingote.
>
> A baleful fortune dogged your offspring's lives,
> It robbed you of your children and your wives,
> But a new wife in painting you did find,
> To beget pictures, children of your mind.
>
> 'Tis to celebrate you we're here. Drink up
> The wine with which Apollinaire fills our cup.
> Drink, for it is time to honour you, so
> Let us all shout together 'Long Live Rousseau!'
>
> O glorious limner of the Republic, on
> Thy name hangs the Independents' proudest badge,
> And gleaming marble, pure Penthelicon
> Will sculpt thy features, banner of our age.
>
> Let each one rise, clink glass and drink it down,
> Let true French life and laughter here revive,
> Away black cares, avaunt you furious frown,
> I drink to Rousseau, may he ever thrive!

Rousseau joined in with a tune on the violin which he had brought with him – one of his own compositions, *Clochettes* – and everybody began to dance. Drowsy with wine and excitement, the guest of honour began to doze off happily, while the wax from a candle dripped unnoticed on to his head and Leo Stein stood by protecting him from the confusion. Neighbours began to drop in and the party went on until three in the morning. Finally the Steins found a cab, packed Rousseau into it with his violin, and took him home. A charming letter of thanks arrived at .the Rue Ravignan soon afterwards. Rousseau was a genuine admirer of Picasso: 'We are the greatest,' he told him, according to Kahnweiler. 'You in the Egyptian style, I in the modern style.'

Rousseau's jungle painting in the Salon d'Automne was not the only work to attract attention. Among the regular visitors to the Paris exhibitions were two immensely rich businessmen from Moscow, Ivan Morosov and Sergei Shtchukin. Both were voracious collectors of all kinds of art. Morosov, who had inherited a fortune amassed from cotton after the Napoleonic invasion, came from a family which numbered the painters Vrubel, Serov, and Pasternak (father of the writer) among its friends, and had presented generous donations to the Tretyakov Museum in Moscow. He was sent abroad to study in Zurich, but returned to mind the business in Tver. In 1900 he moved to Moscow and, in the family tradition, began to collect.

His first purchase in Paris was Sisley's *Frost in Louveciennes*, which he bought in 1903. It was much admired in Russia by Serov and another painter, Korovin, and Morosov went back for more Impressionists, buying Monets, Renoirs and Pissarros. Soon he had progressed to Degas and to the Post-Impressionists – Van Gogh, Gauguin and Cézanne. He became a personal friend of the Symbolist artist Maurice Denis. On his first visits to Paris he would select his purchases at exhibitions; later, however, he got to know dealers like Durand-Ruel and Vollard and bought directly from them. He even used to bid at the Paris auctions without seeing the pictures.

His purchases were housed in a huge eighteenth-century mansion in Prechistenka Street in Moscow; he had had this house altered to hold his collection, which soon numbered 100 Russian and 250 French works, guarded jealously by their owner. The collection was to be nationalized after the 1917 Revolution and Morosov became assistant curator, showing visitors round the house on Sunday mornings. He fled to the west in 1918 and died at Karlsruhe in Germany in 1921.

In this year, 1908, influenced perhaps by Diaghilev's magazine *Mir Iskusstva*, Morosov commissioned Maurice Denis to design a mural for his music room, and the artist duly despatched a set of panels representing the story of Cupid and Psyche. They were criticized in Russia, where Impressionism was still the dominant influence, but Morosov must have been pleased for he went on buying in Paris. His taste progressed gradually from Bonnard and Vuillard and Signac to Fauve artists like Matisse and Marquet; eventually he even bought a Picasso.

Shtchukin was twenty years older than Morosov. He too came from a rich business background – in his case glass and textiles. His father had been not so much a collector as a hoarder, making frequent trips to Italy and France. Sergei's chief interest, however, was in Persian and oriental art and in Russian antiques, of which he used to order cartfuls at a time. He lived in the sumptuous Trubetskoy Palace, but in 1892 he built a special pseudo-Russian-style museum to house his treasures, and in 1897 he added a wing based on the wooden architecture of Kolomenskoe. By that time the collection consisted of over 300,000 items, including Russian silver, ikons and holy relics (he was a reactionary 'Old Believer'), armour, rugs and porcelain from the east, and paintings from Russia and France. As was the custom at the time, antiques and pictures and curios were all jumbled together, and *objets* of widely separated dates and from different countries were displayed side by side.

He had started collecting rather earlier than Morosov, and he seems to have been more adventurous by temperament. In 1895 he opened his collection to the public, sometimes acting as guide himself, and in 1905 he presented the whole enterprise to the Museum of Imperial History in Moscow, with himself as curator. By this time he had already bought a Matisse which he had seen in the 1904 Salon. In the Salon d'Automne of 1908 he was struck by a large canvas in which Matisse had cleverly combined many of his favourite subjects – a domestic, Nabi-style interior with a woman bent over a dinner table; a view of a landscape through a window; a Van Gogh-like chair half hidden, in the Japanese manner borrowed by Lautrec; and an exotic wallpaper of oriental curvaceousness. They were all flattened out into a free decorative design in bold, basic colours, and Matisse called it *The Dessert, a Harmony in Blue*. Shtchukin was much taken with it, and bought it forthwith. But there was an abnormally long delay before the picture arrived from Paris. When it did, and its wooden case was opened, Shtchukin found to his astonishment that the whole work had been repainted. The background was now a vivid scarlet, and its name had been changed to *The Dessert, a Harmony in Red*. Nothing daunted, Shtchukin accepted the change and hung the picture in a central position in his dining-room.

Shtchukin was also to prove a loyal supporter of Picasso. In 1908 he bought his first painting from the Rue Ravignan, and during the next six years he was to buy fifty Picassos. Quiet, awkward and stammering, 'a little man with a big head and a rather porcine face', as Fernande Olivier described him, he was bold and impulsive and took delight in shocking the public. He liked big pictures, and whenever one appeared Kahnweiler used to send him a telegram, often with success.

The two Russian collectors were a prime influence in the first years of what was to become the School of Paris, as the American Gertrude Stein was to be for its second stage. At the Matisse exhibition at Bernheim-Jeune in 1910 – to which Shtchukin and Morosov sent no pictures – almost all the paintings were from the private collections of foreigners. The *Chronique des Arts* remarked: 'We are happy to note that his disciples and active admirers include no one but Russians, Poles and Americans.'

Matisse, together with his fellow Fauves Marquet and Rouault, had been on the selection committee of the Salon d'Automne and had joined in the turning down of six pale, sharp-angled landscapes by a twenty-six-year-old painter – the pioneer Cubist paintings which Braque had brought back from the south of France. The disappointed painter took them off to Kahnweiler who, the day after the Salon closed, exhibited them in a one-man show in his little gallery in Rue Vignon. The catalogue contained a foreword by Apollinaire, in which he wrote, 'Purer than other men, he ignores everything foreign to his art'. If Picasso had opened the door into the Cubist world with *Les Demoiselles d'Avignon*, this was the first completely worked out Cubist exhibition. Louis Vauxcelles wrote in *Gil Blas*: 'M. Braque is an exceedingly bold young man. He despises form and reduces everything, landscapes, figures and houses, to geometrical patterns, to cubes.' The paintings which he and Derain had shown in the Indépendants in April had already been influenced by Picasso – 'strangely formed rather wooden blocked figures', as Gertrude Stein described them. But these new landscapes, painted in Cézanne country,

Georges Braque: *Houses at L'Estaque*, 1908
Kunstmuseum, Berne, Hermann and Margrit Rupf Fund).

seemed to have absorbed some of his careful discipline. This was real Cubism, calm and perfectly carpentered.

In this year appeared a split between the Cubists and Matisse, which was to last for many years. He was now an artist of international reputation; he exhibited this year in Berlin, Moscow, Stockholm and London – where his offering at the New Gallery was described in *The Burlington Magazine* as 'infantile'. In New York's 291 Gallery, run by the photographer Edward Steichen, he was even less warmly received, with comments like 'artistic degeneration', 'loathsome and abnormal', and even 'a cruel temperament'. But on 3 November Bernard Berenson sprang to his defence in *The Nation*, declaring that he was 'a magnificent draughtsman and a great designer'.

Six weeks later Matisse was expressing his own views in public. The Christmas number of *La Grande Revue* published an article entitled 'Notes of a Painter', in which the outwardly serious and professorial artist made some startling statements. 'What I am after, above all, is expression,' he declared, contradicting those who had attacked him as a theorist. 'Composition is the art of arranging in a decorative manner the various elements at a painter's disposal for the expression of his feelings.' He quoted the calm, durable unreality of Greek and Egyptian art, stressed colour as a means of expression, pinned his faith in the human figure, and defined the ideal as 'an art of balance, of purity and serenity devoid of troubling or depressing subject-matter, an art which might be ... something like a good armchair in which to rest.' He added a final shot against the academics: 'Rules have no existence outside of individuals.'

The 'Notes' were an expansion of some remarks he had made to Guillaume Apollinaire, who had published them in his magazine *La Phalange* in 1907. But now Apollinaire had defected to the Cubists and was looking even further ahead. His 'Oreinocritique', which appeared in the same magazine in February, carried more than a hint of Surrealism, and this same year he published an *Introduction to the Works of the Marquis de Sade* – who was later to be a hero of the Surrealists – which spoke of him as 'the most liberated spirit who ever existed'. 'The man who counted for nothing in the nineteenth century may come to dominate the twentieth,' he foretold.

Apart from the sober Cubists, many young painters were now influenced by Matisse's bold palette, perhaps encouraged by two Van Gogh exhibitions – at Bernheim-Jeune and the Galerie Druet – which had started the year. The Fauves were prominent at the Indépendants and featured strongly at a mixed show of twenty-four artists organized by the Galerie Druet in July. The Salon d'Automne in October included a number of Matisses besides the *Dessert* bought by Shtchukin, and featured a retrospective of the Italian Impressionist painter Monticelli.

The sixty-eight-year-old Rodin, by now almost a national monument in his own person, was a faithful supporter of the 'modern' wing of the summer Salons, the so-called National. This year he showed three 'fragments', which were picked out for special praise by Charles Morice in the *Mercure de France*. Rodin had just obtained splendid new studio space in the Hôtel Biron, where Matisse had had his short-lived school,

FOLLOWING PAGES A day at the races. The grandstand at Auteuil during the '*Grande Semaine*'.

Edouard Vuillard: *The Art Dealers*, 1908 (St Louis Art Museum, Gift of Mr and Mrs Richard K. Weil). This portrait of the Bernheim brothers shows that galleries were already installing sophisticated lighting.

an old convent acquired by the state under the new laws nationalizing ecclesiastical property. It had been recently discovered by a sixteen-year-old playing truant from school, Jean Cocteau. Quick, adventurous and romantic by nature, he was enchanted by the deserted rooms and over-grown garden, and persuaded the old *concierge* to admit him to some rooms reserved for music and dancing. 'One door, for which I possessed an enormous key, opened on to an archway and the archway into a garden. Garden park, kitchen garden, Paradise, how can I describe it?' He was to do so later in films like *La Belle et la Bête*.

Rodin and his secretary Rilke temporarily occupied the central rooms of the building, whose future was uncertain. One day Cocteau overheard the *concierge* discussing with some visitors a plan to extend the Rue de Bourgogne southwards across the site occupied by the Hôtel Biron. He rushed off to his literary friends, who made such a fuss in the Press that the scheme was dropped and the building saved. Rodin was the chief benefactor – since it was eventually to become the Rodin Museum. Cocteau had to leave his hiding-place when it was discovered by his mother on an official visit to Rodin's studio as a 'Friend of the Louvre'.

Even at this tender age Cocteau's precocious brilliance and vitality were beginning to make his name known in literary society. He moved in the world of the *soirée* and the artistic hostess – the kind of occasion exemplified by a poetry reading organized by Robert de Montesquiou in June in memory of his beloved secretary and companion, Gabriel de Iturri, who had died three years earlier. The cream of the church, society and the arts – a public which ranged from the Grand Duke Vladimir to Anatole France, Pierre Loti and the ubiquitous Rodin – sat reverently while Montesquiou intoned memorial verses and letters of condolence from distinguished persons, dropping each piece into a bronze bowl as he finished it.

The more serious literary world kept away from such occasions. Proust might have attended, but to his annoyance he was not invited. Montesquiou made up for his slip by calling at Proust's apartment at two in the morning to give him a private rendering of his verse, leaving a bound copy. 'It's just like Bossuet,' wrote Proust, politely. 'I am struggling, without making progress, on days when I'm not too ill, with a novel which will perhaps give you a little more esteem for me, if you have the patience to read it.' His struggle was with his plans for *A La Recherche du Temps Perdu*.

Though he too was inclined to homosexual attachments, the tight-lipped Gide would certainly not have approved of Montesquiou's gesture. He was much occupied in founding, with his friends Jean Schlumberger and Jacques Copeau (later to be the inspired director of the Théâtre du Vieux Colombier), a new magazine designed to uphold the most high-minded literary standards, *La Nouvelle Revue Française*. In the meantime he found time to carry on a brisk correspondence with the Catholic writer Paul Claudel, whose anti-freethinker opinions were hardening. In his journal for June, Claudel described Voltaire as 'imbecile and disgusting, like an old pisspot monkey'. In August he wrote, from Tientsin in China, that a writer he disapproved of 'belongs, like Lamartine, to that class of writer who doesn't even manage to blacken the paper. . . . He thinks himself intoxicated on dewdrops when really he's drunk nothing but a monkey's nose-drips. He likes Renan!' As for Victor Hugo, Claudel admitted in July that he was a great poet, 'if one can be a great poet without intelligence, taste, sensibility, discipline or that highest form of imagination which I call the imagination of proportion. He had simply a huge windy capability arising from the command of a large vocabulary.'

While Proust was sketching out his first pages, another novelist was drawing a line under the last. On 30 August Arnold Bennett, sitting in his room near Fontainebleau, noted with satisfaction: 'Finished *The Old Wives' Tale* at 11.30 today. 200,000 words. Royalty advance of £150 from Chapman Hall.' The length was exactly as he had planned, he was content with the quality, and he gave himself some time off. Visiting the Aviation Exhibition at the Grand Palais, he admired Farman's aeroplane: 'vast and beautiful as a yacht. Same kind of beauty. Yet a new creation of form, a new style.' He was right to perceive that at this time flight was as exciting and pioneering a venture in France as art. The year had opened with a historic achievement by the plane whose beauty had moved him. It was later recorded in an inscription: 'On this spot on 13 January 1908, a closed-circle kilometre was covered by Henri Farman, his biplane being designed and built by Gabriel and Charles Voisin.' In June Farman was to break another record, by achieving a height of ten metres in flight. In spite of his French-sounding name the aviator was in fact English, the son of the Paris correspondent of *The Standard*. For a short time he had studied at the Ecole des Beaux Arts.

In May Europe celebrated the jubilee of Emperor Franz Josef of Austria-Hungary who had succeeded to the throne in 1848. It was quickly followed by Austria's annexation of Bosnia-Herzegovina and Bulgaria's declaration of independence under Ferdinand I. The King of Portugal and the Crown Prince were the victims, in February, of the only major assassination this year. Revolution in Turkey produced tales of horror and brutality in August. *Peter Pan* was presented at the Théâtre Vaudeville and pronounced 'an exquisite fable'. A comet passed over Paris on 1 October, and there were two artistic weddings; Braque married Marthe le Sidaner, and Debussy, after a divorce, married Madame Bardac. Professionally, Debussy had gone to hear Chaliapin at the Opéra.

Feodor Chaliapin in the sumptuous costume designed for him in the name role of *Boris Godunov*. His triumph in Diaghilev's production at the Paris Opéra in 1908 launched him on his world career.

Recitals of Russian music had accompanied Diaghilev's exhibition of Russian art in 1906, and Chaliapin had scored a personal triumph in his Russian concerts of 1907. These successes persuaded Diaghilev and the Paris impresario Gabriel Astruc that the moment had come for a full-scale demonstration of Russian theatrical presentation. Mussorgsky's opera was chosen not because of its popularity in Russia, but because Diaghilev loved it and it offered a huge role for Chaliapin. A deal was struck with the Opéra that it should provide its theatre and back-up artists and extras on condition that the production should become its property afterwards – though in the event it was never used again, and was sold to the Metropolitan Museum in New York.

Preparations in St Petersburg and Moscow were frantic. Diaghilev was in bad odour with both the Tsar and the court, and had only one powerful ally, the big, bluff Grand Duke Vladimir. Bilibin, the designer, and Alexandre Benois, the art historian – who was living in Paris and was familiar with French taste – scoured the markets for old costumes and material. The chorus was to come from Moscow. Two dancers were booked to lead the Parisian *corps de ballet*. The Grand Duke inspected the costumes, modelled by assistants from the sewing-room.

Not surprisingly, enormous difficulties arose when the Russian party arrived in Paris and invaded the Opéra. Some of the scenery would not fit. There was inadequate rehearsal time. The extras gave trouble. 'Two hundred stinking people from the street, with false beards awry and hastily pulled on boyar fur coats and caps' turned the stage into 'an un-controllable orgy', according to Benois. Diaghilev was so alarmed that he called a meeting to ask if the first night should be postponed. 'We Russians must n-not give in!' cried Chaliapin's stammering make-up artist – and the show went on.

When it opened on 19 May the huge, savage, tragic spectacle with Chaliapin at its centre was an unqualified success with the public, though some musicians carped at changes in the score. Here were all the favourite themes run into one – Symbolist exoticism and extravagance in the Moreau style, combined with brilliant colours and bold contrasts. Here in the flesh were the Fauves, made acceptable by being foreign. 'That night,' Benois recalled, 'Chaliapin strode beside me along the *grands boulevards* saying over and over again: "We've done something tonight. I don't know what, but we've really done something!"'

SAISON RUSSE 1909   OPERA ET BALLET

1909
The Invasion of the Ballets Russes

THE YEAR 1909 OPENED with a mixture of promise and foreboding. On New Year's Day Proust returned late along the Boulevard Haussmann to his apartment at No. 122. His biographer, George Painter, wrote:

As he sat reading by his lamp, still shivering with cold, Céline urged her master to take a cup of tea, an unfamiliar beverage to this addict of coffee; and when he idly dipped into it a finger of dry toast and raised the sodden mixture to his lips, he was overwhelmed once more by the mysterious joy which marked an onset of unconscious memory.

The key to his great labyrinth of recollections – to be transposed into that fateful 'madeleine' cake – had presented itself and would soon emerge in the first chapters of *A La Recherche du Temps Perdu*.

Next day the harsh realities of the present jumped into the headlines. A huge earthquake had shaken the island of Sicily and half the town of Messina lay in ruins. At home a quadruple guillotining horrified the inhabitants of Béthune; Paris was shaken by the death of its favourite actor Constant Coquelin, famous for his Cyrano de Bergerac, and, a few days later, of one of its best-known poets, Catulle Mendès. Edward VII was in Berlin again, plotting with the Kaiser. The quarrel between Austria and Serbia seemed at boiling point. On 27 February the correspondent of *L'Illustration* wrote: 'Never at any time has Europe known a period of such critical tension as this last week.' Diagrams of the naval strengths of the big powers began to appear in the papers.

In May it was the turn of domestic affairs to raise hopes and fears. The supreme council of the Trades Union Confederation met in plenary session and decreed a general strike; but it did not monopolize the news. *L'Illustration* noted:

At the very moment when the red posters calling for revolutionary action were going up the theatre lights were going on, and those of the Châtelet more brilliant than all. For it was on its immense fairyland stage that the 'Saison Russe' was making its bow.... That evening, together with the return of Isadora Duncan – these are the great events of the week.

Exactly who should be credited with the idea of bringing the Russian ballet is uncertain; two weeks after the close of *Boris Godunov* Astruc was scribbling on a restaurant menu the names of the dancers he and Diaghilev would bring to Paris the following year. But it was Diaghilev

OPPOSITE The costume designed by Bakst for Karsavina in the *Bluebird* pas-de-deux which formed the highlight of the *divertissement* entitled 'Le Festin'. Diaghilev rechristened the dance *The Firebird* and gave the bird's role to the girl.

who brought the project to life. Now aged twenty-seven, the pushy young country boy from Perm had established himself as an influential figure in artistic circles in St Petersburg. He had edited an art magazine, mounted exhibitions at home and in Paris, organized concerts and now succeeded with *Boris Godunov*. He had energy, imagination, a strong will, incredible self-confidence and talented and influential friends. In St Petersburg he was close to Bakst, Benois and Michael Fokine, the daring young choreographer; in Paris he was familiar with the Grand Duke Cyril, the Princesse de Polignac, Robert de Montesquiou and his wealthy and art-loving cousin Comtesse Greffulhe, president of Astruc's Société Musicale. Diaghilev set to work to bring the two worlds together.

The obstacles were gigantic. The dancers were to be borrowed from the imperial Maryinsky Theatre during their holidays, with Serge Grigoriev, a friend of Fokine's, to supervise them. The idea was to present a mixed programme of ballet and opera, and details were quickly worked out in Diaghilev's apartment. In February, while these discussions were still going on, he attended a concert where he was struck by a scherzo written by a twenty-seven-year-old composer, Igor Stravinsky. Diaghilev immediately introduced himself and became a firm friend.

Diaghilev had contracted to bear the whole cost of the undertaking. Astruc would get a percentage in return for publicity and box-office organization. The cost had been estimated at 265,000 francs for sixteen performances. To finance the project Diaghilev depended largely on the powerful Grand Duke Vladimir, whose son was the lover of the Maryinsky's prima ballerina, Kchessinskaya. On 22 February Diaghilev ran into his first difficulty – the Grand Duke suddenly died. Almost immediately Kchessinskaya, dissatisfied with the roles allotted to her, withdrew, and the Grand Duke's promised subsidy of 100,000 roubles disappeared at the same time. A third blow followed quickly. On 18 March Kchessinskaya's lover wrote to the Tsar, advising him to withhold all support from Diaghilev, and from that moment all co-operation from the imperial theatres was cancelled. The dancers rehearsing in the little theatre in the Hermitage Palace, which had been loaned to them, were ignominiously bundled out, trailing across the town with cabfuls of costumes and props to new premises hastily improvised by Diaghilev.

On 2 April, at four o'clock in the afternoon, Grigoriev assembled the troupe and Diaghilev addressed them:

It gives me great pleasure to make your acquaintance. I trust that we are going to work together in harmony. I am delighted to be showing Paris the Russian Ballet for the first time. Ballet, to my mind, is one of the most lovely of the arts and it exists nowhere else in Europe. It will depend on you all to make it a success and I greatly hope that you will do so.

News of the impending invasion soon reached Paris. 'Diaghilev the impossibilist has launched his *Grande Armée*,' Benois wrote to Montesquiou. Astruc had booked not the Opéra but the Châtelet, the huge, rather run-down theatre that specialized in popular musicals. It was not grand enough for the kind of public at which Diaghilev was aiming, and arrangements were made to have it redecorated, recarpeted, and even partly

Léon Bakst (born Rosenberg)
poses in front of his design
for Nijinsky as 'Le Dieu Bleu'
in 1912. He first met Diaghilev
while still a student at the
St Petersburg Academy of Art
and became, with Alexandre
Benois, one of his closest
collaborators. His success in
Paris launched a new emphasis
on stage design as a serious art.

rebuilt to accommodate a larger orchestra pit. Even at this late date the
programmes were still undecided. The Maryinsky season ended on 1
May. On 2 May the troupe boarded the Paris train. Diaghilev arrived
a day later, announcing to Astruc that he had spent all his funds already
on scenery and costumes.

Rehearsals began in great confusion. Fokine struggled with his mixed
but enthusiastic band – a Moscow contingent arrived late and had to be
taught everything in a fortnight – while carpenters and upholsterers
hammered away deafeningly in the auditorium. Diaghilev meanwhile
carried on his subtle infiltration of the artistic world by inviting influential
friends to watch. Through the snob-telegraph, carried by people like Cocteau, Montesquiou, Alfred Edwards, the wealthy editor of *Le Matin*, and
his wife Misia, later Misia Sert, the word began to get round that something special was about to burst on Paris. By 10 May Astruc could
announce extra performances. On 16 May the orchestra arrived from

Moscow. Finally, on 18 May the papers announced the opening – the habitual *répétition-générale* or open dress-rehearsal – at 8.30 precisely. It was to be a gala evening: 'Evening dress will be obligatory in all parts of the theatre.'

The audience had been carefully assembled, led by the French Foreign Minister escorting the Russian Ambassador, and their wives. There was a lavish spread of ministers and diplomats, society hostesses, portrait painters, musicians, critics and actresses. Astruc, shrewd and enthusiastic behind his Assyrian beard, had gone so far as to invite fifty-two actresses to occupy the front row of the dress circle. All fifty-two accepted and he arranged them, blonde and brunette alternately, like a wreath of beauties across the theatre. Diaghilev's formula – matching dedicated professionalism on one side of the curtain against wealth and influence on the other – was displayed for the first time.

The curtain rose on a minor misfire – *Le Pavillon d'Armide*, a ghostly evocation of Versailles with almost as much mime as dancing, a pastiche score by Tcherepnin, and designs by Benois. The highlight was a *pas de trois* danced by Karsavina, Baldina and Nijinsky, all in pale silk flounces. 'It seemed to me that the hitherto quietly admiring mood of the public burst into enthusiasm when the *pas de trois* . . . was about halfway through,' wrote Karsavina afterwards. The sensation had been unrehearsed. At this point in the dance Nijinsky should have walked off the stage to reappear in a solo. On that night he chose to leap off. He simply rose up, a few yards from the wings, described a parabola in the air, and disappeared from sight. The Nijinsky legend had been born.

After the interval the curtain rose again on an excerpt from Borodin's opera *Prince Igor*, the third act of which culminates in the Polovtsian dances. This was the mood which had so excited the Parisians in *Boris Godunov*, and the barbaric splendour of the music and the virile pyrotechnics of the twenty-five-year old Adolf Bolm sent the elegant audience into ecstasies.

The last ballet was frankly a hotchpotch of numbers arranged to a variety of composers by a variety of choreographers. The highlight was the famous Bluebird *pas de deux* from Petipa's *The Sleeping Beauty*, danced by the twenty-four-year-old Karsavina and the twenty-one-year-old Nijinsky. After the final curtain the cheers were deafening and back-stage all was confusion. Karsavina was the heroine and Nijinsky was the hero. Asked if it were not very difficult to jump so high, he replied, 'No, no. Not difficult. You just have to go up and pause a little up there.'

The reviews – postponed until after the official opening the next night – were rapturous. Karsavina found herself 'La Karsavina', and Willy described in *Commoedia* how, when Nijinsky 'took off so slowly and elegantly, described a trajectory of four and a half metres and landed noiselessly in the wings, an incredulous Ah! burst from the ladies'. The gentlemen were impressed too; he was compared with the great Vestris and was credited with having 'scored a bigger success than the Trades Union orators'. Diaghilev, now his declared protector, took him round the pictures at the Louvre and cautiously introduced him to some of his smart friends. The young dancer was particularly struck by the Gauguins at

OPPOSITE Vaslav Nijinsky in *Giselle*, Act II, 1910. It was Benois' costume for Act I, in which he omitted the obligatory short trunks, which gave offence when worn in St Petersburg in front of the Tsarina and led to Nijinsky's dismissal from the Maryinsky Theatre.

Emmanuel Bibesco's apartment – perhaps an influence when he came to choreograph *L'Après-Midi d'un Faune*.

The completely new charms of the ballet – an art which had fallen into almost total triviality in the city which was once its stronghold – rather overshadowed the opera programmes which alternated with them. Rimsky-Korsakov's *Ivan the Terrible* followed the first ballet programme, and Chaliapin scored another success in it. In the next programme Diaghilev offered the first act from Glinka's *Russlan and Ludmilla*, followed by the première of *Les Sylphides*. Pavlova joined the company for this dreamlike echo of the ballets of the Romantic age, and the combination of her ethereal lightness, Karsavina's charm and Nijinsky's unearthly grace proved another triumph. It was followed by another work which scored a more predictable success, Fokine's *Cléopâtre*, in which the tall,

Auguste Rodin at the unveiling of his memorial to Victor Hugo in the Palais Royal gardens in 1909. The base of the statue, of which part is visible here, was a striking, asymmetrical pile of marble blocks. It was thrown away when the memorial was moved some twenty years later. Rodin enjoyed his status as Grand Old Man and attended social functions gladly.

bony Ida Rubinstein, a rich amateur who had been studying privately under Fokine, scored a personal triumph in a part which related easily to the fantasies of Moreau and the Symbolists.

When the Russian season closed after exactly a month, it had left a permanent mark on Paris society and the arts (and debts of 86,000 francs – Diaghilev's possessions in his hotel were confiscated until a loan could be raised on the sets and costumes). It had represented, paradoxically, not so much a symbol of the new century as a last gallant gesture of the old order. Luxury and foreign exoticism had been the favourite Parisian blend ever since the Romantics, living on in Salon paintings and extravagant furnishings as in the homes of Bernhardt or Montesquiou. *Boris Godunov* had merely introduced the same vision with a new accent. The most popular item on the first night at the Châtelet had been Bolm in the dances from *Prince Igor*, and Rubinstein in *Cléopâtre* offered the same spicy flavour. The first performances of the Ballets Russes trailed their clouds of glory from a vanishing world.

Diaghilev was quick to exploit his success. He commissioned a ballet, *Daphnis and Chloë*, from Ravel, and another, *Masques et Bergamasques*, from Debussy. This composer unfortunately took a dislike to Diaghilev and the work was never finished. Debussy was in poor health – the first signs of cancer were just showing, making him so restless that he began a period of continuous travel. Diaghilev too was constantly on the move in and out of Paris, though he seems to have missed the sumptuous party organized by Montesquiou to celebrate his farewell to his house, the fancifully decorated Pavillon des Muses.

Gustav Mahler was in Paris, where his First Symphony was performed at the Salle Gaveau. It may have been on this occasion that he sat to Rodin for a portrait bust. The sculptor was in the news again. The official memorial monument to Victor Hugo which had been commissioned from him fifteen years earlier, and for which he had received 11,000 francs, had been turned down by the Fine Arts Commission when it was finally proposed to place it in the Panthéon, and now found a home in the Palais Royal gardens. The monument was a rhetorical figure with outstretched arm, reclining on a remarkable modern Constructivist base (left behind when the statue was later moved to Meudon, and broken up in 1935).

The Salon des Indépendants was housed in the Orangerie this year, with – presumably in consequence – a big reduction in exhibits. It included paintings by Utrillo, whose mother had just separated from her husband, leaving her and her son virtually penniless. Utrillo had been obliged to sell all his stock to a dealer at the rate of 500 francs for ten pictures. As usual, Picasso did not submit anything, and now Braque, in accordance with his contract with Kahnweiler, withdrew too. The two painters had become quite intimately connected in their work and at the same time rather detached from their colleagues. They had a steady patron in Kahnweiler and Picasso was able to move out of the decrepit Bateau-Lavoir into a more commodious studio in the Boulevard de Clichy nearby. Here he pushed on with his Cubist researches, devising more and more closely interlocked arrangements of facets and planes to represent the solid forms. At the same time he began to experiment with

Achille Ouvré: *Ravel: Portrait in Pyjamas*, 1909 (Bibliothèque Nationale, Paris). The composer Maurice Ravel seems to have worn a beard only briefly.

the same system in sculpture. Braque meanwhile was beginning to concentrate on still lifes, in which he could deploy the same idiom.

The rest of the Picasso gang must have felt slightly excluded from such fiercely formal researches. Max Jacob was as poor as ever, telling fortunes in his shabby room or painting little pictures from postcards to sell to tourists. Kahnweiler published this year his major work, *L'Enchanteur Pourrissant*, poems illustrated by Derain, with daring images strung on a thread of lyrical imagination.

Henri Rousseau, recently fêted and happy, ran into serious trouble. His earnings had improved – he sold at least 1,800 francs' worth of paintings this year – but his poverty somehow persisted, and worse things threatened. Two years earlier he had been led astray by an acquaintance to try to make a quick profit through a scheme involving some financial trickery. Of course, he was caught out and now he had to appear in court. The case was widely advertised and a big crowd turned up to laugh at the artist's discomfiture. His lawyer emphasized his naïvety – 'an artless,

Pablo Picasso: *Seated Nude*, 1909–10 (Tate Gallery, London). During the summer of 1919 Picasso was in Spain and Braque in the Seine valley. When they returned to Paris they found they had been exploring in the same direction, and for the next few years their Cubist paintings were almost indistinguishable. This painting of Picasso's still retains suggestions of rounded contours.

Georges Braque: *Mandolin*, 1909–10 (Tate Gallery, London). This picture was painted at the same period as Picasso's *Seated Nude* (OPPOSITE). Characteristically, the subject is more smoothly interlocked into the general composition and the picture-planes more lightly flattened than in Picasso's painting.

gentle soul,' he called him. Rousseau declared with surprising spirit: 'If I am condemned it will not be an injustice to me, it will be a loss to art.' The jury retired amid laughter and returned to find both Rousseau and his accomplice guilty; the artist was sentenced to be imprisoned for two years and pay 100 francs' fine, the punishment being suspended. Rousseau rose to his feet exclaiming, 'Thank you, thank you, Mr President. I will paint your wife's portrait!' But for the last year of his life a prison sentence hung over the head of the arch-innocent.

In other spheres, things were moving on rapidly. In July Blériot flew across the Channel. 'The great gesture has been accomplished,' wrote a journalist. 'For the first time a man driving a canvas bird which vomits fire, a veritable terror-rousing legend, has crossed the ocean and left one continent to take possession of another.' The forty-eight-kilometre crossing was made in thirty-eight minutes, from 4.35 to 5.13 pm, averaging seventy-five kilometres an hour. Landing at Dover Blériot broke his undercarriage and propeller, but was greeted by the correspondent of *Le Matin* waving a guiding flag, and by a much-relieved wife, and entertained at the Lord Warden Hotel.

Geographical barriers, too, were being pushed back. On 6 April the American explorer Robert Peary reached the North Pole. The Belgian king, Leopold II, died in Brussels, where Maeterlinck's Symbolist play *The Bluebird* had its première. A Russian émigré, Ilya Ehrenburg, who had arrived in Paris the previous December, attended a demonstration in Montmartre by the wall where members of the Commune had been shot in 1871. He noted, 'At the wall I saw Lenin: he was standing among a group of Bolsheviks and looking at the wall.' The English painter Sickert

A landmark in aviation was created on 25 July 1909 when Louis Blériot flew across the Channel for the first time. ABOVE Blériot leaning contemplatively on the fuselage of his aeroplane; OPPOSITE His plane in mid-flight over the Channel; and BELOW The arrival on the cliffs near Dover.

had a sale of his pictures at the Hôtel Drouot. The Italian painter Modigliani returned home in some confusion, having given up painting after meeting Brancusi. And his compatriot, Severini, handed in to the office of *Le Figaro* one day in February a long manifesto signed 'F. T. Marinetti', which declared in exclamatory style: 'We are young, strong, living – we are FUTURISTS.'

1910
Currents of Change

THE FUTURIST *Manifesto of Destructive Incendiary Violence*, as it called itself, was to bear hideous fruit within a few years. Its glorification of war, 'the only health-giver of the world', and its demands for militarism, patriotism and 'ideas that kill' were to be answered all too soon. The Manifesto's immediate demand for the inundation of all museums ('Let the famous pictures float!') seemed about to be granted even sooner. The winter of 1909–10 was unusually wet and in the new year the Seine began to rise. By the middle of January it had burst its banks and invaded the embankments. By the end of the month it had reached disaster proportions, completely filling the courtyard of the Ecole des Beaux Arts and standing five metres deep in the Quai d'Orsay station. The Métro was put out of action, the bridges were half submerged, the zoo was under water – neighbours feared the crocodiles would swim out of their pools. Sewers burst, looters began to emerge and fifty thousand inhabitants fled their homes and had to be sheltered in public buildings and fed in soup kitchens under the benevolent eye of President Fallières. It was the greatest flood for 150 years. By February it had become a grim joke. 'Even the Seine wants to see *Chantecler*,' wrote a wit, referring to the queues for Rostand's new play. Even the sophisticated Léon Blum pronounced this farmyard comedy, derived from an English pantomime, superior in its best passages to *Cyrano* or *L'Aiglon*. *L'Illustration* published the full text, which was considered to be destined to occupy 'a major place among our great works of literature'.

While water was wreaking havoc in Paris, fire carried out the Futurists' mission even more effectively later in the year in Belgium, where Rodin's group *The Kiss* was almost the only survivor of a disastrous blaze which destroyed the art pavilion in the Brussels Exhibition. The seventy-year-old sculptor was in luck this year, for the Hôtel Biron, where he had his chief studios, was reclaimed by the state and all the inhabitants except himself were forced to leave. Like a venerable Noah he remained among his ever-increasing company of busts, statues, sketches and drawings, a giant survivor of an age which was retreating before the relentless logic of the Cubists, and the racing cars, workshops, slogans and arsenals beloved of the Futurists.

A fellow-survivor from the past departed in the autumn. Henri Rousseau was still chastened by the prison sentence which hung over him,

OPPOSITE Georges Braque in his studio in 1910. There is a feeling of order and calm very different from the dishevelled bohemianism of Picasso's normal working conditions. Happily married, Braque remained faithful to Montmartre, never moving across the river to Montparnasse.

but he did not stop working. To the Salon des Indépendants in March, which this year ran for six weeks, he sent one of his richest jungle scenes, *The Dream*. In it a humble attendant, half buried in a tangle of exotic vegetation among which lions and elephants prowl, serenades a naked lady reclining on a plush sofa. The model for the boldly curvaceous figure was a fifty-four-year-old widow who worked in a draper's shop, Madame Léonie. Rousseau had pursued her in vain, persuading Vollard and Apollinaire to write him references, in the hope that she would marry him. He prepared to make her heir to all his estate, but she obstinately – and, as it turned out, short-sightedly – refused to listen. In August he hurt his leg, which turned septic; he was taken to hospital where he spent his time writing unanswered letters to Madame Léonie. On 2 September his friend Uhde received a message summoning him to the hospital at once. 'I sat beside the bedside and he held my hand, but I knew that there was no hope.' Rousseau died the same day. A year later Robert Delaunay and Rousseau's loyal landlord set up a tombstone on which Apollinaire pencilled a prayer to 'gentle Rousseau' which ended:

> Admit our luggage duty-free at the heavenly gate,
> We will bring you brushes, colours, canvases,
> So that your holy holiday beneath the true light
> May be devoted to painting, as once you got my likeness,
> A portrait of the stars.

When the writing seemed in danger of fading Brancusi engraved it into the stone.

Rousseau had been an outsider and no group ever adopted him. Rouault's new paintings of judges and victims also escaped from any category, but he had briefly been counted as one of the Fauve group which the commercial galleries were now bent on promoting. The Galerie Druet gave Rouault his first one-man show in February, with a catalogue introduction declaring that he 'speaks only of what he knows and feels, nothing more', and this was followed by shows by Othon Friesz, Marquet and Manguin. Matisse had an exhibition simultaneously in the Galerie Bernheim-Jeune. Vlaminck followed the next month at Vollard's, and Berthe Weill showed Van Dongen and Rouault in April. Utrillo, who was never taken on by a gallery, was admitted after an attack of delirium tremens into a clinic at Sannors; but Modigliani, drifting wildly from studio to studio, showed six paintings in the Indépendants.

Cubism had now entered the most intense period of its development. Picasso spent the summer at Cadaqués in Spain with André Derain and his wife. Derain was to be strongly influenced by this contact, though he adopted the manner rather than the genuine method of the Cubists. Braque meanwhile had returned to the south of France; by the autumn both he and Picasso were back in Paris and working on very tightly organized paintings, in which the usual outlines and rounded shapes are broken down into interlocking honeycombs of sharp facets which explore and define the solid forms by showing them from different angles – a style later christened 'analytical Cubism'.

It has been pointed out that this new system, often described as the

OPPOSITE
ABOVE LEFT Pablo Picasso: *Ambroise Vollard*, 1910 (Pushkin Museum, Moscow). Vollard, champion of Cézanne, gave Picasso his first show in 1901.
ABOVE RIGHT Pablo Picasso: *Daniel-Henry Kahnweiler*, 1910 (Courtesy of the Art Institute of Chicago, Gift of Mrs Gilbert W. Chapman). Kahnweiler took Picasso over in 1908 and became his sole dealer and lifelong friend.
BELOW Pierre Bonnard: *Vollard and His Cat*, 1920 (Petit Palais, Paris). A vivid contrast with Picasso's examples of 'analytical Cubism' above. Bonnard painted a large number of pictures on this subject over a period of some twenty-five years.

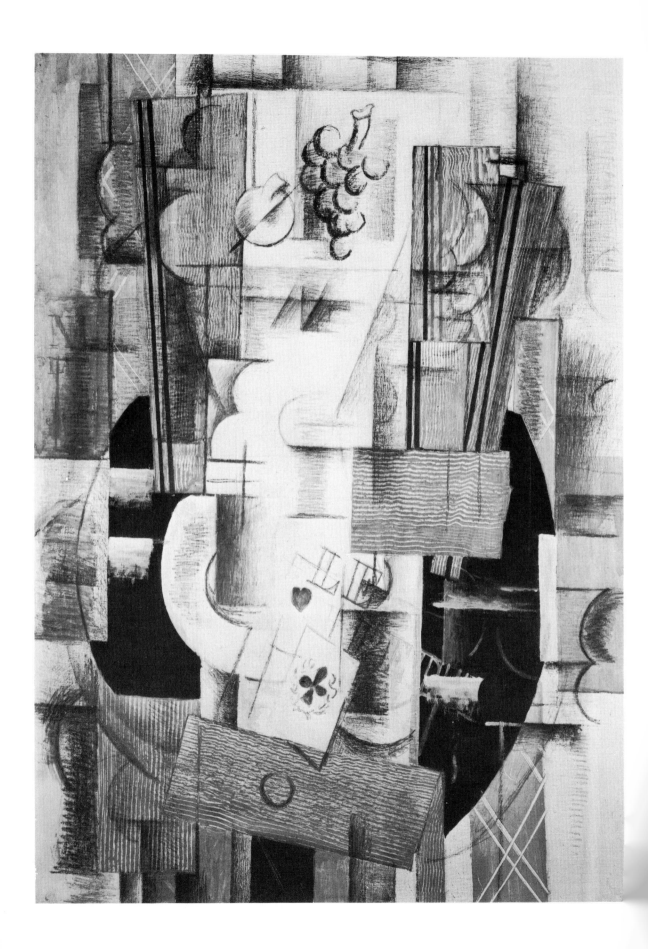

most important revolution in painting since the invention of perspective in the fifteenth century, merely exchanges one idiom for another – both are artificial devices for suggesting three dimensions on a two-dimensional surface – but the exchange was to liberate many future possibilities. In itself it restored attention to the solid, visible world rather than to the impalpable light effects of the Impressionists or the dream fantasies of the Symbolists; it marked a return to realism. It was a democratic art, which renounced idealism for honesty. And as a giant bonus, by the sheer fact of breaking away from a long-held tradition it gave a huge impetus to experiments of all kinds.

The language of Cubism as a method for establishing a logical image of the real world was pursued in its pure sense by very few painters, notably Picasso, Braque and Juan Gris, who had at first supported himself by contributing comic drawings – not at all in the Cubist style – to the magazine *L'Assiette au Beurre*. In this year he began to explore a very austere version of Cubism, was taken up by Kahnweiler, and soon became a passionate devotee of the idiom. Fernand Léger, a tough young twenty-five-year-old, had arrived in Paris from Normandy the previous year, and he too was attracted by the Cubist experiments. He quickly developed a variety of his own, based on interlocking cylinders – a style which was nicknamed 'Tubism'.

Other young artists who began to form a group round Picasso and Braque were Marcel Duchamp, Marcoussis (Louis Markous), Roger de la Fresnaye and André Lhote. Two theoretically orientated painters called Albert Gleizes and Jean Metzinger were much influenced by the mathematical and philosophical talk of an accountant friend of Picasso's, Albert Princet; Einstein's new theories were reflected in the Cubists' effort to penetrate the time-space world by devices such as showing different views of an object at once; while Bergson's renunciation of logic was paralleled by the ambiguities which their method produced. Robert Delaunay developed his own variety of Cubism which was much affected by the dynamic approach of the Italian Futurists.

News of the experiments in Paris spread quickly. Travel was cheap and easy, and reproductions appeared widely in art magazines. In Italy the Futurists were twisting the new theories to their own purposes. In London the first Post-Impressionist exhibition at the Grafton Galleries introduced a startled public to the excitements of modern art and to its perils. 'We have honestly tried and have failed to find any significance of gesture and movement in M. Gauguin's pictures,' wrote *The Times*, thinking that the artist, who had died seven years before, was still alive. 'The artists' aim is to *épater les bourgeois* and this aim is most completely realized by the painter Henri Matisse.' In Russia the seed fell on miraculously receptive soil; disregarding the patient structural researches of the Cubists, the forty-four-year-old Vassily Kandinsky grasped the concepts opened up by the Cubist breakthrough, pushed them forward at headlong speed and this year produced – almost by accident – what seems to be the first ever abstract or non-objective painting.

The most striking pictures to be shown during the year were undoubtedly two enormous canvases exhibited by Matisse at the Salon

OPPOSITE Georges Braque: *Still Life with Ace of Clubs*, 1911 (Musé National d'Art Moderne, Paris). By 1911 both Picasso and Braque had pushed their Cubist experiments further, breaking up the shapes of the subject and reassembling them in new arrangements.

The Spanish painter Juan Gris
became an assiduous Cubist
soon after arriving in Paris,
but at first he earned his
living drawing illustrations
for the anarchist paper *L'Assiette
au Beurre*. This one, dated 1910,
shows a meeting of feminists.

d'Automne. These had been commissioned by Shtchukin the year before
as staircase decorations for his house in Moscow. *The Dance* – a circle
of linked nude figures derived from a background group in *The Joy of
Life* – was finished first, and Shtchukin was delighted. But when he saw
the second panel, *Music*, he was so shocked by the nude male figure that
he countermanded his order, explaining that he had just adopted two
small girls. He asked that the diminutive penis on one figure should be
painted out. Matisse refused; Bernheim-Jeune tried to sell Shtchukin a
large Puvis de Chavannes instead. At the last moment, before leaving
for home, Shtchukin changed his mind. The following spring the two
great panels, examples of Fauvism at its finest, were hung in Moscow
– after some discreet retouching by a local artist – with great effect. 'After
the spicy stuff they get at Shtchukin's how can we hope to tempt people
with the harmless nourishment they get here?' complained the academic
Russian artist, Serov.

   Maurice Denis had been in Moscow on a visit to the home of Shtchukin's rival, Morosov, to inspect his own murals.

A very distinguished house with simple, large, heavy furnishing in a discreet grey, with lots of flowers, lilac, lilies of the valley, cyclamens. My big decoration is a bit isolated in a large, cold room, stone-grey with mouse-grey furnishings. It needs something to 'hold it together'. But it looks quite grand. My colours stand up well as they did in the Salon, but make a more harmonious whole.

An intimate snapshot of Picasso and Fernande Olivier, taken in 1910.

Russia was still a long way from Paris. It took Marc Chagall four days in the train to come from St Petersburg where he had been studying under Bakst in the Svanseva art school. When he arrived at the Gare du Nord he was almost choked by excitement: 'The words fought to get out, eager to shine with this Paris light.' He was met by a compatriot, a painter called Victor Mekler, and installed in Montparnasse in a little hotel next to the Théâtre de l'Odéon. Soon he moved out into a borrowed studio in the Impasse du Maine near the station, where he used to see the sculptor Antoine Bourdelle coming and going from his studio up the street. He began to study at the Palette art school, where Segonzac and the young Cubist Le Fauconnier taught, and he was soon accepted

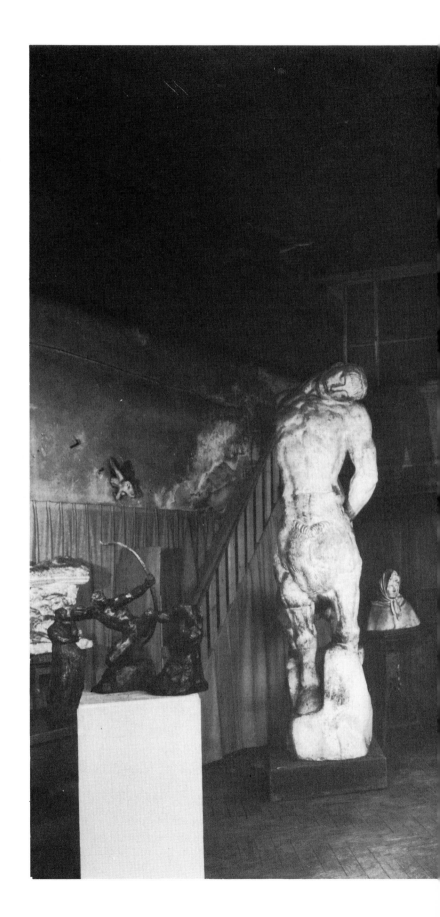

The Montparnasse studio of
the sculptor Emile Bourdelle.

into a circle which included Apollinaire and his poet friend Blaise Cendrars.

Sensitive and quick-witted, Chagall rapidly absorbed the new style to which he was exposed, applying it to subjects which still reflected his origins. 'I brought my objects with me from Russia,' he declared. 'Paris shed its light on them.' Colour was what chiefly attracted him and began to seep into his pictures. 'Colours', he declared, 'which, as Cézanne wanted, mingle at once spontaneously and consciously in a ripple of lines or rule freely as Matisse shows.' He met the Delaunays – Sonia Delaunay being a Russian-born compatriot – at their apartment in the Rue des Grands Augustins, and was much influenced by Robert Delaunay's individual amalgam of Cubism, colour and light. At the Friday parties of the editor of an avant-garde magazine, *Montjoie*, he became acquainted with many of the Cubist circle – Léger and Lhote, Metzinger, La Fresnaye and Marcoussis. He naturally hurried off to the Russian ballet at the Opéra to see his old professor, Léon Bakst, who greeted him warmly but, to Chagall's disappointment, did not recommend him to Diaghilev as a possible designer.

The Ballets Russes, fresh from their first season in Berlin, were having an even greater success than the year before. Owing to the non-cooperation of Chaliapin, Diaghilev had abandoned opera this time; the whole emphasis fell on the dancers and particularly on Karsavina – Pavlova had withdrawn in order to accept an offer from a London music-hall – and

Fernand Léger: *Nudes in a Landscape*, 1910 (Rijksmuseum Kröller-Müller, Otterlo). Cubist woodcutters seem to be at work in a Cubist vision of a Douanier Rousseau jungle.

on his now adored Nijinsky. The young dancer scored a sensational success in a new ballet pitched in the exotic mood of Gustave Moreau and Richard Strauss's *Salome*. Fokine's *Schéhérazade* was a sumptuous plunge into oriental sado-masochism and offered Nijinsky a superb opportunity to display his seductive virtuosities as the Golden Slave – a 'half-human, half-feline animal', 'a flame of lust that sinks and smoulders but never dies', as the critics described him. Benois called him 'half-cat, half-snake, fiendishly agile, feminine and yet wholly terrifying'. The Slave's imperiously sensuous mistress was danced by Ida Rubinstein. She too became the rage of smart Paris with her angular, mannish allure set off by a black panther: Montesquiou and his friend the Italian poet Gabriele d'Annunzio were particularly bowled over by her, and she posed in the nude for the Russian painter Serov in a studio in the Hôtel Biron. Karsavina and Nijinsky were painted more conventionally by Jacques-Emile Blanche in his garden. The season had been the occasion of a different triumph which was almost more remarkable. For the first time in the history of the theatre a designer had won not only attention but fame. Bakst's dazzling sets and costumes, which combined the sumptuousness of Moreau with the brilliance of the Fauves, exploded into Paris fashion and interior design, and remained an influence for years.

The other big success of the season was Stravinsky's ballet *The Firebird*, which brought Karsavina into the headlines. Her appearance with Nijinsky in *Giselle*, a nineteenth-century French classic which had not been danced in Paris for forty years, had been greeted with respect but without enthusiasm. This public wanted something strange and new, and the spicy folk-tale flavour of Fokine's choreography and Stravinsky's magical music – Paris's first taste of this composer – were an instant success.

Bakst's costume for Karsavina as the Firebird, an echo of his 1909 Bluebird design.

Debussy too had been enjoying himself. After hearing *Schéhérazade* for the first time, Colette recorded:

his lips hummed, he made reedy noises through his nose trying to recapture the theme of the oboes, he drummed with his fingers on the lid of the boudoir grand, echoing the deeper notes of the kettle-drum. Still in pursuit, he jumped to his feet, snatched up a cork and rubbed it up and down the windowpane to imitate a pizzicato on the double bass.

Now he was enthusiastic about *The Firebird*, too.

Debussy's appreciation of Stravinsky's score did not extend to the more weighty music of Gustav Mahler. The Austrian composer was in Paris to conduct, among other things, some of his own music. The music publisher Gabriel Pierné arranged a dinner at which Mahler could meet Debussy, as well as Fauré and Dukas. It did not go well. 'Mahler was not at his ease', recorded his wife, 'and he had good reason.' After another dinner with the Comtesse de Greffulhe the party proceeded to the Trocadéro where Mahler was to conduct his Second Symphony. 'In the middle of the second movement', Mahler wrote afterwards, 'I suddenly saw Debussy and Pierné get up and go out. They said afterwards that it was too Schubertian for them – and even Schubert they found too foreign, too Viennese, too Slav.' To be fair, Debussy and Fauré were both influenced by the current strong anti-German public opinion. In September they declined on political grounds an invitation to participate in a French Festival in Munich.

One of the giant setbacks which Diaghilev had had to cope with this year was the sudden death in May, from appendicitis, of King Edward VII – a calamity which put paid to his project for a London season, and which set up more serious shock-waves across the jittery chancelleries of Europe. Announced simply as 'the death of a great king', Edward's demise removed from the power-game a declared friend of the French. Soon they were made even more nervous by a revolution in Portugal.

In America the beloved writer Mark Twain had died, and in the autumn news came from Russia relating the dramatic story of the tragically absurd flight of Tolstoy to his death in a railway station. Scientific progress continued. The suspicion that the future of aviation lay in heavier-than-air machines was underlined by the crashes of two giant Zeppelins during the summer. The cinema was established as a serious art: Bernhardt and Saint-Saëns had condescended to make films. Photo-

The great floods of January 1910 when the Seine burst its banks. A scene down-river in the Rue Gros.

graphy continued to make giant strides. In November came pictures of a bullet passing through a bubble, together with the announcement of a process enabling three-dimensional sculpture to be carried out automatically with the aid of four cameras. In London Bertrand Russell and Alfred Whitehead began to publish their *Principia Mathematica*. Halley's comet swept across the sky and the Earth was declared to be passing through its tail.

No great literary masterpieces were published in Paris during 1910, but T. S. Eliot arrived in Paris and George Moore, 'a dear, rosy baby', as a correspondent described him, 'and very droll', read a paper at the Salle d'Agriculture on Balzac and Shakespeare. Colette, who had published *La Vagabonde*, her first novel under her own name, had begun to write a fortnightly column in *Le Matin* and instantly fell in love with its distinguished editor, Henri de Jouvenel (later ambassador, minister and her husband). She received three votes in this year's competition for the Prix Goncourt, thereby running neck and neck with Apollinaire. The year which had opened with floods ended with torrential rains, threatening fresh inundations.

1911
A Saint and a Suspect

IF CUBISM can be regarded as the most important pictorial discovery of the generation – and perhaps of the century – the year 1911 can be considered its high point. Ever since Picasso had broken with imitative representation in his *Les Demoiselles d'Avignon* in 1907 it had progressed further and further away from recognizable appearances. Step by step the structure of the picture took over from the optical information which had sparked it off; the object dissolved into a symbolic equivalent. Soon both Picasso and Braque were reducing clues to the identity of their subjects to isolated details – an eye or a pipe, the peg of a violin or even a scrap of lettering. Total abstraction seemed imminent, yet neither painter ever gave way to it. Inevitable though it had become as a result of their new approach – as Kandinsky had demonstrated – it was actually the opposite of their aim, which was to achieve more reality, not less. 'When objects splintered into fragments appeared in my painting about 1909, this was for me a way of getting closer to the object,' said Braque. In the unending dialectic between fact and feeling which makes up the history of painting, the Cubists were unshakably factual. 'To evaluate the significance of Cubism we must go back to Gustave Courbet,' Gleizes and Metzinger were to write. The Cubists were intent on recreating the world around them in pictorial terms, not on creating a new one. The tightrope between information and formal demands which Picasso and Braque trod in these months is what gives special excitement to the pictures they painted in the Pyrenees during the summer and in Paris on their return. Braque was living in the Rue Coulaincourt. Picasso was working in his spacious new apartment in the Boulevard de Clichy with its dining-room, aproned maid and Saturday parties. No longer a tentative, exploratory venture, Cubism was now an established style with a coherent syntax and a group of followers. There were whole sections devoted to Cubism both in the Indépendants and in the Salon d'Automne, where Marcel Duchamp exhibited this year for the first time. Yet still *Le Journal* could write: 'Cubism is the swansong of pretentious impotence and smug ignorance.' Critics were as yet unhampered by self-doubt.

The centrepiece of the Indépendants this year was a retrospective collection in honour of Henri Rousseau. Uhde published a monograph on him and Apollinaire wrote perceptively and affectionately of his old friend in the magazine *Les Soirées de Paris*. His own collection of poems, *Le*

Giorgio de Chirico:
The Nostalgia of the Infinite,
1913 (Museum of Modern Art,
New York). In contrast to
the Cubists' search for a
way of portraying the actual
reality of everyday things,
Giorgio de Chirico, who
arrived in Paris from Italy
in 1911, reintroduced an
atmosphere of mystery and
imagination which forms
the basis of Surrealism.

Bestiaire, was published with illustrations by Raoul Dufy, and Apollinaire created a label which was to stick on a whole school of painters when, after a visit to Chagall's studio in Montparnasse to admire *I and the Village* and *Paris through the Window*, he coined the adjective '*surnaturel*' to describe them – a word which he was later, in 1917, to turn into '*surréel*'. Meanwhile the first painter fully to earn that Surrealist label, Giorgio de Chirico, had arrived in Paris. He was a twenty-three-year-old from Florence, and the bundle of paintings under his arm included his characteristically strange and melancholy *The Nostalgia of the Infinite*. Nothing could have been more different from the Cubists; here was the first clue to the next art movement to be born in Paris.

De Chirico's haunting dreams were closely linked to the fantasies of the Symbolists, whose influence was still not dead. It persisted strongly in the theatre. In March Maeterlinck's *The Bluebird* was mounted at the Théâtre Réjane and he was later awarded the Nobel Prize; another prize-winner was Marie Curie. Proust managed to combine modernity and exoticism by listening to *Pélléas et Mélisande* on the theatrephone, a device by which, on payment of a fee, you could listen at home to performances at the Opéra. 'The scent of roses in the score is so strong', he wrote, 'that I have asthma whenever I hear it.' Soon after, he was telephoning sympathetically to St Petersburg where Nijinsky had been dismissed from the Maryinsky for displaying on stage too much of his person to the Tsarina. Proust's gesture seems to have been polite rather than passionate: 'He interests me only as a victim; if he hasn't been victimized then shit to him,' he confided to Reynaldo Hahn.

Two paintings that illustrate the resemblance between the work of Picasso and Braque in the early years of Cubism.
BELOW LEFT Pablo Picasso: *Bottle and Glass*, 1911–12 (Solomon R. Guggenheim Museum, New York).
BELOW Georges Braque: *The Portuguese*, 1911 (Offentliche Kunstsammlung, Basle).

Nijinsky had certainly provoked an exaggerated reaction by the management; the offending costume was the one he had worn the year before in Paris in *Giselle* – a short tunic, but without the regulation Maryinsky trunks. As a result of the fracas Nijinsky became a full-time member of Diaghilev's Ballets Russes, and in June he was back in Paris, at the Théâtre du Châtelet this time, triumphing in a ballet which is the very essence of Symbolism – *Le Spectre de la Rose*. The languorous perfume of this evocation of Mallarmé's poem might also have brought on Proust's asthma. 'Exulting in his rosy ecstasy he seems to impregnate the muslin curtains and take possession of the dreaming girl,' wrote Cocteau, now so much a trusted friend of the company that he had designed its poster for the season.

Through their personal magic (Fokine's original choreography had not seemed inspired), Karsavina and especially Nijinsky had made this slight work a triumph. But the main contribution of the season was a more substantial work, *Petrushka*, with a charming décor by Alexandre Benois which combined the popular Russian savour with French charm. With Fokine's ingenious staging and, above all, Stravinsky's scintillating score, it had an instant success.

Already, however, rifts were appearing in Diaghilev's team. Benois was so enraged at finding a detail of his *Petrushka* scenery – the portrait of the magician – repainted by Bakst that he tendered his resignation as the company's artistic director. To make matters worse, Diaghilev was obliged to postpone the production of a ballet which Cocteau and Hahn had worked out because the proposed designer, Bakst, was busy on another project – a project which, moreover, could prove a rival attraction to the Ballets Russes. This was *Le Martyre de Saint Sébastien*, a spectacle devised for Ida Rubinstein by d'Annunzio, with a score by Debussy. Diaghilev was furious with Bakst. 'We have been completely sacrificed to the work of Rubinstein and d'Annunzio. We are the victims of our too great trust in him,' Diaghilev wrote to his impresario, Astruc. 'Protest violently against responsibilities you try to place on my shoulders,' Bakst wired to Diaghilev in reply.

D'Annunzio had arrived in Paris from Genoa the previous year, leaving behind him a trail of fame, scandal and debts. He moved into the haunt of elegant Italians, the Hôtel Meurice, borrowed 100,000 francs, and plunged into a full-time frenzy of social engagements, enthusiastically acting the part of literary lion with Montesquiou as an adoring trainer. Many of his exotic poems, novels and plays had been translated into French. Tiny, dapper, intelligent and malicious, he joined wholeheartedly in the diversions of the wealthy *salon* set, quickly becoming a familiar landmark in its centrally heated landscape. Into his antique-cluttered rooms poured telegrams and love letters, a fashionable mixture ranging from dinner invitations to a request from a committee presided over by King Ferdinand of Bulgaria to compose a plaque for Wagner's last home in Venice. 'His eye lacks kindness and affection; his voice is more cajoling than really caressing; his mouth less greedy than cruel; his forehead rather beautiful. . . . Less will than calculation; little passion or else cold passion,' decided Gide after lunching with him.

Nijinsky in his make-up for *Le Spectre de la Rose*. 'His face was like that of a celestial insect,' wrote his wife.

Probably encouraged by Montesquiou, d'Annunzio found himself one evening at a performance of the Ballets Russes. It was the first night of *Schéhérazade*. Nijinsky's dusky acrobatics seem to have impressed him little; from his seat in the third row of the stalls he never took his eyes off Ida Rubinstein as the sultry Queen Zobeide. 'Here', he exclaimed to his companion, 'are the legs of Saint Sebastian for which I have been searching in vain all these years!' 'I believe that she lives at the Hôtel Carlton,' he added after the performance, '... I hear that she only leaves to go to the theatre or for solitary motor drives in the forest. ... When she leaves Paris she goes lion-hunting in Africa.'

He called on her, but his project was received frigidly. Undeterred, he began to collect innumerable images of the saint. He retired to the country at Arcachon, and in January 1911 he wrote to her: 'My beloved

« Il faut que chacun
tue son amour pour qu'il revive
sept fois plus ardent. »

Gabriele d'Annunzio

«ST.SEBASTIEN»
(avec IDA RUBINSTEIN)

BAKST

brother. I have done what I had to do: I have worked. You will find the first and third acts complete.... You will, I am sure, have divined the magnitude of my effort. ... You will be nailed to the stake, oh far too beautiful saint!... I think of you incessantly and I love you through the flame of my spirit.' He sent to Paris for a set of bows and arrows; Rubinstein arrived at the local Hôtel Grand and they practised together on the lawn of his villa. On 2 February he wired to her in St Petersburg: 'Work finished. I kiss the wounded knee.'

The producer, Astruc, had been nervous that the mystical-erotic ecstasies of the poetic drama – which was daringly both written by d'Annunzio and acted by Rubinstein in French – might offend Catholic susceptibilities. But the poet had taken the precaution of dedicating it to the highly respected and orthodox Maurice Barrès, who replied to the gesture apparently without reading the manuscript: 'I am dreaming of this still unknown book ... of this inspired companion with whom I shall dwell among all wise men and all foolish women.'

Besides Debussy and Bakst, Fokine also had been seduced away from the Ballets Russes to arrange the dances for Rubinstein. The glamour of all these names raised expectations which were not fulfilled at the première. Proust sat next to Montesquiou, 'wired to the dynamics of your enthusiasm by the electrode of your wrist', as he wrote to him afterwards. But privately he had been disappointed. The angular Rubinstein was as striking as ever – 'She evokes an ibis', Cocteau had written of her – but even he admitted that she 'had not yet grown accustomed to the newly bestowed gift of speech and gesture'. Proust was more outspoken: 'I found the piece very boring despite certain moments, and the music pleasant but thin, insubstantial, crushed by the style. It was a flop for both the poet and the composer. Nobody even took a call.'

It ran for less than a dozen performances. The chief honours seem to have gone to Bakst, who provided yet another sample of his sensuous picturesque orientalism. This production, together with *Le Spectre de la Rose*, formed the swansong of the Symbolist movement, which had deteriorated into a perfumed decadence with the androgynous Rubinstein as the counterpart of Nijinsky, and the stalls filled with the descendants of *fin-de-siècle* dandies and duchesses.

Le Martyre de Saint Sébastien was not approved of by the high-minded *Nouvelle Revue Française*, which also turned a cold shoulder to a submission which Gide, one of its editors, evidently took for a similarly effete enterprise. Labelling its author as 'a snob and a literary amateur', he described the contribution as 'the worst possible thing for our magazine'. The author was Proust and the manuscript was the opening chapter of *A La Recherche du Temps Perdu*.

Debussy was, in fact, already edging into the new artistic mood. In March the Société Indépendante Musicale had, at Ravel's suggestion, performed some early works by the still unrecognized Erik Satie. A few months later Debussy himself conducted Satie's *Gymnopédies* at the Cénâcle Musical. The eccentric, forty-five-year-old composer suddenly found himself accepted. He laid aside his clay pipe and his twelve corduroy outfits and adopted a cigar and a businessman's dark suit. However,

OPPOSITE Bakst's design for Ida Rubinstein in her own production of *Le Martyre de Saint Sébastien*, a last breath of Symbolist decadence. The drawing is accompanied by an extract from d'Annunzio's libretto: 'Each must kill his love, that it may be revived seven times more fierce.'

he kept his pince-nez and his little goatee beard, his sharp tongue and biting wit.

The excitements at the Châtelet in the summer had distracted attention mercifully from a distressing episode in the career of Apollinaire and, to a lesser extent, Picasso. Some years previously, in 1907, a Belgian friend of Apollinaire called Céry-Pieret had sold to Picasso two little Hispano-Roman statues. In fact he had stolen them from the Louvre, and in May this year he helped himself to another, hiding it in Apollinaire's apartment in Auteuil where he was staying. Then in August a thunderbolt dropped from the sky; Leonardo's famous *Monna Lisa* (quickly turned by the popular Press into 'Mona Lisa') had disappeared during the night from the walls of the Louvre. As critic of *L'Intransigeant*, Apollinaire boldly accused the museum of 'laziness, carelessness and indifference', but secretly he suspected Pieret, who in a panic handed in his statue and his story – for a fee – to the *Paris Journal*. The police shared Apollinaire's

Picasso in his studio in the Boulevard de Clichy. Even in this relatively conventional apartment he is surrounded by paintings, pets and bric-à-brac.

thoughts, for they came and searched his apartment. Terrified that Picasso's statuettes might be traced, he and the painter held a hasty conference. Fernande Olivier recalled:

Finally – after a hurried dinner and an interminable evening of waiting – they made up their minds to go out that night and throw the suitcase containing the sculptures into the Seine. They left at midnight but returned still holding the suitcase. They thought they were being followed. Their imaginations dreamed up a thousand possibilities, each more fantastic than the last ... without realizing it they were seeing themselves as characters in a play; so much that though neither of them knew the first thing about cards they had, during the agonizing hours of waiting ... pretended to play cards, like gangsters.

At length they called at the offices of the *Paris Journal* and deposited the statuettes, on condition that the source of their return be kept secret. Apollinaire pressed some money into Pieret's hand and packed him off to the Gare de Lyon. But his precautions were in vain. The police arrived, handcuffed Apollinaire and removed him in a van to La Santé prison on suspicion of stealing the Leonardo. They questioned his *concierge* and threatened to search the homes of his mother and his mistress, Marie Laurencin. In his cell Apollinaire gave way to poetic despair: '*Pauvre maman*, poor brother,' he wrote. 'Forgive me, forgive me! And you, Marie, *chère amie*, forgive me, forgive me.' He ended by incriminating Picasso.

Two days later Picasso was woken up by a plain-clothes policeman and taken off to confront Apollinaire at the Préfecture. 'I thought I was done for,' wrote Apollinaire afterwards. 'But the examining magistrate ... authorized me to interrogate the witness [Picasso] and, using Socrates' favourite *maieutic* I quickly forced him to admit that what I said was true.' What saved Apollinaire in the end was a petition by his fellow-artists, published in the *Paris Journal*, and finally a letter to the paper from Marseille in which Pieret (who was never caught) admitted his guilt. In September the unlucky poet was finally set free and put on probation for a year. But he had suffered a serious setback. The anti-semite Press launched an attack on him, in which traditional right-wing artists joined. *L'Oeuvre* dug up his past history as an editor of pornographic books; and both *Le Passant* and *Le Matin* dropped him completely. The real thief of the Leonardo was to remain unsuspected for another two years.

Picasso was now working in comparative comfort in the Boulevard de Clichy, but the Rue Ravignan, where he kept a few effects, still had its impoverished geniuses. Kahnweiler wrote later:

As I crossed the square before entering No. 13 I often noticed the occupant of the studio which was on the left of the passage inside the front door. In spring and summer the two windows looking on to the square used to be wide open and in one or other of them he would be sitting at work. He was very young and, I thought, handsome, with dark brown hair and an olive complexion. ... It was Picasso who told me that his name was Juan Gris, a name which I had seen below drawings in *L'Assiette au Beurre*. ... I learned that Gris was starting to paint.

His passion for work was unbelievable, and it was probably at this period that he made the remark attributed to him by Max Jacob: 'I only stroke dogs with my left hand, so that if I am bitten I shall have my right hand to paint with.' He began with conventional, naturalistic watercolours, but his first oil paintings, done this year, already showed that he had been looking at the Cubists. Thoughtful and methodical, his cool personal style showed from the start.

The missionary influence of what could already with justification be called the School of Paris was felt everywhere. Amedeo Modigliani, ambitious to become a sculptor, had an exhibition of carvings and drawings in the studio of a friend, but he had virtually no patrons besides a faithful doctor, Paul Alexandre. 'I've only one buyer and he's blind,'

Juan Gris and his wife, Josette, a photograph taken in 1913.

he joked, alluding to an old dealer. Modigliani had changed much since he had arrived in Montmartre as a debonair, elegant young bohemian. Drink and drugs had taken their toll – he was a friend of Utrillo, already an incurable alcoholic. Modigliani's stiff, archaic-looking 'caryatids' of this period already contain the seed of his later style. He was joined in Paris this year by the twenty-one-year-old Ossip Zadkine, who had been born in Russia but studied in London. Meanwhile another Russian, Kandinsky, joined with the German Franz Marc in setting up a group called Der Blaue Reiter (The Blue Rider) in Munich, where the thirty-one-year-old Swiss painter Paul Klee, who was soon to join them, had his first one-man show.

Rodin's bust of Clemenceau. The statesman was not satisfied by it.

The year which had been filled with such heady excitement for the elegant set had sent shivers down the spine of serious politicians. In January a debate in the Chambre had been punctuated by two revolver shots. Shortly afterwards the Premier, Briand, resigned. In July the Germans sent a cruiser, the *Panther*, to anchor off Agadir, a small town in Morocco, with the declared intent of watching over German interests in that country – a defiant insult to its French protectors. In September there were troubles in Spain. In October the Italians and the Turks declared war on each other. Inexorably the clouds of European conflict grew darker and closer. France's most unshakable statesman, the gallant old Georges Clemenceau, sat for a bust by Rodin, but after eighteen sittings Clemenceau was still not satisfied, and demanded that it should be exhibited as 'Portrait of an Unknown Man'. Rouault wrote to a friend from the Moreau Museum: 'I carry within myself an infinite pool of pain and melancholy which life has only increased and of which my art as a painter can, God willing, only be the imperfect expression and the bloom.' In December the critic Vauxcelles wrote of Rouault's second show at the Galerie Druet: 'This is the art of a visionary, of a satirist who tears his victims apart, who suffers and moans.' On 16 December Roald Amundsen planted the Norwegian flag at the South Pole. Earth, water and air seemed to have been conquered, all new dimensions in art discovered – the years of glorious promise were closing in.

1912
The Futurist Explosion

IN 1912 THE SLOWLY DEVELOPING war fever which had raised international temperatures intermittently ever since the turn of the century began to show itself in sinister local symptoms. The year was only two weeks old when news of revolution in China, accompanied by appalling photographs, reached Europe. Within a few days the Franco-German negotiations over Africa, which had been dragging on ever since the Agadir incident, developed alarming signs of breaking down, and the French government fell – the sober businessman Caillaux being replaced by Poincaré (who was quickly to give way to the pacific Briand, and he in turn to Barthou). The mood of France was unstable, with the irresistible rise of socialism pushing some to the right, while it encouraged others, including the powerful railwaymen, to strike; even the *corps de ballet* at the Opéra staged a standstill. Fighting broke out again in Morocco, and soon General Lyautey was on the spot, turning into something of a national hero by the firmness with which he put down the revolt.

More menacing still was the outbreak of overt war in the near east, where the once-powerful Turkey was humiliated by a hostile Balkan League consisting of Bulgaria, Serbia and Greece. Soon, however, Bulgaria was turning against her allies, only to be defeated after a series of atrocities committed in the panic of retreat, which shocked the world. The French were drawing nervously ever closer to Britain; the eighteen-year-old Prince of Wales (thinly disguised as the Comte de Chester) was welcomed in Paris with a warmth which would have astonished Queen Victoria. An apprehensive patriotism was in the air. *L'Illustration* published a chart comparing the relative strengths of the British and German navies, under the heading 'Naval Rivalry'. French uniforms were re-designed to be more practical and less decorative; and Sarah Bernhardt went round the stalls between the acts of *L'Aiglon* to collect money for the air force.

Nerves in Paris were taut – the best possible conditions for the wily Italian poet Filippo Tommaso Marinetti, who had electrified readers of *Le Figaro* in 1909 with the manifesto of his new Futurist creed, which not only accepted war and destruction but positively welcomed them. Ever since, Marinetti had dominated from his rich estate in Milan the movement which he had founded. A well-travelled sophisticate himself, who had chosen the limelight of Paris for his first war-cry, he preached

The real Bal Tabarin, a well-known dance-hall, *c.* 1900.

OPPOSITE Gino Severini: *Dynamic Hieroglyphic of the Bal Tabarin*, 1912 (Museum of Modern Art, New York, acquired through the Lillie F. Bliss Bequest). The Italian Futurists seized on the Cubist idiom as a means of articulating their own very different ideas. The angular pattern here suggests jazz rhythms.

national jingoism and a total break with tradition. He had attracted a faithful circle of admirers, and in 1910 a second manifesto had been issued – characteristically from a theatre stage – on behalf of Futurist painting, followed by a huge exhibition by his disciples in Milan in April 1911.

One of the artists who had signed the manifesto, Gino Severini, was a twenty-nine-year-old who had for some years been working in Paris. When he arrived back in Milan and saw what his colleagues were showing, he was alarmed at their out-of-date style, which was a compound of the Expressionist approach of painters like Munch and the Pointillist experiments of Signac and his followers. Severini returned to Paris with Umberto Boccioni, aged thirty, and Carlo Carrà, aged thirty-three, two of his fellow Futurists, together with Marinetti. They kept up a brave front in the face of their first direct sight of the Cubists and their first meetings with Parisian artists – Fernande Olivier recalled all-night sessions, with Marinetti holding forth while Picasso listened, and on other occasions Marinetti foregathering with his fellow Futurists in a Montmartre café to show off their ostentatious fashions, with odd socks and spectacular ties. 'Parisians mistook this Florentine fancy for absent-mindedness,' commented Apollinaire tartly. But in private the Futurists were impressed, and on their return home they hastily repainted some of their pictures and gave a Cubist twist to new ones.

Marinetti had meanwhile negotiated a showing of his Futurist followers' work at the Galerie Bernheim-Jeune, which was fresh from a show by the increasingly fashionable Van Dongen, famous for his fancy-dress parties, and from yet another optimistic attempt to establish its favourite, René Seyssaud. On 5 February the gallery opened its doors on a large exhibition called 'Italian Futurists'. The ferociously aggressive pronouncements of the group, and its claims – more chronological than stylistic – to be the successors of the Cubist revolutionaries, gave the show a powerful impetus and it received wide attention; the public were agreeably titillated and the critics unexpectedly respectful. 'What we have attempted and done', claimed the Italian artists, 'places us at the head of the European movement in painting.' The popularity of the show was based on the fact that it actually followed the traditional stream, with an emphasis on lively subjects, while dexterously giving it an up-to-date appearance derived from the Cubists. It adopted the new accent without using the new language. A typical example was Severini's *Dynamic Hieroglyphic of the Bal Tabarin*, which presented an impression of a Lautrec scene conveyed in witty, decorative patterns in which the Cubist facets suggested the flounces of flying, brightly coloured petticoats.

The Futurists represented, in fact, a jazzy reaction to the sober exercises of Picasso and Braque, which they rightly found cold and static compared with their own productions. Their aims were diametrically opposed. While the Cubists were intent on finding a logical pictorial equivalent of material reality, the Futurists pursued the expression of what they called 'states of mind'. They stood for a swing back from fact towards feeling and they were justified in detecting an innate hostility between the basically realist ideals of the Cubists and the wild, free, dynamic and basically romantic ideals of the Futurists.

Kees Van Dongen's parties became legendary as he slowly surrendered to society patronage. LEFT The painter in his apartment with some of his own work. BELOW A 1912 photograph of one of Van Dongen's parties. Among the numbered guests are (1) Matisse, (2) Marquet, (5) the designer Paul Poiret, (6) Van Dongen himself, (7) Camoin and (9) Van Dongen's wife.

The Futurists in Paris, 1912.
Marinetti is in the centre;
on his left are Severini
and Boccioni, on his right
Carrà and Russolo.

With the exception of Carrà, all the signatories of the Futurist manifesto were represented in Paris, and Boccioni, Russolo and Balla were
also picked out for praise. French ancestry was emphasized. Gustave
Kahn in the *Mercure de France* traced the influence of Rodin and his
theories of forms – 'The movements of a figure', the sculptor had
pronounced, 'must not stop with the lines of the contour' – while Impressionism was clearly a progenitor, its influence passing down through the
Italian sculptor Rosso. French experiments in the cinema might also have
been mentioned – they were visible in the suggestion of movement by
overlapping images; and behind their concept of interpenetrating entities
lay Henri Bergson's notion of the complex nature of perception, in which
memories of the past blend with the present.

These certainly contributed to the ancestry of the painting and sculpture, but the philosophical attitude of the movement – which, rather than
any aesthetic theories, provided the fuel for its rapid development – was
based directly on the teachings of Nietzsche, who had died twelve years
earlier. The worship of dynamism and virility – female nudes are oddly
rare in Futurist art, and Boccioni was to suggest muscle-man worship
in his *Muscular Dynamism* drawings the next year – had a Nordic origin,
and so had the Expressionist extremism revealed in Boccioni's description
of 'the suffering of an electric lamp which, with spasmodic starts, shrieks
out the great heart-rending expression of colour'. This extremism
emerged equally strongly in the Futurists' inventive literary and musical
experiments, and above all in their consistent love of violence and destruction. The exhibition went on to London, Berlin, Brussels, The Hague,
Amsterdam and Munich, quickly spreading splinter movements over
Europe. The effects of Futurist painting were sensational at the time,
but it can be seen now that it represented not the explosion of a new
kind of art – Picasso had set that off five years before – but the first adaptation of the new style to express traditional ideas and, more importantly,
an omen of the holocaust to be unleashed in Europe two years later,
genuine violence in which Futurist histrionics were to be swallowed up.

Futurism was not the only sign that the Cubist breakthrough was beginning to split into differing streams. Ever since they had exhibited together in 1910, the dozen or so artists who were content to appear under this label at the Salon des Indépendants or the Salon d'Automne began to draw together as a group. The two founders of the movement, Picasso and Braque, still held aloof from these exhibitions at the admonition of their dealer, Kahnweiler. 'In front of certain pictures there would be groups of people writhing with laughter or howling with rage,' he wrote afterwards. 'We had no desire to expose ourselves either to their laughter or to their rage.' But the others stuck together, and were joined this year by Juan Gris, who showed a thoroughly Cubist *Portrait of Picasso*, and was put under contract by Kahnweiler. There was even a *Cubist House* at the Salon d'Automne this year, designed by Duchamp's brother, the sculptor-architect Duchamp-Villon, and decorated by Léger, Duchamp and others of the group. Two of them, Metzinger and Gleizes, published soon afterwards the first monograph on the movement, *Du Cubisme*.

This was a highly theoretical study, very different from the instinctive

Juan Gris: *Portrait of Picasso*, 1912 (Courtesy of the Art Institute of Chicago). Exhibited at the Salon des Indépendants, it was Gris' tribute to Cubism, the style to which he was faithful from first to last.

approach of Picasso and Braque. (Fernande Olivier always maintained
that the only person who could have made Cubism intelligible was
Erik Satie.) It was characteristic of the circle which formed in the
suburban studios occupied by three clever brothers – Marcel Duchamp,
Raymond Duchamp-Villon and 'Jacques Villon' (Gaston Duchamp).
They were joined by Léger, Picabia, Gris, André Lhote and Franz
Kupka, a forty-year-old Czech painter. In October they opened a spe-
cifically Cubist exhibition in a commercial gallery, the Galerie de la
Boétie, under the title 'La Section d'Or'. There were two hundred
exhibits by thirty artists, and special introductory articles had been
written by Apollinaire, André Salmon (another close friend of Picasso)
and the poet Pierre Reverdy. Artists were invited to show works illustrat-
ing their development over the past three years, and the exhibition served
as a useful showcase 'to present the Cubists, no matter of what tendency
... as the most serious and most interesting artists of this epoch', as Apollinaire wrote. His opinions, now given an impressive platform in a half-

defunct magazine *Les Soirées de Paris*, of which he had taken over the editorship, promptly turning it into a serious art journal, were not shared by many of his colleagues. 'May I be allowed to confess', wrote the critic of *Le Journal* that autumn, 'that I do not believe in the future of Cubism. ... Cubism, integral or not, has already had its last word.'

One of the painters diverting the Cubist theory into new channels was Fernand Léger, who had arrived in Paris almost at the same moment as his exact contemporary, Picasso. He had started out as an architect, and was to preserve traces of his training all his life: 'His painting is sister to architecture,' Le Corbusier wrote later. He studied at the Ecole des Arts Décoratifs, having failed to get into the Ecole des Beaux Arts. From the beginning he settled in Montmartre and began to paint in the conventional Impressionist style. Like many of his contemporaries he was converted by the big Cézanne retrospective in 1907. He was soon drawn into the Cubist group which later became the core of the Section d'Or exhibition, but he retained a kind of massive simplicity which owed some-

OPPOSITE Marcel Duchamp: *King and Queen Surrounded by Swift Nudes*, 1912 (Philadelphia Museum of Art, Louise and Walter Arensberg Collection). The suggestion of machines and the use of overlapping forms to convey a sense of movement are closely related to the experiments of the Italian Futurists.
LEFT Fernand Léger: *The Smokers*, 1911–12 (Solomon R. Guggenheim Museum, New York). The puffs of tobacco smoke here become as solid a part of the composition as the landscape behind them.

thing to Henri Rousseau, whose work he first saw in 1909. He greatly admired Rousseau's way of taking over and grasping the subject, and his primitive fervour. 'One of the pure!', he called him. Léger made a curious blend of the styles of Picasso and Rousseau in a huge canvas painted soon afterwards, *Nudes in a Landscape*, in which sharply faceted woodcutters are shown in action in a setting resembling an angular Rousseau jungle.

Slow-moving and big-boned, 'like a piece of wood sculpture', as the young Russian writer Ilya Ehrenburg found him, Léger never quite adopted the full Cubist doctrine – though Kahnweiler, guardian of the movement, gave him a one-man show this year. He always preserved some conventionally modelled corners in his pictures, adding an element of light and colour, with quick rhythms which superficially resembled those used by the Futurists, some of whose interests he shared. 'Why do you go to museums?' he asked Ehrenburg. 'You'd do better to look at aeroplanes, athletes, factories, circus acrobats.'

Such mundane subjects were far from the preoccupations of another deviationist from the Cubist doctrine, a close friend of Léger, Robert Delaunay. By 1912 he had already parted company from the group so far that he did not show in the Section d'Or exhibition. Like Léger, he had been impressed by the innovations of Picasso and Braque when he first saw them in 1910, but he proceeded to develop them in a direction which retained echoes of Impressionism, using inconsequent viewpoints and above all pure, luminous colour to suggest space in a dramatic style which also had something in common with the Futurists. His *Eiffel Tower* pictures of 1910 and 1911 were followed by a series of views from his window in Montparnasse, in which the outlines of buildings disappeared in patchworks of colour which seemed to be floating away from realism towards metaphysical visions – a style christened by Apollinaire 'Orphic Cubism'. By 1912, in *Discs*, a series inspired by the planets, he had already arrived at totally abstract paintings concerned with space, time and light.

The speed with which those first experiments in Montmartre had flashed across the world was amazing. Not only had they produced a variety of cross-currents in Paris itself; the electric charge was already returning to its birthplace from Italy via the Futurists, and this year other painters appeared in Paris from abroad, with far-reaching results. From Moscow, where he had already got to know French painting in the Schtchukin and Morosov collections, came the thirty-four-year-old Kasimir Malevich; he stayed for a month and returned home so intoxicated by the possibilities offered by the Cubist revolution that within the next year he painted what he called 'the expression of non-objectivity', a black square on a white background. By 1918 he was to arrive at what seemed then the ultimate abstract – a similar composition from which even the colour contrast had been eliminated, *White on White*. The forty-year-old Dutchman Piet Mondrian, who had arrived the previous year, showed among the Cubists at the Salon d'Automne this year for the first time, having abandoned his realistic landscapes for good. He was to stay on in Paris until the outbreak of war. From Munich came August Macke and Franz Marc, founders of the Blaue Reiter group, who went back to Germany, after meetings with Picasso and Delaunay, as declared Cubists. Even Paul Klee, arriving from Switzerland, underwent a perceptible change after exposure to the influence of Cubism.

While Cubism reached a peak this year in rapid development and influence, both at home and abroad – there were Cubist exhibitions in Madrid and Amsterdam – art in general remained faithful to earlier styles. The spring Salons were full of late salutes to the Impressionists. The Galerie Druet included in its annual spring miscellany Fauves like Friesz, Marquet and Manguin plus a special show of Utrillo, and Symbolists like Redon and Maurice Denis in its autumn one. The Galerie Bernheim-Jeune followed the Futurists with, first, one of its dark horses, Auguste Chabaud, then Vuillard, Monet (views of Venice), Bonnard, and, in October, a handsome Rousseau retrospective with a catalogue foreword by Uhde. The special feature of the Salon d'Automne this year – whose Cubist section provoked questions in the Chambre des Députés – was a selection of nineteenth-century portraits.

While the tributaries of Cubism were feeding varied individual experiments, the mainstream continued to move forwards in the studio of Juan Gris, who was still working in the Bateau-Lavoir and, in his first oil paintings, was showing himself a faithful and intelligent Cubist disciple. The Salon des Indépendants was a relatively small show this year, housed across the river on the Quai d'Orsay. It included 3,562 works, from which Duchamp's *Nude Descending a Staircase*, which was to be the hit of the New York Armory Show the following year, had been rejected. Gris exhibited a homage to Picasso in the form of a portrait, which was hung next to a near-abstract by Kandinsky. After the Salon d'Automne Kahnweiler took Gris on as one of his Cubist team. Picasso and Braque had pushed forward to the limit their experiments with compositions in which the elements comprising different viewpoints of the subject were broken down and re-assembled – a process which came to be known as 'analytical Cubism'. Afraid that the real presence of the subject might become lost in abstraction, Braque one day introduced into a painting a naturalistic, shadow-throwing nail; and soon afterwards Picasso was sticking on to a painting a piece of oilcloth bearing a simulated chairseat pattern. The pure severity of their early pictures was breaking up and soon they were working with bright colours and mixing degrees of realism. Though more daring than the ostensibly bold ventures of some of their followers, the risks were always strictly pictorial; their mood and subject-matter remained as undramatic as ever. Indeed their appeal to the general public declined as their 'language' became harder to read.

If they were little understood in Paris, they were unintelligible in London, where Cubist paintings by Picasso and Braque were included in the second Post-Impressionist exhibition, in October. Matisse, some months earlier, had been received with equal hostility in New York, where Edward Steichen showed some of his sculptures in his 291 Gallery. 'The work of a madman ... impossible travesties of the human form ... which make one grieve that men should be found who can by any chance regard them with other than feelings of horrible repulsion', wrote the critic of the *New York Globe*.

Revulsion and moral outrage were not confined to New York this year.

Louis Marcoussis: *Portrait of Apollinaire*, 1912. (Philadelphia Museum of Art, Louise and Walter Arensberg Collection). Marcoussis was one of the first young recruits to the Cubist movement.

Paris too had suffered two separate attacks of puritan fever. A visit from the Ballets Russes had become in the last few years a regular part of the summer season. This year they were due at the Théâtre du Châtelet where they had made their début, and the programme looked as though it would be gently attractive. The musical climate was changing – Massenet died this year and in Vienna Schoenberg had hinted at his 'atonal' revolution in *Pierrot Lunaire* – but Diaghilev was still lagging behind the pioneers and took no risks. Besides some old favourites, his novelties would include another Bakst-Fokine bit of oriental exoticism – *Thamar* – and three pieces with music by French composers – *Daphnis and Chloë*, with a score by Ravel, *L'Après-midi d'un Faune*, to Debussy's well-loved evocation of the poem by Mallarmé, and Reynaldo Hahn's *Le Dieu Bleu*, a story devised by Jean Cocteau. But troubles lay behind this ingratiating menu. On 17 April the company's impresario, Astruc, received a telegram from Diaghilev: 'After seeing article front page *Figaro* announcing that Fokine is staging *L'Après-midi Faune* Nijinsky refuses point blank to take part our Paris season.' The ballet had in fact been entrusted, to Fokine's annoyance, to Nijinsky, who had been working on it secretly for months. Nijinsky relented, but Fokine was so angry that he handed in his notice to take effect at the end of the season.

More trouble – though this time of the kind that Diaghilev relished – was to follow. In his very first work Nijinsky, the virtuoso of supple, fluid, bounding movement, a style particularly suitable for Debussy's melting score, had hit on a static, angular idiom which, while strikingly related to the Cubist style, was visibly and violently at odds with the music, and totally unexpected. The divinely ethereal dancer appeared as an awkward half-animal. To make matters worse, the short piece ended with a dramatic gesture in which the faun masturbated into a nymph's forgotten scarf.

Not unnaturally there was an uproar when the curtain fell, in which cheers and boos were mixed. Immediately Diaghilev repeated the ballet. Next morning the critics, who had greeted the Hahn ballet on its opening night amiably enough, were laudatory again – with one notable exception. Gaston Calmette, the director of the powerful *Le Figaro*, took over its front page himself. On 30 May he wrote:

Our readers will not find in its usual place on the theatre page an account by my esteemed colleague Robert Brussel of the first performance of *L'Après-midi d'un Faune*, a choreographic scene by Nijinsky, arranged and danced by that amazing artist. I am not printing the account.... I am, however, certain that any of our readers who were present yesterday at the Châtelet will join with me in protesting against the extraordinary exhibition which they had the audacity to serve up to us in the guise of serious work.... We are shown a lecherous faun, whose movements are filthy and bestial in their eroticism and whose gestures are as crude as they are indecent. That is all. And the over-explicit miming of this mis-shapen beast ... was greeted with the boos it deserved.

Diaghilev's reply to this massive broadside aimed at his favourite was surprisingly calm, but effective. He merely quoted at length the very different reaction of two artists. The first was Odilon Redon, Diaghilev's

OPPOSITE Robert Delaunay: *Eiffel Tower*, 1910 (Solomon R. Guggenheim Museum, New York). The artist has expressed a feeling of universality by showing the structure from several viewpoints and by allowing the light and space to interpenetrate the buildings.

FOLLOWING PAGES
LEFT Henri Rousseau: *The Muse Inspiring the Poet*, 1909 (Musée de Basle). This portrait was commissioned by Guillaume Apollinaire, and the muse represents his painter friend, Marie Laurencin. Rousseau carefully measured the poet's features with a tape and, on second thoughts, changed the foreground from wallflowers to sweet williams.
RIGHT Max Jacob: *Apollinaire* 1909 (Musée d'Orleans). The setting of this fanciful portrait suggests a hashish-smoking establishment, but poetry has replaced the pipe as an intoxicant.

first choice as designer for the ballet, and a close friend of Mallarmé. 'How happy he would have been to recognize, in that living frieze we have just been watching, his faun's very dream,' Redon wrote, praising the ballet as a 'wonderful evocation of his thought'.

Diaghilev's second ally was even more powerful, Auguste Rodin. He had certainly been appreciative but he was now persuaded to sign an article in *Le Matin*, actually written by Roger Marx. The article declared:

Nijinsky has never been so remarkable as in his latest role. His beauty is that of antique frescoes and sculpture; he is the ideal model, whom one longs to draw and sculpt. . . . I wish that such a noble endeavour could be understood as a whole and that . . . the Théâtre du Châtelet would arrange others to which all our artists might come for inspiration and to communicate with beauty.

Stung by this opposition, Calmette counter-attacked with a piece against the sculptor. 'I need only recall that in contempt of all propriety he exhibits in a former chapel of the Sacred Heart and in bedrooms vacated by the nuns expelled from the Hôtel Biron series of libidinous pencil drawings. It is inconceivable that the French state should have paid five million . . . solely to provide free lodging for the richest of our sculptors.' Fearful that his project for a Rodin Museum might be destroyed, the sculptor timidly disavowed his signature. But already champions had sprung into the arena both on his behalf and for Nijinsky. The Russian Embassy, suspecting a plot against the Franco-Russian pact, supported Diaghilev. Rumours of police intervention circulated, but the ballet went on and the publicity did wonders for the box office.

This episode had a curious echo in a very different setting – not a theatre, but a cemetery. A few years earlier, the sculptor Jacob Epstein, who had arrived in Paris from America in 1902, had moved on to London where, in 1909, he was entrusted with the task of designing a memorial to Oscar Wilde, to be set up over a new tomb for the writer in the Père Lachaise cemetery. Selecting a twenty-ton block of stone from a quarry in Derbyshire, the sculptor set to work at once and laboured for nine months, finally producing a male, winged figure in vaguely Assyrian style, with the face of what he called 'a demon-angel'. It was unveiled to the London public in 1912 and received high praise. The *Evening Standard*, remarking that it was 'as reserved in execution as it is monumental in conception', described it as 'a rectangular block of stone that has felt itself into expression'. It was transported across the Channel shortly afterwards, but its reception by supposedly more liberal-minded and advanced French opinion was very different. Sexual organs were deemed unseemly in a cemetery. 'I was still at work putting the finishing carving to the head,' wrote Epstein later, 'when, arriving one morning, I found the tomb covered with an enormous tarpaulin and a *gendarme* standing beside it. He informed me that the tomb was banned.' Shortly afterwards *Commoedia* reported:

When the monument was just being placed into position the sculptor, Jacob Epstein, went up to inspect the work when his notice was at once drawn to a huge mass of plaster – a good kilo of it – covering up a certain part of the

OPPOSITE Sonia Delaunay: *Prisms and Discs*, 1914 (Musée National d'Art Moderne, Paris). The artist was fascinated by the colour and light, particularly the bright new electric street lighting in Paris.

statue.... The joke has gone far enough.... We ask M. le Préfèt de Police or M. le Préfèt de la Seine to go and see the monument in person – to examine it in detail and impartially – and then to state frankly whether a fig-leaf or a stroke of the chisel would produce the more ridiculous effect.

The case produced a spate of protests and manifestos in the Press. By March *Commoedia* was writing: 'Today it is not from the clutches of English judges that Oscar Wilde has to be wrested but from the hypocrisy that is holding his "Geni" a prisoner.' Rodin, when appealed to, again behaved timidly, and held back. In the end, according to Epstein, Wilde's executor, Robert Ross, 'had a large plaque modelled and cast in bronze and fitted to the figure as a fig-leaf is applied'. What Marinetti and his *machismo*-minded colleagues thought of the precaution is not known; they and their Cubist rivals were too busy fighting their own

Jacob Epstein with his tombstone for Oscar Wilde in his London studio in 1912. The offending detail has apparently been blacked out by the photographer.

OPPOSITE
ABOVE Bakst's sketch for a costume design for Ravel's ballet *Daphnis and Chloë*.
BELOW Nijinsky as the Faun in his controversial production, *L'Après-midi d'un Faune* choreographed to Debussy's music.

RIGHT The elderly Degas,
nearly blind, taking a rare
stroll in the streets of Paris.

BELOW Marc Chagall:
The Green Donkey, 1911
(Tate Gallery, London).
Most of the pictures
painted by Chagall during
his first visit to Paris
were based on memories
of his native Vitebsk.

battle to spare a thought for the *démodé* English writer. His embattled memorial bore the words: 'And alien tears shall fill for him pity's long-broken urn/For his mourners will be outcast men, and outcasts always mourn.'

In retrospect 1912 itself seems to stand like a monument, at the summit of the creative years in Paris. The great artistic momentum had reached a peak, and suddenly a feeling of change came over the scene. Picasso broke with his faithful companion of the Bateau-Lavoir, Fernande Olivier, and took up with a new girl. While he was away in the summer he wrote to Kahnweiler asking him to move all his belongings from Montmartre and install them on the other side of the river, in the Boulevard Raspail. His old companion and fellow-explorer, Braque, married. Apollinaire parted from Marie Laurencin – who, illogically, had often been included in Cubist shows on his account – and flirted with the Futurists. Leo Stein, unable to follow his sister Gertrude in her enthusiasm for the Cubists, and increasingly out of sympathy with her expanding social life, moved out of the studio in the Rue de Fleurus and left Paris altogether. Even the nearly blind, seventy-two-year-old Edgar Degas was driven out of his old studio by property developers.

The Cubist set was splitting up and portents of a new phase began to appear – glimmers of a return to romanticism. A ragged Jewish sixteen-year-old, Chaim Soutine, arrived from Minsk in Russia and quickly made friends with his compatriot, Marc Chagall, who had shown a dream-like *The Cattle Dealer* at the Indépendants, and with his friend Modigliani. In the Salon d'Automne de Chirico exhibited other visionary scenes, southern ones this time – *Enigma of an Autumn Afternoon* and *Enigma of the Oracle*. Standing in the Gustave Moreau Museum a young poet, André Breton, had a vision which would one day knit these dreams into a complete new art movement, Surrealism.

1913
The Move to Montparnasse

PICASSO'S FIERCELY INDEPENDENT and somewhat secretive temperament – he never once submitted a work to any mixed show in Paris – made him a legendary figure from an early age. His move from the Boulevard de Clichy to the Boulevard Raspail was at the same time a cause and a symptom of a new phase in the story of the School of Paris. Matisse was already on the Left Bank, on the Quai St-Michel. Apollinaire was receiving every Sunday in a new apartment in the Boulevard St-Germain. Léger was living just off it. The office of Apollinaire's *Les Soirées de Paris* was only a few blocks away from Picasso's new home. Gertrude Stein's studio attracted artists and art-lovers to the Rue de Fleurus every Saturday, and a whole colony of young artists from abroad had sprung up around the Gare Montparnasse. The centre of gravity of the Parisian art world had moved. 'The truth is that Montparnasse has replaced Montmartre,' wrote Apollinaire in the *Mercure de France*, 'that old Montmartre of artists, entertainers, windmills and cabarets, not to mention hashishovores and the first opiomanes.'

The publicity which followed the successes of the Cubists and their friends was turning the village on top of the Butte of Montmartre, already a popular haunt for patrons of music-halls and night-clubs on its lower slopes, into a tourist attraction. The little Place du Tertre with its narrow streets and tiny cafés no longer offered the intimacy and privacy which stimulated artistic discussion and creative work. By comparison, Montparnasse was still unexploited. Its university connections had bequeathed to it a combination of learning and high spirits. The Closerie des Lilas café, where Paul Fort in his high collar and black stock had once lorded it over the Symbolist poets on the first floor and which still offered free writing paper to aspiring geniuses, together with the Moorish-style Bal Bullier dance-hall almost opposite it in the Boulevard de Montparnasse, vividly symbolized its atmosphere of serious but light-hearted adventure.

The district had venerable artistic traditions – it was in the thirteenth century that Jehan de Meung had composed the *Roman de la Rose* in a building which is now 218 Rue St-Jacques, and countless writers and painters, from Delacroix to Gauguin and Vuillard, had lived there. It bordered not on night-clubs, like Montmartre, but on the respectable homes of the St-Germain nobility. At one end Rodin was installed majestically in the Hôtel Biron, and at the other there were plenty

OPPOSITE Amedeo Modigliani: *Self-Portrait*, c. 1913 (Private Collection). Modigliani in typical pose behind a glass.

of cheap studios and cafés to provide amusement for the young artists who, drawn by the spreading fame of the School of Paris, arrived from all over the world.

Many of them landed up in a curious building which was almost exactly the equivalent of the Bateau-Lavoir in Montmartre. This was a cluster of dilapidated studios far out beyond Montparnasse near the Vaugirard abattoirs, reached from a narrow street called the Passage de Dantzig. Like its northern counterpart it was known by a nickname earned by its appearance – it was called 'La Ruche' because of the beehive shape of the central building. It had been built out of material left over from the 1900 Exhibition by a successful old sculptor as a workshop for his assistants – the 'beehive' had housed the wine-growers' section in the Exhibition. The buildings had been converted into the focus of a vast conglomeration of studios – nearly 140 of them; unlike the Bateau-Lavoir, which burnt down in 1970, it is still in active use today. In those days there was no gas or running water, and sanitation was primitive – Soutine recalled placing saucers of water round the floor to attract the beetles. But the accommodation was cheap and it provided a lively communal centre for lonely young artists arriving from abroad. They were a different lot from those in the Bateau-Lavoir ten years earlier. Many of them came from Russia and central Europe, and a number of these were Jewish – Yiddish was in common use. Other languages spoken included Italian, Russian, Polish, Norwegian, Swedish, German and even Japanese. One of the most successful youngsters to arrive there was Foujita, 'charming, with hair like a Laplander and a blue boiler-suit', the son of a wealthy official. He studied dancing with Isadora Duncan's brother Raymond, and soon found a market for his oriental-flavoured painting.

La Ruche served as a kind of reception-room for indigent art immigrants, many of whom later moved out into another tumbledown collection of studios nearer to the centre, known as the Cité Falguière. The list of those who passed through La Ruche is impressive and international. It included Léger, Alexander Archipenko, who had moved in in the year of his arrival from Russia, 1908, and came under the influence of the Cubists; his fellow-sculptors Henri Laurens and Jacques Lipchitz from Romania; the Delaunays; Moise Kisling from Poland; Marc Chagall and Chaim Soutine from Russia; poets like Max Jacob, Pierre Reverdy and Blaise Cendrars – who wrote a poem about the place significantly ending 'Empty bottles, bottles'; and many other writers, musicians, actors and artists of varied persuasions, nationalities and talents.

They used to meet in the local cafés, particularly in Le Dôme and La Rotonde on the Boulevard Montparnasse. Ilya Ehrenburg wrote of La Rotonde:

The café was like a hundred others. Cabbies and taxi-drivers stood at the zinc counter. Clerks drank coffee and apéritifs. At the back there was a dark room impregnated for all time with the smell of smoke, where stood ten or a dozen tables. At night this room would fill with people and noise ... some-one would always get drunk and be thrown out. At two o'clock in the morning the Rotonde would close for an hour.... At 3 am the café would open and men were free to continue their joyless talk.

The proprietor, Libion, fat, good-natured and grey-haired, kept a kindly eye on his eccentric clientele. 'Here's five francs,' he would say. 'Go and find yourself a woman, you've a mad look in your eyes.'

Modigliani was a regular customer, hawking round his drawings in a sky-blue folder – he would sell a drawing for a glass of absinthe, or paint a portrait for ten francs. By now he had rejected his elegant 'bohemian' costume of velvet suit, red scarf and big black hat for rags, since drink and drugs and tuberculosis were taking their toll of his handsome frame. His friends were now chiefly Soutine, who lived an equally disordered life, and Utrillo, who was a complete alcoholic but, cared for by a kindly bar-keeper who sometimes kept him locked in his room, was producing some of his best impressions of his beloved Montmartre. 'You may find Utrillo drunk anywhere,' Picasso remarked drily, 'but Modigliani is always drunk right in front of the Rotonde or the Dôme.'

The Picasso gang was often to be found there – not only the painter himself but also Gris and Apollinaire and Salmon. Léger would be drinking with Gleizes and Metzinger and the always dapper Jacob – he came from a family of tailors. Cocteau, still only twenty-two, and destined to act as the connecting link between this scene and the elegant world of Diaghilev, would be there, and so would Blaise Cendrars, who had a Scottish father but had spent years in Russia. He was naturally friendly with the huge and emotional Mexican Diego Rivera, who had a Russian wife. Soutine and his young childhood friend Kremegne would be together in a dark corner. Chagall would be talking to Lipchitz, Archipenko to Zadkine, Kisling or Goncharova. The twenty-two-year-old Max Ernst, who arrived from Germany this summer on a short visit after meeting

Two dandies painted by a well-known society artist. LEFT Jacques-Emile Blanche: *Portrait of Marcel Proust*, 1895 (Mante-Proust Collection). BELOW Jacques-Emile Blanche: *Portrait of Jean Cocteau*, 1912 (Musée des Beaux Arts, Rouen).

Delaunay and Apollinaire in Macke's house, became friends with Jules Pascin. It was a curious evocation of the desperate, struggling world which Picasso had portrayed ten years earlier in his Blue Period. Nearly all these people were lonely, far from home, cut off by language and pitifully poor. Most of them were social outcasts, many of them were Jews: 'If anyone wants to understand Modigliani, let him remember not the hashish-den but the gas-chamber,' remarked Ehrenburg later.

A different Russian circle could be found further south, where Bolshevik exiles used to meet in a café near the Lion de Belfort. In 1911, Ehrenburg attended a meeting in a nearby hall, where he found them gathered soberly round a table drinking soft drinks, except for Lenin who ordered a mug of beer.

He was dressed in a dark suit with a stiff white collar and looked very respectable. ... When the meeting was over he came up to me. 'Are you from Moscow?' he asked.... He told me to come and see him. I found the house in a little street near the Parc Montsouris, Rue Beaunier.... The door was opened by Krupskaya. Lenin was working. He sat deep in thought over a long sheet of paper, his eyes narrowed a little.... I was struck by the order in the flat; the books stood on the shelves, Lenin's desk was tidy.... I was fascinated by his head.... It made one think not of anatomy but of architecture.

A centre of this polyglot society was the apartment of Robert and Sonia Delaunay, who were full of crazy ideas. Apollinaire wrote:

Every Thursday and Saturday they would 'reform costume'. They don't try to change the shape or cut of clothes, following the fashion of the moment, but they try to make their influence felt by using new materials in an infinity of colours. Here, for example, is a costume of Monsieur Delaunay – violet coat, beige waistcoat, nigger-brown trousers. Here's another: red cloak, with a blue collar, yellow and black socks, black trousers, sky-blue waistcoat, minute red tie. ... If you visit the Bal Bullier you won't spot them at once. The costume-reformers generally sit near the band, respectfully observing the monotonous clothes of the dancers.

The Delaunays were in the throes of working out abstract paintings of pure contrasted colours, aiming at what they called 'simultaneous sensations' rather than blended ones. Apollinaire had christened their style 'Orphism'.

Two figures held aloof from this noisy café society. Matisse, now forty-four, had been spending many months during the last two years in Morocco and in the country; the results were shown in a much admired exhibition at Bernheim-Jeune in April. The southern sun had further developed his colourful hedonism. 'If one felt obliged to compare the art of Henri Matisse to something one would have to choose an orange,' wrote Apollinaire in L'Intransigeant, '... the work of Henri Matisse is a fruit of radiant lustre.' To the Salon d'Automne Matisse sent only one canvas, but a splendid one, a portrait of his wife.

By now successfully embarked on a style of his own, he had little in common with the struggling artists of La Ruche. Constantin Brancusi, on the other hand, though he had lived in Paris for nine years, was still virtually unknown, though he had many friends among his central European compatriots in Montparnasse. Brancusi was of an austere and retir-

Marc Chagall: *Russian Scene or Man in the Snow*, 1913 (Musée National d'Art Moderne, Paris). One of Chagall's Russian-inspired pictures painted in Paris.

ing temperament. 'He never went to cafés,' wrote Epstein, who met him in 1912. 'He was in the habit of keeping a number of bottles of milk maturing – evidently for yoghourt, in the Romanian style – and rows of these bottles stood in the passage of his studio. He would exclaim against café life and say that one lost one's force there. No matter what time one called on Brancusi, he was always at work.'

Improbably, he had become an intimate of Modigliani when he first arrived, and introduced him to sculpture a few years later. By 1910 Modigliani was already carving heads in the elongated style which soon crept into his painting. 'At night he would place candles on the top of each one and the effect was that of a primitive temple,' Epstein related. ' A legend of the quarter said that Modigliani, when under the influence of hashish, would embrace these sculptures.' This year Modigliani had his first real exhibition, at the Galerie Weill. But his nudes with their explicit pubic hair proved so shocking that the police intervened and the show had to be taken off.

Few people could have been more opposite to Modigliani in character and artistic aims than his compatriot Giorgio de Chirico. He had trained as an artist in Greece, the country of his birth, and in Munich where he had read Nietzsche's writings. He drew from them a very different inspiration from that drawn by the Futurists; he was fascinated by Nietzsche's conception of the artist's 'oneness with the primal source of the universe which reveals itself to him in a symbolical dream picture'. These calm, nostalgic visions, which exaggerated rather than denied the traditional use of perspective, were totally alien to the main painting trends in Paris, but when they were exhibited they were admired by both Apollinaire and Picasso, who, however, called de Chirico a 'painter of railway stations'. De Chirico, for his part, was sympathetic to his young Parisian colleagues, but seems to have remained totally unaffected by the Futurists – though one of them, Carrà, was to become a close collaborator later on. In the Indépendants this year de Chirico showed three accomplished examples of his hallucinatory style, in which empty Renaissance squares are rendered mysterious by romantic lighting and curious,

Robert Delaunay: *Homage to Blériot*, 1913–14 (Musée National d'Art Moderne, Paris). With its aeroplanes and suggestions of propellers whirling in front of the Eiffel Tower, this painting catches the excitement of pre-First World War Paris.

menacing statues. He sent some similar paintings to the Salon d'Automne, where Apollinaire praised them as 'metaphysical landscapes'. He was not the type to mix freely with the boisterous café crowd, but he did become a regular attender of Apollinaire's Sundays in his Boulevard St-Germain apartment, and through him met poets, painters and – most important of all – a dealer who appeared on the scene at this time, Paul Guillaume.

Apollinaire's influence was at its peak at this moment. He contributed art criticism to several journals, and in March he had published *Les Peintres Cubistes*, in which he not only commented perceptively on the painting of many of his friends, but tried to divide them into four categories. Always faintly bourgeois in temperament, Apollinaire was now reasonably secure financially as well, and a respected as well as a popular figure. 'His face is full and yet oblong, his eyes are gentle but have a strange light,' wrote *Le Figaro* of him. 'His mouth appears too small for laughter and yet opens up with great bursts of mirth and then closes tightly again. His lips are so red that they give his otherwise tranquil face a suggestion of blood, the vivacious blood of a voluptuary but also the blood of cruelty.'

In fact Cubism was changing even as Apollinaire was writing his book. Picasso and Braque were at this moment experimenting with pictures in which line and colour were separated to serve different functions – a technique which was accompanied by *collage*, the action of sticking scraps of paper, cardboard or other material on to the canvas as elements in a cocktail of ingredients which took the label 'synthetic Cubism'. The breaking up of the painted surface – unknown since Gothic art – was to prove another venture which would have far-reaching results in the future.

One of those who remarked on Apollinaire's changed circumstances with amusement was Gertrude Stein, whose own Saturday receptions had taken on a more cosmopolitan and fashionable tone. Jacques-Emile Blanche, an emissary from the *salon* world, became a regular visitor. From London came Epstein; Wyndham Lewis, who was just launching his Cubist-orientated Vorticist movement in England; the critics Roger Fry and Clive Bell, the latter with his painter wife Vanessa; and the wealthy hostesses Lady Ottoline Morrell and Lady Cunard. Americans began to appear in large numbers – not so much artists, though there were plenty of them, as connoisseurs, collectors and patrons like Mildred Aldridge and Mabel Dodge, William Cook from Chicago and Prichard from Boston. Severini brought some of his dashing Italian friends, but, according to Gertrude Stein, 'Everybody found the Futurists very dull.'

The reputation of the Stein collection and the Stein Saturdays had received a huge boost in America by the opening in February of what came to be known as the Armory Show. In the autumn of 1912 two keen art-lovers, Walt Kuhn and Arthur B. Davies, had done a whirlwind tour of Europe with the idea of putting on a big international art show in New York. They had been impressed by the Sonderbund Exhibition in Cologne and Fry's second Post-Impressionist show in London. They had visited the Steins and noted pictures and sculpture by many of the Paris

avant-garde. There were several American painters in France who were working in the modern tradition – men like Arthur Dove, Alfred Maurer, Max Weber and Patrick Bruce, while Edward Steichen had introduced New York to some Parisian artists in his 291 Gallery. But this was to be a giant demonstration which would, the organizers hoped, be 'a red-letter night in the history not only of America but of all modern art'.

It turned out to be so – for it was the beginning of the School of New York. Its influence stemmed not only from its quality but also from its size. Held in an old regimental armoury in Lexington Avenue, it displayed the work of nearly three hundred artists, two-thirds of them American, in eighteen rooms. The exhibition started, perceptively, with Goya and proceeded via Ingres, Delacroix and the Impressionists to Cézanne, Van Gogh and the Fauves and Cubists. It received massive publicity. Duchamp, with his relatively unadventurous Futuristic *Nude Descending a Staircase* – he had not seen a Futurist work in the flesh when he painted it – gained the most attention, Matisse the most abuse. 'We may as well say in the first place that his pictures are ugly, that they are coarse, that they are narrow, that to us they are revolting in their inhumanity,' wrote the critic of the *New York Times*. But modern art was on the map, even if it had won its place there mainly through scandal.

Nobody knew how to use offence as a public relations exercise better than Diaghilev, and in his 1913 season he succeeded again in bringing blood to the cheek of the Paris public. His Ballets Russes appeared this year in a fresh setting – the striking new Théâtre des Champs Elysées, into which his impresario, Gabriel Astruc, had poured years of work and hundreds of thousands of francs. Astruc wrote:

Since that morning in 1906 when Louis Barthou, to whom I applied at the Ministry of Works, accompanied me to M. de Selves, prefect of the Seine, to support my demand for the concession up to 30 March 1913, the date of the inaugural Gala, there were never twenty-four hours in which, whatever my preoccupation, 'my theatre' did not occupy my total attention.

It was a huge and handsome theatre, or rather complex of theatres, standing in what is now the Avenue Montaigne. Designed by the Perret brothers, decorated outside with sculptures by Bourdelle and inside with murals by Maurice Denis, its severe style was found un-French, indeed Germanic by some critics. It opened with a triumphant revival of Berlioz's *Benvenuto Cellini*, followed by *Der Freischütz* and other operas. Debussy, Fauré, Paul Dukas, Saint-Saëns and Vincent d'Indy conducted their own works. Loie Fuller, still popular thirteen years after her exploits in the 1900 Exhibition, danced to Debussy's *Nuages* and *La Mer* with a troupe of children. Finally, in May, came Diaghilev with both ballet and opera.

His season opened quietly with what can now be seen as a revolutionary work – a ballet by Nijinsky set to Debussy's score *Jeux*. Deserting not only classical arabesques and pirouettes as he had done in his *L'Aprèsmidi d'un Faune*, but also the whole world of myth and romantic drama, Nijinsky composed his ballet about a subject perhaps inspired by the Futurists – athletes playing a game, a kind of tennis, in modern clothes.

ABOVE Maurice Utrillo, photographed *c.* 1912.
OPPOSITE Maurice Utrillo: *Impasse Cottin, c.* 1911 (Private Collection). One of Utrillo's typical Montmartre street scenes with a flight of steps leading up towards the Sacré Coeur.

International Exhibition Modern Art
New York

To our Friends and Enemies of the Press

The Association of American Painters and Sculptors, Inc.

March 8th **BEEFSTEAK DINNER** **1913**
Healy's—66th St. and Columbus Ave.

MENU

ALL YOU CAN EAT AND DRINK

Souvenir of a dinner celebrating the
opening of the Armory Show in New York.
Arthur B. Davies heads the signatures,
with Walt Kuhn bringing up the rear.
Duchamp's *Nude Descending a Staircase*
is already being promoted.

Not surprisingly few people, certainly not the composer, approved and the piece – probably not very well worked out – disappeared. Its successor was to prove equally short-lived but equally daring, this time on its musical side. Gertrude Stein, now moving in smarter circles, was at the première of *The Rite of Spring*, and wrote:

We arrived in the box and sat down in the three front chairs, leaving one chair behind. Just in front of us in the seats below was Guillaume Apollinaire. He was dressed in evening clothes and he was industriously kissing various important looking ladies' hands. He was the first one of his crowd to come into the great world wearing evening clothes and kissing hands. . . . No sooner did the music begin and the dancing than they began to hiss. The defenders began to applaud. We could hear nothing . . . one literally could not, throughout the whole performance, hear the sound of music. . . . Our attention was constantly distracted by a man in the box next to us flourishing his cane and finally in a violent altercation with an enthusiast in the box next to him, his cane came down and smashed the opera hat the other had just put on in defiance.

'After the "performance",' Stravinsky recalled, 'we were excited, angry,

Immediately it arrived in America Cubism became a popular target for cartoonists. This drawing ingeniously relates it to traditional native patchwork quilts.

disgusted and . . . happy.' Next morning the critics dismissed the strange, primitive dances which Nijinsky had arranged to the immensely complicated rhythms – he had stood on a chair during the ballet, shouting out the counts to the dancers – and concentrated their attacks on the music, many of them enjoying the same pun on the French title (*Le Sacré du Printemps*), calling it: 'Le Massacre du Printemps.' The ballet had only three more performances, which were received more calmly, and when the score was played at a concert soon afterwards it scored a distinct success. In November Diaghilev got word from South America that Nijinsky had married, and instantly dismissed him. For better or worse, the Ballets Russes were never the same again.

The fashionable world of Diaghilev and his aristocratic patrons and that of the scruffy artists from Montmartre were beginning to interlock. The delicate Proust would hardly have joined in the vociferations after *The Rite of Spring*, though he already knew Diaghilev and Stravinsky and was temperamentally on the side of the avant-garde. But he had pressing preoccupations of his own. He had finished the first part of his novel, but after its rejection by *La Nouvelle Revue Française* he could not find a publisher. It was turned down twice more before he finally signed a contract with Grasset for it to be published at his own expense. Gallantly author and publisher struggled with the proofs – nearly a hundred sheets which grew steadily with corrections and pasted-on additions. In November *Du Côté de Chez Swann* was finally published, dedicated to Calmette, editor of *Le Figaro*, who had been a loyal supporter. 'My dear Proust,' he wrote, 'For several days I have never left your book: I am supersaturating myself in it with rapture, revelling in it.' *La Nouvelle Revue Française* now offered to buy the rights from Grasset and publish the remaining two volumes, but Proust declined.

Gide, who had so memorably rejected Proust's first chapters, had himself just published a new novel, *Les Caves du Vatican*. Alain-Fournier's delicate study of adolescence, *Le Grand Meaulnes*, had also appeared. In England D. H. Lawrence brought out *Sons and Lovers*, and in Ireland James Joyce finished *Dubliners*.

The year ended with a mixture of comedy and menace. In December the news suddenly broke that, after two years of complete mystery, the missing picture from the Louvre, Leonardo's *Monna Lisa*, had been found in Florence. A local Italian second-hand dealer, who had once been the famous actress Eleonora Duse's stage manager, had put an advertisement in a French paper for '*objets d'art* of all kinds'. It was spotted by a thirty-two-year-old artisan living in Paris called Vincenzo Peruvio, who promptly pulled out a parcel kept in his cheap hotel room near the Gare de l'Est, wrote to the dealer to say that he was coming to offer him the Leonardo, and set off for Florence. 'A thin young man arrived and offered to show me the picture,' the dealer wrote, 'saying that he wanted 500,000 francs for it.' An inspection was arranged for the next day; accompanied by an expert, the dealer arrived at the Tripoli Italia Hotel and climbed up to the third floor. The stranger shut the door and 'drew from under his bed a plain wooden box in which were revealed a confusion of paintbrushes, plasterer's tools, white overalls and even a mandolin. Removing the top layer he uncovered an object wrapped in red velvet. We took it, placed it on the bed and to our astonished and delighted gaze the "Gioconda" appeared, intact and marvellously preserved.' It turned out that the thief, who had been working in the Louvre as a glazier, had removed it after hours under his coat, leaving the frame behind. This had contained an excellent thumb-print but unfortunately of the left thumb, while the museum records included only right thumb-prints. There were some red faces at the Louvre, much amusement, and, after the picture had been put on show for a month in Italy, where it had not been seen since it was painted, it was safely returned to Paris. The thief seemed confused about the motive for his crime: he declared it to be patriotic, but cash reward seems not to have been ruled out.

This happy ending brought light relief to a scene which was becoming increasingly gloomy. The year had started with troubles in the Balkans, sparked off by a coup d'état by the Young Turks. Poincaré, the new President of France, paid an anxious visit to London to sign the *entente cordiale*. Britain had internal troubles – a suffragette had thrown herself under the King's horse during the Derby and had been killed. In July Bulgaria attacked Greece and committed atrocities which shocked the world. Pressures were building up dangerously and the prospect of a general conflagration came nearer and nearer. In July *Le Matin* published a poem by Rudyard Kipling, called simply *La France*:

Furious in luxury, merciless in toil,
Terrible with strength that draws from her tireless soil. . . .
Now we count our keels afloat, and new hosts on land
Massed like then (remembrest thou?), when our strokes were planned,
We were schooled for dear life's sake to know each other's blade,
What can Blood and Iron make more than we have made?

1914
The End of the
Beginning

IN RETROSPECT A SHADOW lies like a cloud over the first half of the year 1914. It opened cheerfully enough with rejoicings over the safe return to the Louvre of the *Monna Lisa*; Sarah Bernhardt rolling her 'golden voice' in celebration of the award of the Cross of the Légion d'Honneur; and a revival, after fifteen years, of the annual fancy-dress ball at the Opéra – a red-and-yellow occasion attended with delight by d'Annunzio and hundreds of society ladies in masks and paper streamers.

But the fun was soon interrupted by an event which brought all conversation to a standstill. On 16 March the second wife of the Minister of Finance, Joseph Caillaux, after having her nails manicured, called at the offices of *Le Figaro* and asked to see the editor, Gaston Calmette. She was kept waiting for almost an hour while he talked to the eminent writer Paul Bourget. When at last she gained admission, she drew a revolver from her muff and shot Calmette three times. He died of his wounds within a few hours.

The motive for the assassination was a mixture of politics and feminine jealousy. *Le Figaro* was conducting a ruthless and somewhat scurrilous campaign against Caillaux, who was threatening to introduce both income tax and a capital tax. The minister's ex-wife had sent to Calmette some letters she had discovered, which contained indiscreet political comments. Fearing that more were to be published, the current Madame Caillaux took a dramatic step – the immediate result of which was, naturally, what she had hoped to avert – the resignation of her husband. Public indignation at this example of women's activism was coupled with shock at the unexpected violence, and dismay at the feebleness and corruption in the government which the incident revealed.

Nerves were, in fact, under strain. The fighting in North Africa was rumbling on in spite of Lyautey's efforts. Machine guns were tried out as armaments on aeroplanes. George V of England paid a state visit to Paris, accompanied by the Queen and the Prince of Wales, and reassuring pictures of French warships kept appearing in the papers. Quarrels seemed to break out easily. Claudel wrote furiously to Gide about his new book, *Les Caves du Vatican:* 'You have done a great wrong by inserting in your novel a scandalous passage. . . . May God, whom you mock, be with you.' Jean-Louis Forain, the formidable right-wing cartoonist, accused Frantz Jourdain, the President of the 1913 Salon d'Automne,

OPPOSITE Life went on in spite of threats of war. The hobble skirt appears at a Longchamp race meeting in 1914, to distract male attention from more serious concerns.

221

Three survivors.
ABOVE Clemenceau with the
veteran Claude Monet in
the garden at Giverny which
Monet loved to paint.
RIGHT Pierre-Auguste Renoir,
crippled with arthritis and
holding a brush with difficulty,
still kept painting in his
studio at Cagnes. The picture he is
working on is a portrait of Madame
Tilladurieux. Behind is a portrait of
Madame Colonna Romaro.

of giving it a pro-German twist, but it was a popular success – 'There is no place in Paris where good humour reigns more completely than at the Grand Palais,' *L'Illustration* had reported. Modern art was becoming accepted even if not approved.

It seemed on the surface that painting had indeed settled down. The old men patiently carried on their established styles. Redon was exploring his new colourful decorations. Monet was obsessed by his water lilies at Giverny. Rodin, recovering from an illness and worried about his efforts to leave his works in the Hôtel Biron intact to the nation, was recuperating in the south of France. All these veterans were seventy-four. Renoir, a year younger, was crippled with arthritis but still painting in his house at Cagnes. Degas, on the other hand, was now too blind to work; he was eighty. Of the Nabis, Bonnard was forty-seven, Vuillard forty-six and Denis forty-four – all now secure and reasonably prosperous. The Fauve group were also by now well represented by commercial dealers, especially by the Galerie Druet, which this year featured Camoin, Friesz, Manguin and Marquet in its annual mixed exhibition. Matisse showed regularly with Bernheim-Jeune. He was working quietly in his studio on the Quai St-Michel, painting this year some of the few works in which a Cubist influence is traceable.

The Cubists themselves had moved far away from the austere beginnings of the movement. Picasso and Braque were exploring the possibilities opened up by their invention of *collage*, in new, bright and cheerful paintings which also included effects of texture and playful mixtures of real and painted motifs. They left Paris together in the summer for Céret in the south of France, where they were joined by Derain, who had by now abandoned Cubism for his own slightly quirkish figure studies and landscapes. The dour, melancholy Gris, still working in the Bateau-Lavoir, was left as the most faithful and painstaking practitioner of the Cubist doctrine. Crudely expressed, this can be summed up as the assertion that the viewer does not look through a Cubist painting into a space suggested by perspective or other optical illusions; instead, different aspects of the subject are stacked up against the surface like pictures against a wall. The honest base of the picture remains the canvas, on which scraps of information are presented in the form of signs.

The most obvious reaction against this austerely intellectual approach – which, paradoxically, was born in picturesque Montmartre – was being provided by the neo-romantic artists of Montparnasse, many of whom showed traces of central European Expressionism. Modigliani was at this time immersed mainly in sculpture, to which he had been attracted after meeting Brancusi and Archipenko, and after seeing an exhibition by an American sculptor, Elie Nadelman. He did not follow

As the dangers of war approached, the British fleet became increasingly important to France. The Entente is cemented as George V is greeted on a visit to France.

the tradition of sensitive modelling represented by Rodin, but aimed to return to something more primitive by carving on stone, apparently sometimes using pieces he found lying around. He thought there was 'too much modelling in clay, too much mud', related Jacques Lipchitz, who had arrived from Lithuania in 1913 and moved into La Ruche. Rouault was also taking time off from painting, devoting himself mainly to pottery at his studio in Versailles.

Modigliani was lucky enough to be introduced this year by Max Jacob to the dealer Paul Guillaume, who took him on. Chagall had also benefitted by an introduction from one of the old Montmartre gang: Apollinaire had arranged for him to meet Herwarth Walden, owner of the main gallery showing modern art in Berlin; in 1912 Chagall had dedicated a weird painting to both of them, adding the names of his friend Cendrars and the Italian writer Ricciardo Canudo for good measure. In this year

Georges Braque: *Oval Still Life (The Violin)*, 1914 (Courtesy of the Museum of Modern Art, New York, Gift of the Advisory Committee). The apotheosis of Cubism.

Walden arranged a one-man show in his Der Sturm gallery, and in mid-May Chagall left Paris to be present at the opening. He was not to return for ten years, having spent most of the interim back in Russia.

Chagall had been influenced in many of his pictures – which, with the exception of a view of Paris through a window, were mostly nostalgic recollections of his native Vitebsk – by the paintings of the 'dissident Cubists' and particularly by one of them, Robert Delaunay. Reverting to the neo-Pointillists and through them to the Impressionists, Delaunay was trying to restore light as the leading character in his paintings, allowing it to 'interpenetrate' solid shapes like buildings or the Eiffel Tower, and expressing it through patches of colour. He presented these, not blended in the Pointillist manner, but frankly laid out in vivid contrasts – a development of the famous theory of simultaneous contrasts put forward by the chemist Chevreul as far back as 1839.

In their big, comfortable studio in the Rue des Grands Augustins on the Left Bank the Delaunays became hosts and friends to many of the young artists. Robert Delaunay had an adventurous and independent mind with the assurance bred of a well-to-do family. He had been one of Douanier Rousseau's firmest friends and after his death he bought ten paintings from the artist's daughter to pay for a worthy tomb. He developed his own theories with extraordinary single-mindedness, helped by his gifts as a lyrical colourist. Already in 1912, in his *Windows*, patchworks of singing colour, the references to the Eiffel Tower and other landmarks had dwindled to mere clues. His *Disc* of the same year, though derived from the idea of the planets, is totally abstract – as much so as Kandinsky's famous pioneer non-figurative painting of 1910. Delaunay's work was known to Kandinsky as early as 1911 and he contributed to the first Blaue Reiter show in Munich the same year: he sold three pictures in two days and became a prime influence on German painting. August Macke and Franz Marc visited him in Paris and Klee was to show clear traces of his visit to Delaunay's studio the next year.

Though friendly with most of the 'dissident' Cubist artists who organized the Section d'Or group, he was too independent to join in their show. He was not a member of the tight group centred round the Duchamp brothers in Puteaux. These intelligent and ingenious artists – men like Metzinger and Gleizes, Herbin, Lhote and Jacques Villon (Gaston Duchamp) – already represented the tributaries of the Cubist mainstream. But in their midst lurked two figures who were to plant a milestone in the progress of art as decisive as Picasso's *Les Demoiselles d'Avignon* – Marcel Duchamp and Francis Picabia. Revolutionary though the Cubist adventure had been, it stayed within the limits laid down by custom. Not only did Picasso and Braque accept the conventional arrangements of pigment on a canvas as the framework of their experiments – they actually accentuated its character, insisting on its physical existence. They worked away at re-forming and reforming the traditional image – they did not reject it. They both belonged to the artisan class and preserved a certain humility towards their craft.

The two new revolutionaries were of a different breed. They both came from well-off families – Picabia's father was Cuban consul in Paris and

Amedeo Modigliani: *Portrait of Paul Guillaume, c.* 1914. Guillaume was a dealer who began to support the modern schools of painters just before World War I. Modigliani was one of his protégés.

Amedeo Modigliani: *Caryatid,* 1914–15 (Private Collection). At this period Modigliani considered himself a sculptor, and this drawing, like many similar ones done at the time, was probably derived from a sculpture.

The three talented Duchamp brothers. The painter Marcel Duchamp is on the right.

Duchamp's father was a lawyer – and they came to share a contemptuous view of the art world with its cliques and quarrels, its hangers-on and commercial dealers. Doubts had been planted in Picabia's head at an early age; his grandfather was a friend of Daguerre, and held strongly that the invention of a practical process of photography had put an end to the usefulness of art. However, Francis became a fairly successful young artist in the Impressionist style, and was given a one-man show by the Galerie Haussmann in 1905, when he was twenty-six. He promptly quarrelled with the gallery and, encouraged by the girl who was to become his wife, began to make exploratory sketches in a style which was nearly abstract. In 1909 he painted a picture he called *Rubber*, in which the subject, a plateful of oranges, was so fiercely stylized that it virtually disappeared – a rival to Kandinsky's 'pioneer' abstract painting.

The next year he met Duchamp who, though eight years younger, was close to him in spirit. They both became friends of Apollinaire, the lightning conductor of his age, who took them along to see a revival of a provocatively iconoclastic play by Raymond Roussel, called *Impressions d'Afrique*. Something in the tradition of Jarry's *Ubu Roi*, it seems to have sparked off the rebellious and sarcastic streak in the artists, a mood encouraged by the anti-establishment manifestos of the Futurists. Picabia was also attracted by the emphasis laid by the Futurists not only on machines – which were featured also by some of the Section d'Or Cubists – but on mechanics. In 1913 he sailed for New York, where he very successfully promoted his own work and that of his Paris colleagues.

Marcel Duchamp, the youngest of the three brothers who formed the core of the Section d'Or group, experienced the same influences as Picabia, but the rejection by the 1911 Salon d'Automne of his mildly Futuristic *Nude Descending a Staircase*, immediately followed by a visit to Munich, seem to have precipitated an even more drastic revulsion against tradition. Curiously Duchamp, who had participated in the intellectual discussions of the Section d'Or group and observed the development of the decidedly conceptual theories of the Cubists, felt painting was still too 'retinal' and dominated by manual dexterity. He set out on what Picabia's wife called 'forays of demoralization' – exercises in the break-up of the whole traditional concept of art, similar to those carried out by writers like Jarry and Laforgue and musicians like Satie. In Munich he began the series which was to lead to his weird *Large Glass*, a transparent construction featuring mechanical symbols for sex. In 1912 he was mocking 'real standards' with personalized measuring rods, and in 1913 he found a vivid way of expressing his disdain for 'high art'. He attached an ordinary bicycle wheel to an ordinary kitchen stool, and claimed it as a sculpture – 'a pleasant gadget', as he sarcastically described it. This was followed soon after by a 'painting' consisting of a popular lithograph of a landscape to which he added a green dot and a red dot, renaming it *Pharmacy*. And in 1914 he presented the ultimate insult to sensitive art-lovers, an arrangement of plain, everyday bottle-racks called *Bottle-Rack*. The brutal anti-art campaign which was to congeal into the Dada movement a few years later had been born, planting an explosive charge which was to undermine even Picasso's experiments and to open up in the basic foundation of art a crack which was to grow wider and wider. It is possible to detect in this nihilistic attitude a touch of bourgeois *ennui*, an echo of the yawning aesthetes of the *fin de siècle*, but it also hinted at a Nordic worship of the irrational, derived perhaps from Munch and certainly stimulated by the discoveries of Freud. De Chirico's architectural dream-pictures of this year also explored the world of the subconscious, hiding menace beneath a gentle nostalgia in paintings which join with Henri Rousseau's poetic visions to form the base from which Surrealism was to spring.

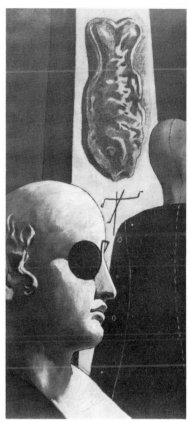

ABOVE Giorgio de Chirico: *The Dream of the Poet*, 1914 (Peggy Guggenheim Foundation, Venice). In contrast to the homely subjects of the Cubist painters, these mysterious symbols offer a foretaste of Surrealism.
LEFT Francis Picabia: *Udnie*, 1913 (Musée National d'Art Moderne, Paris).

The presence of Germany with its Gothic associations of nightmare and violence permeated politics as well as art, and it is possible now to detect symbols of an age passing. In May the eighty-three-year-old and apparently indestructible Emperor of Austria, Franz Josef, suffered a severe illness. The Atlantic and the Pacific Oceans were joined by a canal driven through Panama. The French forces in Morocco were equipped with portable radios as well as bayonets. Proust's beloved chauffeur Agostelli was killed in a flying accident, to be transmuted in his novel into Albertine. Antoine resigned from the Théâtre de l'Odéon after a final, lavish production of Molière's *Psyché*. Even the Russian season, back this year at the Opéra, seemed to be taking a breather. With Nijinsky gone, and the dashing experiments of Cocteau and Picasso still in the future, the new offerings, a mixture of opera and ballet in Rimsky-Korsakov's *Le Coq d'Or* and another exotic piece, *La Légende de Joseph*, with a score by Richard Strauss and a new young star, Léonide Massine, failed to excite the public in spite of the loan of d'Annunzio's greyhound to Potiphar's wife. The Archbishop of Paris banned the tango. In Los Angeles Charles Chaplin made his first film in baggy trousers.

In June the government fell again, and a new Premier, Ribot, took over – he was a veteran vigorously attacked by the Left for his militarism. The old order clung on, but precariously. Never again would there be such a dazzling concatenation of wealth, talent and tradition as was revealed in the Parisian receptions of this time, when the Princesse Murat would have to bang the piano lid to command silence for Caruso, Kubelik or Paderewski, when Madame Ephrussi could hire Pavlova and a whole *corps de ballet* to dance in the moonlight in her garden, and the American Mrs Moore offer Chaliapin – according to Astruc – the biggest fee he had ever received. It was a last flowering of *la belle époque*. Jean Porel, son of the actress Réjane, recalled it all later:

All those beards, both the fashionable ones and the political ones, those watch-chains, those symbolic stomachs, those carriages, those gloved salutations, those top hats, those diplomatic visits, those edged visiting cards, and oh, those flowered terraces, the ladies' hats! Those royal visits, those frock-coated duels, those striped footmen's waistcoats, those secret treaties, those nurses' bonnets, those receptions at the Elysée, those horse buses, those rows between the President and the government, those parties where it took longer to undress a girl than to have her, those restaurants as red as mucous membrane, those unheated apartments, those officers in white gloves, those *salon* canaries, those colonial complications – those button boots, those affairs – all that human bric-à-brac, touching rather than funny, of an age getting ready to die, head held high, in a single war!

This was a society which was indeed to die; but by now it was only an inessential ornament, resting on Paris like one of Worth's hats, due to be thrown away in the post-war season. Life in Paris was not all balls and dinner parties. 'The capital of the world was singularly provincial,' Porel continued. 'Paris was composed of *quartiers* with their many shopping streets, their little theatres and dance-halls. Everybody knew one another, chatted on the street, gossiped about the baker. You could go about in any clothes, do whatever you pleased.' Houses were regularly locked at 10 pm, but every spring there was a ball organized by the students of the Ecole des Beaux Arts, where custom allowed carnival licence to sweep across Paris all night. Heads were still exhibited publicly after a guillotine execution. Rioting would break out suddenly; a shot would ring out, making Anatole France look up from the stall on the *quai* where he was peering at bargains, 'holding a book in his hands as a gardener holds a pear', as Ehrenburg recorded. Old men providing a cartload of hot water and a tin bath – subsequently emptied down a pipe through the window – would call on the many respectable apartments that lacked washing facilities. The miserable studios and attics where young artists and sculptors and writers lived were as primitive as they had been in the fifteenth century.

But it was in that world that the twentieth century had been born. Within fifteen years the whole relationship between man and appearances, the whole way men thought about what they knew and saw and felt, had been changed. Virtually every subsequent way of tackling the craft of image-making, every variety of and attitude towards art, had been invented. Impressionists, Symbolists, Neo-Classicists, Fauvists, Cubists, Futurists, Orphists and finally Abstractionists and the ancestors of Surrealism, Dada and anti-art had offered their new-born brain-children to their successors, reaching heights of achievement which were not to be surpassed. Paris, in the first fifteen years of the century, had been the cradle of the whole vast, varied and troublesome family of modern art.

One of the most significant aspects of this unequalled activity was the speed at which it moved. New ideas emerged, flowered and were superseded at a pace which was symbolized by the new methods of locomotion – the horse gave way to the car and the car to the aeroplane during those brief years. Science was leaping forward with comparable strides and art was connected to science more closely than ever before. The new discoveries in physics and psychology were paralleled almost instantly in art, and painters followed the achievements of France's pioneer racing-cars and aeroplanes with excitement: it was not by accident that Picasso introduced into some of his 1912 paintings the newspaper headline 'Our Future is in the Air' or compared his wood-and-string constructions with primitive aircraft. Even more remarkable was the fact that art suddenly outgrew national frontiers. Modern art may have been born in Paris but its parents were mostly foreign and its godparents almost entirely patrons from abroad. A glance at the names in the index of any book on modern art shows the preponderance of un-French names – with Matisse and Braque as splendid exceptions; and the buyers of their work were almost all foreigners. The School of Paris was, as it happened, not really a French phenomenon – its last great French representative, Duchamp, made his reputation in New York – but a symbol of the new order in which art is truly international, with ideas flashing from Tokyo to Stockholm within a few weeks.

This was in its way a tribute to Paris. No other city in the world could have provided the conditions for such an outburst of international talent, an environment which offered the security, the freedom, the lifestyle and the intellectual stimulus which acted as the forcing-bed into which so many fateful seeds blew in from abroad, germinated, grew and burst into flower. 'Paris was the place that suited those of us that were to create the twentieth-century art and literature naturally enough,' wrote Gertrude Stein later. 'France could be civilized without having progress on her mind, she could believe in civilization in and for itself.' The 'capital of the world', as Porel had called it, was in fact the launching platform of our century.

On 28 June Parisians were shaken by another alarming report from the Balkans. The heir to the Austrian throne, the Archduke Ferdinand, and his wife had been assassinated by a nineteen-year-old Serbian student at Sarajevo. 'Never in the last forty years has the peace of all Europe stood in such peril,' wrote *L'Illustration*. It was grave news, but grave news had become a commonplace. The next week the journalists were scratching their heads to find new adjectives to describe the brilliant Jewellery Ball given by the Princesse de Broglie in her home. It was followed by the fashionable opening of the Camondo collection of Old Masters at the Louvre. President Poincaré flew off on a state visit to Russia.

The next week, domestic drama dominated even the chilling course of events in the Balkans. The trial of Madame Caillaux for the murder of Calmette opened with the accused handsome, smart and defiant in the dock. There was the promise of sensational private letters, and a succession of witnesses who missed no chance of hitting the headlines even if some of the blows landed below the belt. Referring to the imminent general call-up to the army Henry Bernstein, the playwright, declaimed, 'I don't know which day Monsieur Caillaux goes. I must warn him that in a war one cannot use a female substitute to do the shooting!' The letters proved disappointingly harmless and grisly evidence suggested that the shots need not have been fatal to a healthy man. Madame Caillaux was acquitted.

But outside France events were moving inexorably to a climax. On 23 July Austria declared war on Serbia. 'We are getting ready to enter a long tunnel of blood and darkness,' wrote Gide in his diary on 31 July in Normandy. 'Georges [his gardener] has received orders for the requisition of carts and horses. The savings banks refuse to give out more than 50 francs at a time.... The weather is very threatening; a grey film floats between sky and earth.' News came from Paris that the left-wing leader Juarès, who had just returned from a peacemaking trip to Brussels, had been shot in the back in a café. Russia had ordered general mobilization. Everybody knew that the long-awaited crisis had come; war between France and Germany was manifestly inevitable. The whole nation held its breath. 'A day of painful watching,' recorded Gide next day. 'Why don't we mobilize? Every moment we delay is that much more advantage for Germany.' At about three o'clock in the afternoon the church bell in the village began to toll. Gide ran to warn his wife and found her in the garden, her face drawn. ' "Yes, it's the alarm.... The order to mobilize has been posted...." The bell was silent now; after the great alarm through the countryside there was nothing but an oppressive silence. A fine rain fell intermittently.'

On 1 August Germany declared war on Russia; two days later it was the turn of France. Gide boarded the last civilian train to Paris. 'A crowd

on the platform, both serious and vibrant. A workman shouts as he goes by: "All aboard for Berlin! And what fun we'll have there!" People smiled but did not applaud.' France's foreign colony suddenly became nervous. While Gide was rumbling up to Paris from Normandy Jean Arp, who had a German passport, was approaching the city by train from Strasbourg, to take refuge for a few months in the old Bateau-Lavoir in Montmartre before leaving for Switzerland. On 3 August Gris wrote in agitation from Collioure in the south of France to Kahnweiler in Rome: '*Mon cher ami*, I have been more or less ordered to leave. That is to say I have been advised to go, and when I said that I didn't want to unless formally ordered to do so I was told to be prepared even for that. But where shall I go to?'

Matisse immediately reported for military duty at his house at Issy, but to his annoyance was turned down. Picasso was in the house he rented outside Avignon, together with Braque, Derain and their wives. He drove into Avignon with his friends to see them off to join their regiments; as they said goodbye on the little station they must have known that a heroic age was over. 'I never saw them again,' Picasso told Kahnweiler afterwards. 'It was not true,' the dealer explained, 'but it contained a truth. Nothing was ever the same again.'

The death sentence of an age, 1 August 1914. Crowds gather round the general mobilization order, pasted up in a street in Paris.

Bibliography

Monographs on virtually every artist, musician, writer, dancer or politician mentioned in this book are readily available. The list below is selected from works covering some aspect of the period from a more general point of view. It does not include histories of art, of which there is a wide choice.

Bell, Clive, *Old Friends* (London, 1956).
Blanche, Jacques-Emile, *Portraits of a Lifetime* (London, 1937).
Carco, Francis, *De Montmartre au Quartier Latin* (Paris, 1927).
    L'Ami des Peintres (Paris, 1953).
Chasse, Charles, *Le Mouvement Symboliste* (Paris, 1947).
    Les Nabis et Leurs Temps (Paris, 1960).
Cocteau, Jean, *Paris-Album* (Paris, 1956).
Cooper, Douglas, *The Cubist Epoch* (London, 1971).
Coquiot, Georges, *Les Indépendants* (Paris, 1920).
Crespelle, Jean-Paul, *Montmartre Vivant* (Paris, 1964).
    Montparnasse Vivant (Paris, 1962).
    La Folle Epoque (Paris, 1968).
Dunlop, Ian, *The Shock of the New* (London, 1972).
Duthuit, Georges, *The Fauvist Painters* (London, 1950).
Ehrenburg, Ilya, *People and Life* (London, 1961).
Gide, André, *Journal* (London, 1951).
Hobhouse, Janet, *Everybody who was Anybody: A Biography of Gertrude Stein* (London, 1975).
Jakowski, Anatole, *Les Feux de Montparnasse* (Paris, 1957).
Jeanne, René, *Le Cinéma Français* (Paris, 1947).
Jourdain, Franz, *Le Salon d'Automne* (Paris, 1928).
Jullian, Philippe, *The Symbolists* (London, 1973).
    The Triumph of Art Nouveau (London, 1974).
    Montmartre (London, 1977).
Kahnweiler, Daniel-Henry, *Conversations* (London, 1971).
Leymarie, Jean, *Les Fauves* (Paris, 1959).
MacOrlan, Pierre, *Montmartre* (Brussels, 1946).
Olivier, Fernande, *Picasso et Ses Amis* (Paris, 1933).
Salmon, André, *Montparnasse* (Paris, 1950).
    Souvenirs sans Fin (Paris, 1955).
Shattuck, Roger, *The Banquet Years* (London, 1959).
Stein, Gertrude, *Autobiography of Alice B. Toklas* (London, 1933).
Vollard, Ambroise, *Recollections of a Picture Dealer* (London, 1936).
Warnod, André, *Ceux de la Butte* (Paris, n.d.).
    Le Bateau-Lavoir (Paris, 1975).
Wilenski, R. H., *Modern French Painters* (London, 1939).

Acknowledgments

The author and publisher would like to thank the following museums, collections and individuals by whose kind permission the illustrations are reproduced. Sources without parentheses indicate the owners of paintings and photographs; those within parentheses refer to illustration sources only.

Endpapers View of Paris. Mansell Collection, London.

1 Montmartre, *c.* 1900, photograph by Charles Puyo. Royal Photographic Society, London.

2–3 View towards Arc de Triomphe. Roger-Viollet, Paris.

6 Street in Paris. Roger-Viollet, Paris.

12 Universal Exhibition, from *Encyclopédie du Siècle*. Snark International, Paris.

14 Burning of the Théâtre Français. Rousseau Collection (Snark International, Paris).

15 Sarah Bernhardt. Mander and Mitchenson Theatre Collection, London.

17 Blanche: *André Gide and Friends*. Musée des Beaux Arts, Rouen (Snark International, Paris), © SPADEM Paris 1978.

18 **above** Universal Exhibition, photograph by Zola. Paul Elek Ltd, London.

18 **below** Moving platform at Exhibition. Snark International, Paris.

20 Loie Fuller. Bibliothèque Nationale, Paris.

21 Béraud: *The Châlet du Cycle in the Bois de Boulogne*. Musée de Sceaux, © SPADEM Paris 1978.

22 Lithograph by Carrière for Rodin Pavilion. Private Collection (Snark International, Paris).

23 *The Fauns Who Went to the Exhibition*. (From H. Gerbault: *Boum ... Voilà!*)

24–5 Sculpture Hall of Grand Palais. Mansell Collection, London.

25 Eiffel Tower and River Seine. Bibliothèque Nationale, Paris.

28 Picasso: *Self-Portrait Arriving in Paris*. Mrs E. Heywood-Lonsdale Collection (from Roland Penrose: *Portrait of Picasso*, Lund Humphries), © SPADEM Paris 1978.

29 Picasso: *La Diseuse*. Museo Picasso, Barcelona (Roger-Viollet, Paris), © SPADEM Paris 1978.

30 Boldini: *Young Woman Undressing*.

(Weidenfeld and Nicolson Archives, London), © SPADEM Paris 1978.

31 *L'Impudique Albion*, from *L'Assiette au Beurre*, 1901. Mansell Collection, London.

32 Huysmans and others, 1900. Sirot-Angel Collection, Paris.

33 Matisse: *Notre Dame*. Tate Gallery, London, © SPADEM Paris 1978.

35 Forain: *Comtesse Anna de Noailles*. (Giraudon, Paris), © SPADEM Paris 1978.

36 Catulle Mendès. Roger-Viollet, Paris.

37 **left** Sem caricature of Jean Lorrain. (Roger-Viollet, Paris), © SPADEM Paris 1978.

37 **right** Cartoon from *L'Assiette au Beurre*, 1901. Mansell Collection, London.

38–9 Woman in Bois de Boulogne, photograph by Lartigue. John Hillelson, London.

40 Bonnard: *The Bourgeois Afternoon*. Private Collection, Paris (Giraudon, Paris), © SPADEM Paris 1978.

41 Vuillard: *The Painter Ker-Xavier Roussel and His Daughter*. Albright-Knox Art Gallery, Buffalo, New York, © SPADEM Paris 1978.

42–3 Denis: *Homage to Cézanne*. Musée National d'Art Moderne, Paris (Bulloz, Paris), © SPADEM Paris 1978.

44 Picasso: *Seated Nude*. Musée National d'Art Moderne, Paris, © SPADEM Paris 1978.

46 Picasso: *Self-Portrait*. Apollinaire Collection (Snark International, Paris), © SPADEM Paris 1978.

47 Toulouse-Lautrec: *Cocyte in 'La Belle Hélène'*. Musée Toulouse-Lautrec, Albi.

48 Poster advertising *Claudine in Paris*. Brisgaud Collection (Weidenfeld and Nicolson Archives, London).

50 **above** Debussy. Radio Times Hulton Picture Library, London.

50 **below** Cartoon from *L'Assiette au Beurre*, 1901. Mansell Collection, London.

51 Sabattier: *The Motor Mask in Paris*. Radio Times Hulton Picture Library, London.

52 Matisse: *Studio under the Eaves*. Fitzwilliam Museum, Cambridge, © SPADEM Paris 1978.

53 Marquet: *Matisse Painting*. Musée National d'Art Moderne, Paris (Giraudon, Paris), © ADAGP Paris 1978.

54 Colette. Roger-Viollet, Paris.

55 Polaire. Roger-Viollet, Paris.

56–7 Tsar Nicholas II, state visit. Caisse Nationale des Monuments Historiques, Paris.

58 Picasso: *Life*. Grand Palais, Paris (Giraudon, Paris), © SPADEM Paris 1978.

61 Picasso: *Two Women Seated at a Bar*. Walter Chrysler Collection, New York (Giraudon, Paris), © SPADEM Paris 1978.

62–3 Rue Castiglione. Bibliothèque Nationale, Paris.

65 Isadora Duncan. Radio Times Hulton Picture Library, London.

66 Lapin Agile sign. Private Collection (*Le Figaro*/Snark International, Paris).

68 **above** Moulin de la Galette. J. Warnod Archives (Snark International, Paris).

68 **below** Moulin de la Galette, interior. (From J. Crespelle, *Montmartre Vivant*, Hachette.)

69 **above** Rue Lepu. Bibliothèque Nationale, Paris (Snark, International, Paris).

69 **below** Rue Laffitte. (*Le Figaro*/Snark International, Paris.)

71 **above** Bateau-Lavoir, back. (From J. Crespelle, *Montmartre Vivant*, Hachette.)

71 **below** Bateau-Lavoir. Roger-Viollet, Paris.

72 **left above** Picasso: *Portrait of Max Jacob*. Marcel Lecomte Collection (J. Warnod Archives), © SPADEM Paris 1978.

72 **left below** Jacob: *Pablo Picasso*. Modern Art Foundation, Geneva (J. Warnod Archives), © SPADEM Paris 1978.

72 **right** Picasso. René Jacques Collection (Snark International, Paris).

73 Alfred Jarry. Roger-Viollet, Paris.

74 **above** Lapin Agile, interior. J. Warnod Archives.

74 **below** Père Frédé. J. Warnod Archives.

75 Lapin Agile. Roger-Viollet, Paris.

76 Bouguereau's studio. Sirot-Angel Collection, Paris.

77 **above** Helleu: *Woman at a Gallery*. (Weidenfeld and Nicolson Archives, London), © SPADEM Paris 1978.

77 **below** Grun: *Friday at the Salon* (print). Musée des Beaux Arts, Rouen.

78 Béraud: *The Night Moths*. Musée Carnavalet, Paris (Bulloz, Paris), © SPADEM Paris 1978.

80 Redon: *Pegasus*. Private Collection (Bulloz, Paris).

81 Picasso: *The Two Sisters*. Private Collection (Bulloz, Paris), © SPADEM Paris 1978.

82 Matisse: *Nude in the Studio*. Private Collection (Snark International, Paris), © SPADEM Paris 1978.

84 Frédé's donkey. J. Warnod Archives (Snark International, Paris).

85 Salon d'Automne catalogue, 1905. (Weidenfeld and Nicolson Archives, London.)

86 Marquet: *The Fourteenth of July at Le Havre*. Private Collection (Mansell Collection, London), © SPADEM 1978.

87 above Camoin: *Portrait of Marquet*. Musée National d'Art Moderne, Paris (Snark International, Paris), © SPADEM Paris 1978.

87 below Matisse, Camoin and Marquet. (From J. Crespelle, *Montmartre Vivant*, Hachette.)

88 above Matisse: *The Open Window, Collioure*. John Hay Whitney Collection, New York (Weidenfeld and Nicolson Archives, London), © SPADEM Paris 1978.

88 below Derain: *Collioure*. Pierre Lévy Collection, Troyes (Weidenfeld and Nicolson Archives, London), © ADAGP Paris 1978.

89 Page from *L'Illustration*, 1905. (Weidenfeld and Nicolson Archives, London.)

90 Cézanne and *The Bathers*. Sirot-Angel Collection, Paris.

93 Matisse: *Portrait of Madame Matisse (Portrait with the Green Stripe)*. State Art Museum, Copenhagen, © SPADEM Paris 1978.

94 above Matisse: *André Derain*. Tate Gallery, London, © SPADEM Paris 1978.

94 below Derain: *Portrait of Vlaminck*. Private Collection (Giraudon, Paris), © SPADEM Paris 1978.

95 above Derain: *Self-Portrait in a Black Hat*. (Giraudon, Paris), © ADAGP Paris 1978.

95 below Matisse: *Self-Portrait*. State Art Museum, Copenhagen, © SPADEM Paris 1978.

96 Matisse: *Luxe, Calme et Volupté*. Musée National d'Art Moderne, Paris, © SPADEM Paris 1978.

98 Picasso: *La Toilette*. Albright-Knox Art Gallery, Buffalo (Snark International, Paris), © SPADEM Paris 1978.

101 Picasso: *Self-Portrait*. Philadelphia Museum of Art (Weidenfeld and Nicolson Archives, London), © SPADEM Paris 1978.

102 Vlaminck: *The Dancer at the 'Rat Mort'*. Private Collection (Bulloz, Paris), © SPADEM Paris 1978.

103 Braque: *The Landing-stage at L'Estaque*. Musée National d'Art Moderne, Paris (Bulloz, Paris), © ADAGP Paris 1978.

104 Marie Laurencin. P. M. Mosena Collection, Paris (J. Warnod Archives).

105 Laurencin: *Apollinaire and His Friends*. Apollinaire Collection (Snark International, Paris), © ADAGP Paris 1978.

106 Rouault: *At the Salon*. (Giraudon, Paris), © SPADEM Paris 1978.

108 Rodin drawing Cambodian dancer, from *L'Illustration*, 1906. Mansell Collection, London.

109 Rodin drawing of Cambodian dancer, from *L'Illustration*, 1906. Mansell Collection, London.

110 Modigliani, photograph by Marc Vaux. J. Warnod Archives.

110–11 Matisse and students. Snark International, Paris.

113 Rouault: *Girl, a Nude with Pink Garters*. Musée de la Ville de Paris (Bulloz, Paris), © SPADEM Paris 1978.

114 above left Picasso: Sketch of a single figure for *Les Demoiselles d'Avignon*. F. Graindonge Collection (J. Warnod Archives), © SPADEM Paris 1978.

114 above right African mask. Museum of Modern Art, New York, Abby Aldrich Rockefeller Purchase Fund.

114 below Picasso: Group sketch for *Les Demoiselles d'Avignon*. Kunstmuseum, Basle (Snark International, Paris), © SPADEM Paris 1978.

114–15 Picasso: *Les Demoiselles d'Avignon*. Museum of Modern Art, New York, acquired through the Lillie P. Bliss Bequest, © SPADEM Paris 1978.

116 Bonnard: *Moulin Rouge at Night*. Private Collection, Aix-en-Provence (Giraudon, Paris), © SPADEM and ADAGP Paris 1978.

118 above Matisse: *The Blue Nude*. Cone Collection, Baltimore Museum of Art, © SPADEM Paris 1978.

118 below Braque: *Nude*. (Snark International, Paris), © ADAGP Paris 1978.

119 Braque: *L'Estaque*. Musée National d'Art Moderne, Paris (Snark International, Paris), © ADAGP Paris 1978.

120 Fernande Olivier and Dolly Van Dongen. Dolly Van Dongen Collection (J. Warnod Archives).

122 Postcard from Picasso to Apollinaire. (J. Warnod Archives.)

124 27 Rue de Fleurus. Collection of American Literature, Beinecke Rare Book and Manuscript Library, Yale University.

125 Picasso: *Portrait of Gertrude Stein*. Metropolitan Museum, New York (Snark International, Paris), © SPADEM Paris 1978.

126 left Fernande Olivier and Dolly Van Dongen in the Bateau-Lavoir. Dolly Van Dongen Collection (J. Warnod Archives).

126 right Van Dongen: *Portrait of Fernande Olivier*. Private Collection (Snark International, Paris), © SPADEM Paris 1978.

127 Van Dongen and others. Dolly Van Dongen Collection (J. Warnod Archives).

128 Bakst: *Diaghilev and His Old Nurse*. Courtesy of *Dancing Times* (Snark International, Paris).

130–1 Paris–Peking motor race. Radio Times Hulton Picture Library, London.

132–3 Rousseau. J. Warnod Archives (Snark International, Paris).

135 Rousseau: *The Artist Painting His Wife*. N. Kandinsky Collection, Paris (Snark International, Paris).

136 Rousseau soirée programme. Musée de Montparnasse, Paris (J. Warnod Archives).

140 Braque: *Houses at L'Estaque*. Kunst-museum, Berne, Hermann and Margrit Rupf Fund, © ADAGP Paris 1978.

142–3 Auteuil races, from *L'Illustration*, 1908. Mansell Collection, London.

144 Vuillard: *The Art Dealers*. St Louis Art Museum, Gift of Mr and Mrs Richard K. Weil, © SPADEM Paris 1978.

146 Chaliapin. Radio Times Hulton Picture Library, London.

148 Bakst programme cover. Bibliothèque de l'Opéra, Paris (Bulloz, Paris).

151 Bakst, photograph by Oppé. Mansell Collection, London.

153 Nijinsky. Roger-Viollet, Paris.

154 Rodin. Radio Times Hulton Picture Library, London.

155 Ouvré: *Ravel: Portrait in Pyjamas*. Bibliothèque Nationale, Paris (Snark International, Paris).

156 Picasso: *Seated Nude*. Tate Gallery, London, © SPADEM Paris 1978.

157 Braque: *Mandolin*. Tate Gallery, London, © ADAGP Paris 1978.

158 Blériot's plane in mid-flight. Mansell Collection, London.

159 above Blériot in cockpit. Mansell Collection, London.

159 below Blériot on arrival in England. Mansell Collection, London.

160 Braque. L. Laurens Collection (*Le Figaro*/Snark International, Paris).

163 above left Picasso: *Ambroise Vollard*. Pushkin Museum, Moscow (Giraudon, Paris), © SPADEM Paris 1978.

163 above right Picasso: *Daniel-Henry Kahnweiler*. Courtesy of the Art Institute of Chicago, Gift of Mrs Gilbert W. Chapman, © SPADEM Paris 1978.

163 below Bonnard: *Vollard and His Cat*. Petit Palais, Paris (Bulloz, Paris), © SPADEM and ADAGP Paris 1978.

164 Braque: *Still Life with Ace of Clubs*. Musée National d'Art Moderne, Paris (Bulloz, Paris), © ADAGP Paris 1978.

166 Gris drawing from *L'Assiette au Beurre*. Bibliothèque Nationale, Paris (Snark International, Paris).

167 Picasso and Fernande Olivier. Dolly Van Dongen Collection (J. Warnod Archives).

168–9 Bourdelle's studio. Musée Bourdelle, Paris (Giraudon, Paris).

170 Léger: *Nudes in a Landscape*. Rijksmuseum Kröller-Müller, Otterlo, © SPADEM Paris 1978.

171 Bakst's 'Firebird' costume design. Musée des Arts Décoratifs, Paris (Snark International, Paris).

172 Paris floods. Radio Times Hulton Picture Library, London.

174 *Monna Lisa* photograph. Bibliothèque Nationale, Paris.

176 de Chirico: *The Nostalgia of the Infinite*. Museum of Modern Art, New York, © SPADEM Paris 1978.

177 left Picasso: *Bottle and Glass*. Solomon R. Guggenheim Museum, New York, © SPADEM Paris 1978.

177 right Braque: *The Portuguese*. Offentliche Kunstsammlung, Basle, © ADAGP Paris 1978.

179 Nijinsky in *Le Spectre de la Rose*. Mansell Collection, London.

180 Bakst's 'Saint Sébastien' costume design. Bibliothèque de l'Opéra, Paris (Snark International, Paris).

182 Picasso in his studio. René Jacques Collection (from J. Crespelle, *Montmartre Vivant*, Hachette).

184 Gris and wife. Josette Gris Collection, Paris (*Le Figaro*/Snark International, Paris).

185 Bust of Clemenceau by Rodin. Radio Times Hulton Picture Library, London.

186 Severini: *Dynamic Hieroglyphic of the Bal Tabarin*. Museum of Modern Art, New York, acquired through the Lillie P. Bliss Bequest, © ADAGP Paris 1978.

187 Bal Tabarin. Snark International, Paris.

189 above Van Dongen. Weidenfeld and Nicolson Archives, London.

189 below Van Dongen party. Roger-Viollet, Paris.

190 Futurists. (From J. Crespelle, *Montmartre Vivant*, Hachette.)

191 Gris: *Portrait of Picasso*. Courtesy of the Art Institute of Chicago (Snark International, Paris), © ADAGP Paris 1978.

192 Duchamp: *King and Queen Surrounded by Swift Nudes*. Philadelphia Museum of Art, Louise and Walter Arensberg Collection, © ADAGP Paris 1978.

193 Léger: *The Smokers*. Solomon R. Guggenheim Museum, New York, © SPADEM Paris 1978.

195 Marcoussis: *Portrait of Apollinaire*. Philadelphia Museum of Art, Louise and Walter Arensberg Collection (Snark International, Paris), © SPADEM Paris 1978.

197 R. Delaunay: *Eiffel Tower*. Solomon R. Guggenheim Museum, New York, © ADAGP Paris 1978.

198 Rousseau: *The Muse Inspiring the Poet*. Musée de Basle (Giraudon, Paris).

199 Jacob: *Apollinaire*. Musée d'Orléans (Snark International, Paris), © SPADEM Paris 1978.

200 S. Delaunay: *Prisms and Discs*. Musée National d'Art Moderne, Paris (Giraudon, Paris), © ADAGP Paris 1978.

202 above Bakst's 'Chloë' costume design. Musée des Arts Décoratifs, Paris, Serge Lifar Collection (Snark International, Paris).

202 below Nijinsky in *L'Après-midi d'un Faune*. Radio Times Hulton Picture Library, London.

203 Epstein. Mansell Collection, London.

204 above Degas. Bibliothèque Nationale, Paris (Weidenfeld and Nicolson Archives, London).

204 below Chagall: *The Green Donkey*. Tate Gallery, London, © ADAGP Paris 1978.

206 Modigliani: *Self-Portrait*. Private Collection (Bulloz, Paris), © ADAGP Paris 1978.

209 left Blanche: *Portrait of Marcel Proust*. Mante-Proust Collection (Giraudon, Paris), © SPADEM Paris 1978.

209 right Blanche: *Portrait of Jean Cocteau*. Musée des Beaux Arts, Rouen (Giraudon, Paris), © SPADEM Paris 1978.

211 Chagall: *Russian Scene or Man in the Snow*. Musée National d'Art Moderne, Paris (Snark International, Paris), © ADAGP Paris 1978.

212 R. Delaunay: *Homage to Blériot*. Musée National d'Art Moderne, Paris (Giraudon, Paris), © ADAGP Paris 1978.

214 Utrillo: *Impasse Cottin*. Private Collection (Snark International, Paris), © SPADEM Paris 1978.

215 Utrillo. Radio Times Hulton Picture Library, London.

216 Armory Show dinner menu. Armory Show Papers, Archives of American

Art, Smithsonian Institution, Washington DC.

217 Cartoon on Cubism. Armory Show Papers, Archives of American Art, Smithsonian Institution, Washington DC.

220 Longchamp races. Radio Times Hulton Picture Library, London.

222 left Monet and Clemenceau at Giverny. Durand-Ruel Collection (Snark International, Paris).

222 right Renoir. Snark International, Paris.

223 George V at Calais. Roger-Viollet, Paris.

224 Braque: *Oval Still Life (The Violin)*. Museum of Modern Art, New York, Gift of the Advisory Committee, © ADAGP Paris 1978.

225 above Modigliani: *Portrait of Paul Guillaume*. J. Warnod Archives (Snark International, Paris), © ADAGP Paris 1978.

225 below Modigliani: *Caryatid*. Private Collection (Snark International, Paris), © ADAGP Paris 1978.

226 Duchamp brothers. Armory Show Papers, Archives of American Art, Smithsonian Institution, Washington DC.

227 above de Chirico: *The Dream of the Poet*. Peggy Guggenheim Foundation, Venice, © SPADEM Paris 1978.

227 below Picabia: *Udnie*. Musée National d'Art Moderne, Paris (Bulloz, Paris), © SPADEM Paris 1978.

231 Mobilization order, Paris 1914. Bibliothèque Nationale, Paris.

The publisher has taken all possible care to trace and acknowledge the ownership of all the illustrations. If by chance we have made an incorrect attribution we apologise most sincerely and will be happy to correct the entry in any future reprint, provided that we receive notification.

Index